D0840907

We live in an era that is flooding us with books that present various types of claims about Jesus. They seek to undercut the idea that we have a trustworthy portrait of him. So it is refreshing to see a volume clear away the seeming fog. *Reinventing Jesus* effectively presents the other side of the public debate about Jesus, where seemingly glitzy speculation is shown to be more like virtual reality than the history it often claims to be.

—DARRELL BOCK
Author, *Breaking the Da Vinci Code*
and *The Missing Gospels*
Research Professor of New Testament Studies,
Dallas Theological Seminary

This carefully argued book offers a detailed and very helpful critique of many of the recent extreme approaches to the Gospels (from the Jesus Seminar to *The Da Vinci Code*). It explains the issues of Jesus scholarship, text criticism, and other subjects on a level that all readers who read the book through can grasp. Komoszewski, Sawyer, and Wallace have made a significant contribution!

—CRAIG KEENER
Author, *A Commentary on the Gospel of Matthew*
and *The Gospel of John*
Professor of New Testament,
Palmer Theological Seminary of Eastern University

Many college students, unfortunately, enroll in a university religion class only to have their faith shattered. And in the last few years, dozens of radio and TV news programs have also been demolishing Christian faith by citing researchers with the Jesus Seminar or proponents of *The Da Vinci Code*. Fortunately, *Reinventing Jesus* provides sound, biblical answers to these questions being raised on campus and in the culture. This book answers the major questions being raised today about the Bible and Jesus Christ, yet it provides those answers in a way that is easy for the layperson to understand. *Reinventing Jesus* will answer your questions and help you answer the questions others may have about the truthfulness of Christianity.

—KERBY ANDERSON
National Director for Probe Ministries
Cohost of *Point of View* (USA Radio Network)

For the past decade Jesus has been a major figure in the news. The popular media have tended to showcase a few radical scholars whose "new views" have been presented as "new discoveries." Was the real Jesus different from what the New Testament reports? Were other books with a negative picture of Jesus banned from the Bible to repress the truth? These are the new questions being asked and they deserve fresh answers. *Reinventing Jesus* answers the call and reflects scholarship that is both sound and honest. No attempt is made to ignore or dismiss skeptical arguments too quickly. Instead, these three scholars present solid reasons for holding that the New Testament presents the most accurate portrait of the real Jesus available. Readers will be pleasantly surprised by how clearly the authors have presented the data, some of which is seen for the first time!

—MICHAEL LICONA
Author, *The Case for the Resurrection of Jesus*
and *Paul Meets Muhammad*
Director of Apologetics Evangelism,
North American Mission Board,
Southern Baptist Convention

Reinventing Jesus puts top-flight scholarship on the bottom shelf. Komoszewski, Sawyer, and Wallace have crafted a book that is carefully researched, copiously documented, and clearly written. It will handsomely repay the effort of any serious reader looking for the real evidence behind historic belief in the deity of Christ.

—JOSH MCDOWELL
International author and speaker

Whatever problems orthodox Christians have in demonstrating either historical reliability or historical integrity, the problem does not reside in whether or not the New Testament itself contains what was originally written. The facts are that, in spite of a welter of variations, the evidence that survives permits us to know with utter certitude that we are in touch with the original Gospels, letters, and writings of the first century. Recent skepticism advocating that the orthodox corrupted the text is proven in *Reinventing Jesus* to be an overstated conclusion driven by other-than-historical forces.

—SCOT MCKNIGHT
Karl A. Olsson Professor in Religious Studies,
North Park University

Never in the history of the Christian faith has unbelief had the tools at its disposal that it has today. Every kind of argument against the Bible and its portrait of Jesus is picked up and repeated endlessly in published works and on the Internet. Christians are often hit with "scholarly" arguments indicating that we can't have any knowledge of what the Bible originally said or who Jesus really was. We are told Christianity is not unique and the story of Jesus is patterned after pagan myths. *Reinventing Jesus* cuts through the rhetoric of radical skepticism and provides a clear, understandable, and compelling response to those attempting to rewrite the history of early Christianity. People loosely slap "must read" on just about anything these days. But when it comes to *Reinventing Jesus*, the label sticks!

—JAMES WHITE
Author, *The King James Only Controversy*
and *The Forgotten Trinity*
Director, Alpha and Omega Ministries

Perhaps like never before, some radical reinterpreters of the historical Jesus have tried to do a makeover of Jesus' public image, turning him into a politically correct guru who echoes snippets of today's popular cultural agenda. It seems that any Gospel data that do not fit this image are automatically jettisoned. The authors of *Reinventing Jesus* march into this morass in order to sift the evidence for the New Testament reports. Their careful, painstaking analyses invite us to study the data for ourselves and compare the ancient, accredited records with today's reconstructions. The endnotes alone are worth the cost of the book! Bravo, Kregel Publications, for this fine entry into the fray!

—GARY R. HABERMAS
Author, *The Historical Jesus*
Distinguished Research Professor,
Liberty University

We are living in a day when "truth is up for grabs" both within and outside the church. Ed Komoszewski, Jim Sawyer, and Dan Wallace have done a superb job of writing an in-depth, yet accessible, book that challenges the radical skepticism about Jesus flooding popular culture. I highly recommend it!

—CHIP INGRAM
President and CEO, Walk Thru the Bible
Teaching Pastor, *Living on the Edge* radio broadcast

"Who do men say that I am?" is a question Jesus asked his disciples, and it is one that is still being asked today. In *Reinventing Jesus*, the authors answer this question, addressing some of the most well-known arguments offered by those who do not confess that Jesus is Lord. They do so in a respectful way, with academic rigor and clarity of prose.

—FRANCIS J. BECKWITH
Associate Professor of Church-State Studies,
Baylor University

The authors of *Reinventing Jesus* convincingly demonstrate that the Jesus of faith and the Jesus of history are one and the same. Amidst the swirl of misinformation and myth assaulting the popular culture today, here is a clear, digestible explanation for anyone wanting to know the facts about how the New Testament and the church's earliest teachings were developed and transmitted.

—DAVID GREGORY
Author, *Dinner with a Perfect Stranger*

REINVENTING
JESUS

REINVENTING JESUS

HOW CONTEMPORARY SKEPTICS MISS THE REAL JESUS AND MISLEAD POPULAR CULTURE

J. ED KOMOSZEWSKI

M. JAMES SAWYER

DANIEL B. WALLACE

Kregel
Publications

Reinventing Jesus: How Contemporary Skeptics Miss the Real Jesus and Mislead Popular Culture

Published by Kregel Publications, a division of Kregel, Inc., P.O. Box 2607, Grand Rapids, MI 49501.

Cover photograph: 11th-century Greek manuscript of Luke 22.69 owned by the Center for the Study of New Testament Manuscripts, www.csntm.org. Image modified by Dave Lenz.

Library of Congress Cataloging-in-Publication Data
Komoszewski, J. Ed.
    Reinventing Jesus / by J. Ed Komoszewski, M. James Sawyer, and Daniel B. Wallace.
        p. cm.
    Includes bibliographical references and index.
    1. Apologetics. 2. Popular culture—Religious aspects—Christianity.
3. Jesus Christ—Historicity. 4. Bible—Evidences, authority, etc. I. Sawyer, M. James. II. Wallace, Daniel B. III. Title.
BT1103.K66   2006
239—dc22   2006012241

ISBN 10: 0-8254-2982-X
ISBN 13: 978-0-8254-2982-8

Printed in the United States of America

16 / 9 8

To our children:

Katie and Emily
Dan, Jon, Joel, and Josh
Noah, Ben, Andy, and Zack

May you always know
that you never need fear
the pursuit of truth.

CONTENTS

ACKNOWLEDGMENTS

We can't take credit for the substance of this book. Though we've tucked a few new (and we hope helpful!) insights into the pages, our priority has been to acquaint a vast audience with the best scholarship. What is of value in this volume is the work of great minds—past and present—that have wrestled vigorously and honestly with the historical data. We stand on the shoulders of giants.

We can only take partial credit for the shape of this book. Profound thanks go to the following: Jim Weaver, director of Academic and Professional Books at Kregel Publications, who caught the vision for the project, got it off the ground, and gave it direction; Jarl Waggoner, our editor, whose keen eye made the manuscript cleaner and clearer; Robert M. Bowman Jr., Dan Lioy, and Glenn L. Weaver, who made helpful suggestions for improving the manuscript; Grant Edwards, Eric Montgomery, and Ivan Yong (Dan Wallace's interns at Dallas Seminary during the 2004–05 academic year), who dug up vital information on the pseudepigrapha, Gnostic gospels, and canon; and other folks at Kregel Publications, whose patience, support, and guidance saw this book to completion. Keeping authors, who sometimes live too close to the data, moving down the right path was no small feat.

We accept responsibility for the shortcomings of this book. Because the evidence for historic Christianity is plentiful, though sometimes complex, we were frequently torn over what to say (or not say) and how to say it. No doubt we missed some things in our aim to pare a massive amount of evidence down to manageable size. And we know we didn't entirely escape our professorial tendencies to lapse into shoptalk or long-windedness. Fortunately, our wives—Shelley, Kay, and Pati—repeatedly read the pages of this book and constantly reminded us that not everyone has the inclination (or endurance!) to decipher the complex ramblings of men who live for this stuff. If anything we've written is judged to be clear and concise, they are owed a large share of the credit.

REINVENTING JESUS?

Attempts to reinvent Jesus are nothing new. The vines of radical skepticism toward the biblical Christ have been creeping up the walls of the ivory tower for two centuries.[1] But only in recent years has such intense cynicism sprouted at the grassroots. And it has spread quickly.

This comes as no surprise. After all, our culture is ripe for conspiracies about Jesus.

The seeds of radical skepticism have been widely sown by mass media for over a decade. From the Jesus Seminar—a fringe group of scholars whose color-coded version of the Gospels repeatedly made headlines in the 1990s—to the recent blockbuster novel and now movie *The Da Vinci Code*, skeptics of all stripes have used the popular media to promote their demoted versions of Jesus.

Distrust spawned in the media has taken firm root in our postmodern society, where the quest for truth has been replaced by a convenient tolerance for every idea. "That's just your interpretation!" has become the tired mantra of hurried people who can't be bothered by a thoughtful evaluation of evidence. It's simply easier to pretend all interpretations are created equal.

The radical skepticism sown in the media and rooted in postmodernism has been cultivated in an environment of biblical ignorance. As New Testament scholar Luke Timothy Johnson notes:

Americans generally have an abysmal level of knowledge of the Bible. In this world of mass ignorance, to have headlines proclaim that this or that fact about [Jesus] has been declared untrue by supposedly scientific inquiry has the effect of gospel. There is no basis on which most people can counter these authoritative-sounding statements.[2]

The media's assault on the biblical Jesus, postmodernism's laissez-faire attitude toward truth, and America's collective ignorance of Scripture have joined to create a culture of cynicism. In short, society has been conditioned to doubt.

To be sure, an open mind is a good thing. But a mind is open only as long as it is closing in on truth. Our hope is that you will approach the evidence in this book with an open mind, whether it's opened *completely* or *cautiously.*

If you are skeptical of the Jesus of the Bible, we hope you'll discover that a step toward him doesn't require leaving your brain behind. If you embrace the biblical Christ but think faith isn't concerned with matters of the mind, we want you to see that belief in the Incarnation—God entering the time-space world as a man two millennia ago—compels you to take history seriously. And if you are a Christian already committed to loving God with your heart *and* mind, we trust your faith will be strengthened and you'll be equipped to share it more compellingly.

This book is not written for scholars but for laypersons—*motivated* laypersons. While we have tried to capture the essence of arguments and avoid technical jargon, we realize that the material will stretch many of our readers. For one thing, much of it will be new. What's more, it will be far-reaching. Since the most probable interpretation of Jesus is grounded in the totality of evidence, it's essential to see the broad landscape. This may seem a bit much, but as one automotive manufacturer says, "It's not more than you need. It's just more than you're used to."

We have not endeavored to critique or review the various attempts at reinventing Jesus. Counterfeits are legion, and the list is growing.

Rather, our primary objective is to build a positive argument for the historical validity of Christianity. We contend that a progressive case, built on the following sequence of questions, undermines novel reconstructions of Jesus and underscores the enduring essence of the Christian faith:

- If the first Gospels were written decades after the life of Jesus, how do we know the writers got the story right? We'll tackle this question in our first section, "I Believe in Yesterday."
- If the writers got the story right, how do we know the Gospels and other New Testament documents were copied faithfully? Is what we have now what they wrote then? This will be addressed in "Politically Corrupt? The Tainting of Ancient New Testament Texts."
- If the writers got the story right and the documents were copied faithfully, how do we know the right documents were included in the Bible? How did the church decide which ones to include? Was there a conspiracy to hide competing books? Our third section explores the question "Did the Early Church Muzzle the Canon?"
- If the writers got the story right, the documents were copied faithfully, and the right documents were included in the Bible, what does this say about earliest belief in Jesus? Did Jesus' followers view him as more than a man from the onset of Christianity? Or was Jesus' divinity the invention of a fourth-century church council? We'll get to the bottom line in "The Divinity of Jesus: Early Tradition or Late Superstition?"
- If the writers got the story right, the documents were copied faithfully, the right documents were included in the Bible, and the Bible reveals belief in the divinity of Jesus, how do we know the whole thing wasn't plagiarized from other religions? Our case concludes with "Stealing Thunder: Did Christianity Rip Off Mythical Gods?"[3]

Our focus is mainly on the integrity of the New Testament text as it bears witness to historic belief in the divinity of Jesus. As such, our approach is primarily *historical* rather than *theological*. Of course, history and theology are inextricably linked. But our starting point is *not* belief in the Bible as divinely inspired or infallible—or anything similar. We believe that when the tools of the historian are applied to the biblical text, it builds its own case for its unique character. Or as one British scholar said, "We treat the Bible like any other book to show that it is *not like* any other book."

As you make your way through the pages of this volume, we invite you to recall the story of Thomas in John 20:24–28. Despite the testimony of the other disciples, Thomas doubted that Jesus had indeed risen from the dead. In fact, Thomas insisted, "Unless I see the wounds from the nails in his hands, and put my finger into the wounds from the nails, and put my hand into his side, I will never believe it!" (v. 25b). The living Jesus appeared to Thomas eight days later, saying, "Put your finger here, and examine my hands. Extend your hand and put it into my side. Do not continue in your unbelief, but believe" (v. 27). Interestingly, Jesus didn't scold Thomas for his doubt. Rather, he called him to examine the evidence. He invites you to do the same.

I BELIEVE IN YESTERDAY

Chapter 1

THE GOSPEL BEHIND
THE GOSPELS

The Jesus of the gospels is an imaginative theological construct, into which has been woven traces of that enigmatic sage from Nazareth— traces that cry out for recognition and liberation from the firm grip of those whose faith overpowered their memories. The search for the authentic Jesus is a search for the forgotten Jesus.

—ROBERT W. FUNK, ROY W. HOOVER, AND THE
JESUS SEMINAR, *The Five Gospels*, 4

How do we know the Gospel writers got it right? Why was the writing of the Gospels delayed for decades? What happened in the meantime? Isn't it likely that the Gospel writers (or Evangelists, as they are sometimes called) simply forgot most of the details about what Jesus said and did by the time they put pen to papyrus? Since all the Gospel writers were obviously people of faith, how do we know their faith didn't get in the way of accurate historical reporting? Since they were writing to specific communities, how do we know they didn't radically rework the material to meet the needs of their audiences? These and other questions will be explored in this section.

Defining Our Terms

As a preliminary task, it might be good to begin with some basic definitions, because these terms will be used throughout this section by scholars we are quoting. It's helpful to get some of the basic terminology down so that you can understand what they are saying.

We begin with the expression *Synoptic Gospels. Synoptic* refers to those works that take a similar point of view. The synoptics are the Gospels that look at Jesus in approximately the same way. Three Gospels seem to have quite a bit of overlap of material (both in wording and arrangement of narratives); hence they are known as the Synoptic Gospels—Matthew, Mark, and Luke. John's view of Jesus is so different that it has been estimated that 90 percent of the material in John is unique to that Gospel, while less than 10 percent of Mark is unique to his Gospel. Hence, John is *not* one of the Synoptic Gospels.

When thinking about the Synoptic Gospels, scholars are concerned about *source criticism*. This has to do especially with the *written* sources that the Evangelists used when writing their Gospels. "Criticism" in this sense relates to "research," or critical assessment; it has nothing to do with a critical *attitude*.

When it comes to source criticism, most scholars consider two starting points for a discussion. First, they are of the opinion that there is a *literary relationship* among the Synoptic Gospels. That is, Matthew, Mark, and Luke were not written in total isolation from each other; their authors engaged in literary borrowing. (We might call it plagiarism *to some degree*, but that is a modern concept. Besides, each Evangelist made his own contribution to his Gospel by selecting, arranging, and editing the material. The scholarly examination of such editing is known as *redaction criticism*.)

Second, in terms of literary relationship, most scholars hold to *Markan priority*. The usual formulation of this is that Mark was the first Gospel, and Matthew and Luke independently used Mark for their own Gospels. There is, however, a vocal minority of scholars who hold to *Matthean priority*. The usual formulation of this is that

Matthew wrote first, and Luke wrote later but independently of Matthew. Mark then utilized both Matthew and Luke to write his Gospel.

One other point about source criticism needs to be mentioned: those who hold to Markan priority generally hold to the *four-source hypothesis*. Essentially, this means that Matthew and Luke used four different sources to write their Gospels. These four sources are designated:

- Mark: The Gospel of Mark.
- Q: Either a written source that no longer exists or an oral source (i.e., the passing on of the life and especially teachings of Jesus through the spoken word rather than the written text), or a little of both.
- M: Material unique to Matthew. Some scholars think of it as a written source, while others think of it as oral; still others consider the Evangelist as his own source of information, if he was an eyewitness.
- L: Material unique to Luke. Since Luke's Gospel was definitely *not* written by an eyewitness (in Luke 1:1–4 the author mentions that he used sources for his Gospel), this has to be sources other than the Evangelist himself.

All of this terminology can be quite bewildering, and the issues involved are rather complex. But the basic concepts are relatively simple. As an imperfect illustration, consider modern translations of the Bible. Most Christians do not realize that many modern translations are conscious revisions of the King James Version of 1611. It started in 1885 with the Revised Version. Then, in 1901 the American Standard Version appeared. In 1952, the Revised Standard Version was published. After that, the New American Standard, New Revised Standard, and English Standard Version all came out. All of these modern translations are revisions of the KJV, as their prefaces note.

Now suppose these Bibles did not have prefaces or title pages. Could you tell which ones were earlier translations and which were later? Certainly, most readers would be able to recognize the KJV as the oldest translation. As well, the Revised Version and American Standard Version would be recognized as archaic in their language. But even the Revised Standard Version and the New American Standard would probably stand out because of the "thees" and "thous"— used in these translations only in prayers to God. And an expert in English would notice other shifts in language usage, helping to pinpoint when each Bible was produced.

Detecting the relationship between these translations is *source criticism.* Obviously, catching all the nuances of the literary relationships between the modern translations requires very detailed study. But only a basic knowledge of the history of the English Bible is needed to see that multiple sources do indeed stand behind our modern translations.

By pressing the analogy further, a couple of other points become clear. First, the modern translations do not differ from the KJV only in the mere updating of the language. There are also *interpretive* differences. The KJV at times interprets the Greek or Hebrew in a way that is ambiguous or misleading to the modern reader. Modern translations try to clarify the wording. At other times, the KJV simply missed the point of the original Greek or Hebrew, and modern translations correct the wording.

Second, there are *textual* differences. The KJV is based on later manuscripts, while modern translations utilize manuscripts that are many centuries older than those used for the KJV. We will discuss these matters in the next section of this book.

Certainly modern translations that are revisions of the King James Version do not simply duplicate KJV wording. They alter the wording, correct misleading impressions, and offer a different rendering based on different manuscripts. In short, even though there is literary dependence, it is not wholesale dependence. But the very fact that they begin by revising the KJV shows a great deal of respect for the old translation. However, the differences in interpretation and text also show their own emphases for their own, modern-day readers.

No doubt, by now you see many parallels between the Synoptic Gospels and Bible translations: *source criticism, redaction criticism,* and *literary dependence* are all relevant terms to both areas of study. The basic concepts of scholarly study of the Gospels are not difficult to grasp, even though the terminology may seem foreign to you.

There are many other terms we could discuss, but these should be enough to get you into the discussion without feeling like you're in a foreign country.

Now, let's return to the issue in this chapter. There are some skeptics who think that the faith of the early Christians somehow corrupted their memory of Jesus and transformed him into something that he was not. If true, the transformation was carried out in a coherent fashion and caught on throughout the Greco-Roman world with breathtaking speed.

The arguments of skeptics have been amply answered.[1] Our objective is simply to focus on a few things relevant to the person and work of Jesus Christ. Since so many of the questions that relate to the historical Jesus are more about what happened *after* the Gospels were written, we will focus on those issues in this book as well. Here we want to address the primary question: Did the Gospel writers get it right when it came to Jesus?

This means exploring the issue of the gospel behind the Gospels. That is, we will address the proclamation of the words and deeds of Jesus *before* they were written down in the Gospels. This is known as *oral tradition.* We will also look at the criteria that scholars use to determine what Jesus said. We need to know the *criteria of authenticity.* But what we need to keep in our frontal lobes in all this is the question, Were the Gospel writers faithful in recording what Jesus said and did?

WHY THE WAIT? THE DELAY OF THE WRITTEN GOSPELS

The Gospels, by any reckoning, were written some decades after Jesus lived. Several skeptics consider this an embarrassment to the historical roots of the Christian faith and argue that during these decades of silence Christians were fomenting a conspiracy. Earl Doherty boldly claims, "When one looks behind the Gospel curtain, the mosaic of Jesus of Nazareth very quickly disintegrates into component pieces and unrecognizable antecedents."[2] The Jesus Seminar is even more to the point: "The Jesus of the gospels is an imaginative theological construct, into which has been woven traces of that enigmatic sage from Nazareth—traces that cry out for recognition and liberation from the firm grip of those whose faith overpowered their memories. The search for the authentic Jesus is a search for the forgotten Jesus."[3]

At issue is what happened in the decades between the time Jesus lived and the writing of the Gospels. This issue involves two questions: Why was there such a delay in writing the Gospels? And, What happened in the interval between the life of Jesus and the written Gospels?

Many reasons could be given for the delay of the written Gospels, but even thinking about the question this way is perhaps looking at it from the wrong perspective. It might be better to ask, Why were the Gospels written at all? If we think in categories of *delay*, then this presupposes that the writing of the Gospels was in the minds of these authors from the beginning. However, that is almost certainly not the case. What was paramount in the apostles' earliest motives was *oral proclamation* of the gospel. They wanted to disseminate the word as quickly as possible. Starting in Jerusalem, and traveling throughout Judea, Galilee, and Samaria, the good news about Jesus Christ became known. When the Pharisee Paul became a Christian, the gospel then spread rapidly to other regions of the Mediterranean. By the time he got to Thessalonica in the late 40s, the Jews who opposed his message complained to the city council that Paul and Silas had "stirred up trouble throughout the world" (Acts 17:6).

In the book of Acts a common refrain is that the gospel was spreading and the young church was growing rapidly (Acts 2:47; 6:7; 9:31; 12:24; 13:49; 16:5; 19:20; 28:31). Paul confirms this in his letters. He commends the Thessalonians for making known the gospel he preached to them (1 Thess. 1:8–10) and tells the Romans that their faith "is proclaimed throughout the whole world" (Rom. 1:8). We also see strong evidence of the spread of the gospel in other letters (e.g., James 1:1; 1 Peter 1:1; Jude 3).

In other words, the apostles and leaders of the young church were preoccupied with broadcasting the gospel orally. There was no need to think about a written gospel at this time. The remarkable speed with which the good news of Jesus Christ became known throughout the Roman Empire in the first few years of the church's existence is testimony to the apostles' success in the task of oral proclamation.

Scholars often point to two catalysts that prompted the writing of the Gospels. First, the apostles started to die off. And second, the Lord's return was evidently not going to happen within the first few decades of the church's existence. These two factors are often suggested as the main reasons why the Gospels began to be written.

However, if the Gospels were written because the apostles were dying off, we would expect them to be written to *their* communities. However, at least two of the four Gospels (Mark and Luke), and probably three (John), were written to Gentile Christians, and the principal apostle to the Gentiles was Paul, not one of the original Twelve. Paul was never in a position to write a Gospel in the first place because he did not know Jesus in his earthly existence.[4] And if the Gospels were written before the Jewish War (66–70)—a possibility we will consider next—then thoughts about the delay of the Lord's return might not have been as prominent. In reality, each one of the Gospels has its own reasons for being written when it was written and to whom. But the fundamental point that the oral proclamation of the gospel was of primary concern to the leaders of the church in the first few decades is vital to remember.

What kind of delay are we actually talking about? How long did it take for the four Gospels to be written? Most scholars regard Mark as the first Gospel, written no later than the 60s. If Jesus died in 30 or 33 (there is some debate between these two dates), then the first Gospel would have been written within four decades of the death of Jesus.

Even if Mark were written this late, there would have been plenty of eyewitnesses still living to confirm the truth of what he wrote. But there is significant evidence to suggest that he wrote earlier than this. The dating of the New Testament books can be rather involved. Without trying to make the matter too simplistic, we wish to highlight just a few points.

First, if Luke used Mark to write his Gospel (as most scholars believe), then Mark, of course, must have been written prior to Luke's Gospel.

Second, Luke is in reality the first volume of a two-volume work; Acts is the second volume. And there is increasing evidence that Acts was written in the early 60s, prior to Paul's trial in Rome. (After all, the book begins with a bang but ends with a whimper—dragging on for chapter after chapter in anticipation of the trial that *never* comes. But if Acts is meant, in part, as some sort of "trial brief," then the reason it doesn't get to the trial makes sense.)[5]

Third, the Olivet discourse, in which Jesus predicts the destruction of Jerusalem, is found in Mark 13. Many scholars simply deny the possibility of true prophecy in the Bible and hence demand a date after 70 for Mark (as well as Matthew and Luke). But J. A. T. Robinson, in *Redating the New Testament*, made the interesting case that the prophecy in Mark 13 actually argues for a date prior to 66. He points out that the specifics of the Olivet discourse do not altogether match what we know of the Jewish War: "'The abomination of desolation' cannot itself refer to the destruction of the sanctuary in August 70 or to its desecration by Titus' soldiers in sacrificing to their standards. [Furthermore,] by that time it was far too late for anyone in Judaea to take to the hills, which had been in enemy hands since the end of 67."[6] Yet in Mark 13:14, Jesus tells his disciples, "But when you see *the abomination of desolation* standing where it should not be (let the reader understand), then those in Judea must flee to the mountains." Robinson concludes, "I fail to see any motive for preserving, let alone inventing, prophecies long after the dust had settled in Judaea, unless it be to present Jesus as prognosticator of uncanny accuracy *(in which case the evangelists have defeated the exercise by including palpably unfulfilled predictions).*"[7]

Robinson is correct that the prophecy in Mark 13 was not fulfilled exactly as it was recorded. But whether the Jewish War is all that was envisioned in the prophecy is a different matter. Nevertheless, his fundamental point is solid, increasing the likelihood that Mark was written prior to 70.

What all this means for Matthew and Luke is simply that they too were most likely written before 70. Again, the two basic reasons to argue this are that (1) Luke is the first volume of Luke-Acts and Acts was most likely written in the early 60s; and (2) the argument that the Gospels must be written after 70 because predictive prophecy is impossible backfires in the Olivet discourse (recorded in all three Synoptic Gospels) since the prophecy was not completely fulfilled at that time.[8]

WHAT HAPPENED IN THE MEANTIME?

A fundamental disagreement in scholarly circles over the life of Jesus concerns the role that oral tradition played. Skeptics such as Robert W. Funk and the Jesus Seminar argue implicitly that the oral tradition behind the Gospels was isolated and faulty to the extreme:

> Scholars of the gospels are faced with a similar problem: Much of the lore recorded in the gospels and elsewhere in the Bible is folklore, which means that it is wrapped in memories that have been edited, deleted, augmented, and combined many times over many years.[9]

As we noted above, the interval between Jesus and the written Gospels was not dormant. The apostles and other eyewitnesses were proclaiming the good news about Jesus Christ wherever they went. This, of course, would have happened both in public settings and in private meetings. People hungry to know about the Lord would inquire of the apostles. The stories about Jesus and the sayings of Jesus would have been repeated hundreds, perhaps thousands, of times by dozens of eyewitnesses before the first Gospel was ever penned.

The period of oral proclamation involves some implications for the accuracy of the written Gospels. If the earliest proclamation about Jesus was altered in later years, then surely first-generation *Christians* would know about the changes and would object to them. It would not even take outsiders to object to the "new and improved Christianity," since those who were already believers would have serious problems with the differences in the content of their belief. Not only this, but the rapid spread of the gospel message meant that *there were no longer controls on the content.* That is, once the gospel spread beyond Jerusalem, the apostles were no longer in a position to alter it without notice. And the gospel indeed spread from day one of the church's existence—the Day of Pentecost—since Peter proclaimed the message to Jews who had traveled from as far away as Rome (Acts 2:9–11). So, if there was some sort of conspiracy—or a faith that "overpowered their memories," as the Jesus Seminar argues—then it had to have been formulated before the Day of Pentecost.

The problem with this hypothesis is twofold. First, it is hardly conceivable that the apostles could have forgotten so much about the "real" Jesus in a matter of fifty days after his crucifixion and allowed their faith in him to overpower their memories of him. Second, they were not the only witnesses to Jesus Christ. Hundreds of other followers of Jesus knew him well, had seen his miracles, and had heard his messages. What Jesus taught and what Jesus did were not things done in secret. This hypothesis is so full of holes that no scholar holds to it.

This leaves us with only two alternatives: either the gospel message changed dramatically over several *years,* or it remained stable over several years—until the time it was written down. The first alternative, as we noticed above, is improbable in the extreme. British scholar Vincent Taylor noted this long ago. His insights are still worth quoting today. In discussing form criticism (the view that the Gospels were patchwork efforts that invented situations in which to place stories about Jesus[10]), he does not mince words:

> It is on this question of eyewitnesses that Form-Criticism presents a very vulnerable front. If the Form-Critics are

right, the disciples must have been translated to heaven immediately after the Resurrection. As Bultmann sees it, the primitive community exists *in vacuo* [in isolation], cut off from its founders by the walls of an inexplicable ignorance. Like Robinson Crusoe it must do the best it can. Unable to turn to any one for information, it must invent situations for the words of Jesus, and put into His lips sayings which personal memory cannot check. All this is absurd. . . . However disturbing to the smooth working of theories the influence of eyewitnesses on the formation of the tradition cannot possibly be ignored. The one hundred and twenty at Pentecost did not go into permanent retreat; for at least a generation they moved among the young Palestinian communities, and through preaching and fellowship their recollections were at the disposal of those who sought information. . . . But when all qualifications have been made, the presence of personal testimony is an element in the formative process which it is folly to ignore.[11]

Taylor wrote these words in 1933. Sixty years later, the Jesus Seminar proclaimed that faith in Jesus overpowered the apostles' memories and that the real Jesus had been forgotten—the very points that Taylor debunked! And the fact is, Taylor's argument has been repeated by other scholars for decades. They have added other arguments as well, but his fundamental tenets have not been answered.

We are left with one alternative: the proclamation of the gospel had a stable core that was reproduced in public and private settings and confirmed by eyewitnesses. We need to examine *how* faithfully an "oral culture" would have been able to remember Jesus Christ, which is the subject of chapter 2.

Chapter 2

ORAL TRADITION AND A
MEMORIZING CULTURE

*. . . memory is as much or more creative reconstruction as accurate
recollection.*

—JOHN DOMINIC CROSSAN,
The Birth of Christianity, 59

REMEMBERING JESUS

How accurate were the disciples in transmitting the proclamation about Jesus? Opinions vary about the disciples' memory
of Jesus—from almost zero ability to exacting duplication. Those
who argue that the disciples simply forgot (such as John Dominic
Crossan[1]) or that their faith overpowered their memories (such as
the Jesus Seminar[2]) have some roadblocks in their way.

As we mentioned in chapter 1 (pp. 29–31), their recollections were
not individual memories but *collective* ones—confirmed by other
eyewitnesses and burned into their minds by the constant retelling
of the story. Thus, both the repetition of the stories about Jesus
and the verification of such by other eyewitnesses served as checks

and balances on the apostles' accuracy.[3] *Memory in community* is a deathblow to the view that the disciples simply forgot the real Jesus.

Another deficiency in Crossan's approach is that his anecdotes for faulty memories simply do not relate to *deifying* a man or anything like it! They involve such instances as forgetting where one was when he or she learned of the *Challenger* explosion in 1986 or forgetting the lines of a memorized poem. Yet, though some people forgot where *they* were when the *Challenger* exploded, did they forget that the *Challenger* was lost in an explosion or embellish the story? Applying this to the Gospels, Crossan's illustrations show only that the time and place of Jesus' miracles or sayings could have gotten muddled in the disciples' minds; there would have been no hint of changing a non-miracle into a miracle. Consider that this was memory in community, in which the disciples would surely have been talking with each other immediately after one of Jesus' miracles or messages. Also remember that the disciples were eyewitnesses to the events. Given this situation, Crossan's entire construct becomes largely irrelevant when applied to the Gospels.

Remarkably, the Jesus Seminar (of which Crossan was a member) seems to recognize that faulty memory is not an adequate explanation for the Jesus of the written Gospels. For them, *faith* has trumped memory. At least this is a better explanation for what we see in the Gospels, but it involves, as we have seen, a conspiracy theory that leaves too many loose ends.

On the other end of the spectrum are those who believe that the disciples reproduced verbatim what Jesus said. Birger Gerhardsson has brought together a massive amount of data to show how deeply entrenched the culture of memory was in the ancient Jewish world.[4] He shows that Jesus would have been regarded as a rabbi and his followers as disciples. In such a relationship memorizing the master's words would have been completely natural. He notes, for example:

> A well-known saying of Hillel is reproduced in b. Ḥag. 9b (bar.): "The man who repeats his chapter ... one hundred times is not to be compared with the man who repeats it

one hundred and one times." And when the question of the Rabbis' repetition for their pupils is taken up, it is the tireless Rabbi who is praised. Thus R. Perida is treated as exemplary; he used to repeat every passage "four hundred times" for a dull pupil, and once when the pupil in question had still not absorbed the passage, R. Perida proceeded to repeat it "four hundred times" more. This hyperbolical description gives us a most eloquent picture of the simple, yet effective, methods used by teachers when they wished to pass on doctrinal passages to their pupils.[5]

The problem is that the verbatim quotation view doesn't square completely with the written Gospels. Many scholars point out that ancient historians were not concerned with quoting the very words of a person but were very much concerned with getting the gist of what he had to say.[6] This is almost surely the case with the Gospel writers as well.[7] For now, we simply need to point out that the Gospels don't always record the words of Jesus (or others) in exactly the same way—even for sayings that must surely have been uttered on only one occasion (e.g., Jesus' cry from the cross or the heavenly voice at Jesus' baptism). In the least, this suggests that Gerhardsson's view is somewhat overstated.

At the same time, Gerhardsson has put forth real parallels from the culture of the ancient Jewish rabbis and their disciples.[8] This contrasts with the general tenor of those who see memory as individual and untrustworthy. Crossan, for example, brings in many anecdotes from modern society to show how our memories play tricks on us. Even apart from the probability that the differences in abilities to memorize between modern and ancient cultures must surely be significant, almost all of his illustrations are of individuals whose memory is based on hearing something said, rather than of communities (or groups of individuals) who were eyewitnesses.[9] His anecdotes are seriously deficient as true and proper parallels.[10]

GETTING IT RIGHT

Perhaps the best model for what the disciples actually did in re-membering Jesus was developed by Kenneth Bailey. He speaks of an "informal controlled oral tradition."[11] He argues that, although there was some flexibility in the retelling of stories in an oral culture such as that of ancient Palestine, a stable core was invariably repeated exactly the same. In his epic volume, *Jesus Remembered*, New Testament scholar James D. G. Dunn affirms Bailey's insights:

> The crucial question, of course, is whether such an under-standing of oral tradition provides an explanatory model for the Jesus tradition, and in particular, whether we can find the marks of such "informal, controlled oral tradition" in the Synoptic tradition itself. I believe it does and think we can.[12]

A similar viewpoint is put forth by Darrell Bock in his essay, "The Words of Jesus in the Gospels: Live, Jive, or Memorex?"[13] He argues that "each evangelist retells the living and powerful words of Jesus in a fresh way for his readers, while faithfully and accurately presenting the 'gist' of what Jesus said. I call this approach one that recognizes the Jesus tradition as 'live' in its dynamic and quality."[14]

We have argued that the apostles and other eyewitnesses would surely have told the story of Jesus repeatedly by the time the Gospels were written. This repetition by multiple witnesses would provide quality control over the tradition that was passed on. But four other things should be noted. First, as Gerhardsson observes:

> In the tradition of western culture it is only in our own day that the memory has been *effectively* unloaded into books. Not until our own day have we learned to accept a form of education which to a great extent consists of being able to find the material which is required in the right books, with-out needing to carry it all in the memory. Not until our day

has the pedagogical revolution taken place which has been called "the dethronement of memory."[15]

This is such an important point—though largely ignored by those who assume that the disciples forgot Jesus—that it needs to be stated differently (lest you forget!). Dunn puts it this way:

> One of the most striking flaws in the quest of the historical Jesus results from the fact that it was undertaken in the age of the printed word. Gutenberg and Caxton had instituted a revolution in human perspective in sixteenth-century Europe much more significant in its outworkings than the revolution associated with the names of Copernicus and Galileo.... Consequently, we in the West simply take it for granted that the basis of a sound education is the ability to read and write.... In a word, we are all children of Gutenberg.[16]

In terms of a deteriorating memory, there are actually three great epics: the period before the printing press; the centuries from the printing press to the personal computer; and the present age of the personal computer. It may well be that some day the names of Jobs and Gates will be mentioned in the same breath with Gutenberg. Anyone who teaches Greek or Hebrew knows how increasingly difficult it is today to convince students of the need to memorize paradigms and vocabulary! Regardless, memorization has been de-emphasized for a long time in education due to the availability of the printed page.

Second, as Bock noted, "If the role of oral tradition was important to the ancients in general, it was especially important to Jewish culture."[17] This is the point that Gerhardsson underscores with ample illustrations.

Third, Jesus' instructions were often, if not usually, uttered in rhythmic or otherwise memorable fashion. As Barnett notes, "Much of his teaching is cast in poetic form, employing alliteration [repetition of same sounds or letters], paronomasia [puns, word-plays], assonance [resemblance of sound], parallelism, and rhyme. According to R. Riesner, 80 percent of Jesus' teaching is cast in poetic form."[18] At the least, this suggests that Jesus *expected* his disciples to learn from him, and learn well, both the content and the form of much of his instruction.

Fourth, some of Jesus' disciples may well have taken notes during his lifetime.[19] Along these lines, an interesting parallel is found in the Dead Sea Scrolls, where "attention is drawn to the Teacher of Righteousness, founder of the Qumran sect, whose teachings appear to have been written down during his lifetime."[20] There is no reason why some of the disciples could not have taken notes, though there is also no proof that they did.

In conclusion, the ancient Jewish culture, the relation of the disciples to Jesus as their rabbi, the multiple witnesses, and the repetition of the stories about Jesus from the very beginning all point to a strong oral tradition behind the written Gospels. Although this oral culture does not suggest that the Evangelists always wrote down verbatim what Jesus said, they certainly got the essence right. (And this is in line with ancient historical reporting.) But besides the general evidence from oral tradition, there is the specific evidence known as the criteria of authenticity. These criteria also point to the faithfulness of the Gospels in the proclamation about Jesus. We will look at these criteria in our next chapter.

Chapter 3

AN ECCENTRIC JESUS AND THE CRITERIA OF AUTHENTICITY

Beware of finding a Jesus entirely congenial to you.
—ROBERT W. FUNK, ROY W. HOOVER, AND THE
JESUS SEMINAR, *The Five Gospels,* 5

How do critical scholars go about determining whether Jesus said something recorded in the Gospels? They utilize what are called *the criteria of authenticity.* Although there are several such criteria, we will look specifically at four of the most important ones.

THE CRITERION OF DISSIMILARITY

First is the criterion of *dissimilarity.* This criterion essentially says that if a saying attributed to Jesus differed from the teachings of the Judaism of his day and from what the early church later taught, then the saying must be authentic. The reason for this is easy to understand: If such a saying cannot be found in Judaism prior to Jesus, then there is good reason to think that it really goes back to him and not earlier. And if the early church did not pick up on it, then obviously they did not invent the saying and put it on Jesus' lips. The Jesus Seminar states as a *fact* that "we know that the evangelists not infrequently ascribed Christian words to Jesus—they made him talk like a Christian."[1] Whether such dogmatism is warranted is a matter we will not take up here. We simply want to note that it is an important criterion that Jesus said things that were *unique*.

Application of this criterion usually is restricted to Jesus' difference from Judaism rather than Christianity. For example, the Jesus Seminar notes that the saying in Mark 7:15 ("There is nothing outside of a person that can defile him by going into him. Rather, it is what comes out of a person that defiles him") surely must be an authentic saying of Jesus because this is "a broadside against his own religious traditions."[2] But this principle was picked up by early Christianity (e.g., 1 Tim. 4:4: "For every creation of God is good and no food is to be rejected if it is received with thanksgiving"), so it is not absolutely unique to Jesus.

A major problem with the criterion of dissimilarity is that if it is observed rigidly, the only Jesus we have left is an eccentric Jesus— one who had nothing in common with the Judaism of his day and had no influence on his followers! As Darrell Bock observes, "If both sides of the dissimilarity are affirmed, so that Jesus differs from *both* Judaism *and* the early church, then Jesus becomes a decidedly odd figure, totally detached from his cultural heritage *and* ideologically estranged from the movement he is responsible for founding. One wonders how he ever came to be taken seriously."[3]

A second problem with this criterion is that scholars often use it to make a *negative* assessment on whether Jesus could have said something. But in light of its first inherent weakness, this criterion really can legitimately be used only to make a positive assessment. That is, it should not be used to deny that Jesus said something (since what he said could indeed be similar to the Judaism of his day or the early church). This is true of virtually all of the criteria of authenticity: *these criteria should not be used to deny what Jesus might have said, but only to confirm it.* Unfortunately, critical scholarship applies these criteria in ways they are not designed for. If we were to apply this criterion to the work of the Jesus Seminar, one wonders what would be left of their work—for what they say has been said by many others before them and after them.

A third problem is that the Jesus Seminar and others often apply this criterion inconsistently. That is, even when a saying passes the most rigorous dissimilarity test, its authenticity might still be reject-ed. For example, Jesus seems to be the only person in ancient Judaism to have placed an "amen" at the beginning of his own statements. In Judaism, *amen* was used almost exclusively to affirm God's will or to agree with statements about his character.[4] But in the Gospels, Jesus used "amen" at the *beginning of his own statements*—as if to say that what he is about to declare is the will and word of God. And in the twenty-five times that such an "amen" occurs in John, it is always doubled (thus, "amen, amen, I say to you . . ."). The usage in both the Synoptic Gospels and in John is dissimilar to anything in Judaism or early Christianity. Almost invariably, Jesus' use of *amen* signals a solemn statement about "the history of the kingdom of God bound up with His person. Thus in the ἀμήν [*amēn*, 'amen'] preceding the λέγω ὑμῖν [*legō humin*, 'I say to you'] of Jesus we have the whole of Christology *in nuce* ['in a nutshell']."[5] These sayings are both unique to Jesus and have a consistent content—a content that addresses what he thought of himself in relation to God's kingdom.

Before we discuss what the Jesus Seminar does with these unique sayings of Jesus, a word should be said about their colored beads. The Jesus Seminar made international headlines for the use of these beads, most likely because the general public could easily grasp the concept. Each member of the Jesus Seminar cast a vote by placing a bead into a box. Each bead was red, pink, gray, or black, with the following meanings:

> **red:** **Jesus undoubtedly said this or something very like it.**
>
> **pink:** **Jesus probably said something like this.**

> gray: Jesus did not say this, but the ideas contained
>   in it are close to his own.
>
> black: Jesus did not say this; it represents the per-
>   spective or content of a later or different
>   tradition.[6]

How does the Jesus Seminar deal with such a unique saying? Of the seventy-five "amen"-prefixed sayings of Jesus, only *four* are considered likely to go back to Jesus in some sense (all get the color pink). In addition there are twenty "gray" sayings. The rest (fifty-one) are black.[7] What would cause the Jesus Seminar to reject the majority of "amen"-prefixed sayings of Jesus? Some other criterion is apparently overriding the criterion of dissimilarity. We will look at another example to see what it is.

According to the four Gospels, *"the* Son of Man" was Jesus' favorite self-designation. What is unusual about the phrase is that it is almost never found in ancient Judaism or early Christian literature—except when it appears on the lips of Jesus. The British scholar C. F. D. Moule draws the conclusion that

> the simplest explanation of the almost entire consistency
> with which the definite singular is confined to Christian
> sayings is to postulate that Jesus did refer to Dan 7, speaking
> of "*the* Son of man [whom you know from that vision]." . . .
> To attribute the phrase to Jesus himself is not to deny that
> some of the Son of Man sayings in the Gospels may well be
> an addition modeled on the original sayings; but I can think
> of no reason why there should not be a dominical origin for
> each of the main types of sayings.[8]

At the least, Moule is arguing from the criterion of dissimilarity for the authenticity of such "Son of Man" sayings in the Gospels.

What does the Jesus Seminar do with these sayings? Bock notes that they "are excluded as being authentic, except when they describe humans as the son of man, a usage attested to in Judaism through its use in the Psalter and Ezekiel! The reason why the title 'Son of Man' is excluded is the fact that it expresses such a high Christological view of Jesus."[9]

Regarding the Jesus Seminar's inconsistent application of this criterion, Bock observes:

> What this "Son of Man" example reveals perhaps is a hidden criterion—a Christological standard—in the Seminar's evaluation of sayings: If a saying says Jesus is more than a sage and a teller of parables, then it is not authentic. But this approach begs the question. If, on the other hand, the critical criteria are not consistently applied by the Seminar's scholars, then certainly a claim of bias may be justified. On the other hand, if Jesus was merely a sage and teller of parables, then why all the fuss over him? Where did the severe animosity surrounding him come from? How can they explain his rejection, given their slight portion of authentic sayings on mostly proverbial topics?[10]

Bock raises several significant points here. Not only is the Jesus Seminar inconsistent in applying its own principles due to a strong bias against seeing Jesus as more than a man, but such bias also leaves them with a Jesus whose death as a *criminal* is a huge mystery. All historians know that an effect must have a sufficient cause. But in the Jesus Seminar's reconstructed and tamed Jesus, the cause is not sufficient for the effect of his crucifixion.

We might add one other point here that we will address more fully in the rest of this book. In the first century A.D., the state of Jewish monotheism was remarkably strong. But the Gospels present Jesus as claiming to be more than merely a prophet, more than a sage, more than a storyteller. His actions as well as his words show him coming perilously close to claiming to be divine. The Judaism of Jesus' day certainly would have an aversion to this—and did! But would the first Christians readily accept it? Since the first Christians were Jews, they too would have the same problems with this idea as the rest of their Jewish culture. To the extent that the Gospels are rooted in Palestinian soil, the criterion of dissimilarity reveals Jesus to be more than a mere man. But if someone is simply not open to this possibility, only then will this criterion—and thus, Jesus' divinity—be rejected.

CRITERION OF MULTIPLE ATTESTATION

Second is the criterion of *multiple attestation.* This criterion says that "when a saying appears either in multiple sources (M, L, Q, Mark) or in multiple forms ([e.g.], in a miracle account, a parable, and/or apocalyptic settings)" then it has multiple attestation.[11] As a reminder of what we said at the beginning of this section, M, L, Q, and Mark refer to the four sources that are used by Matthew and Luke. M simply means material unique to Matthew, L is material unique to Luke, and Mark is the Gospel of Mark. Q refers to the common material between Luke and Matthew and may have been a written or an oral source or a combination of the two.

As with the criterion of dissimilarity, the rigorous application of this criterion would give us a truncated Jesus, accepting only those sayings that he repeated in different contexts and in different ways. What it leaves out are many sayings uttered in unique situations or said only once. Like the criterion of dissimilarity, this criterion is limited in that it should be used only for *positive* affirmations of what Jesus said. If a saying of Jesus is recorded just once, does this mean that he did not really say it? If we were to apply that criterion to most other ancient historical figures, we would have to throw out most of what we know of ancient history! As Bock notes, "This criterion is helpful for what it includes, though one must be careful not to suggest that failure of a saying to be attested in multiple sources is adequate reason for rejecting it."[12]

Sadly, the Jesus Seminar and others use this criterion both positively *and negatively.* Yet, if we were to apply this criterion to the writings attributed to Robert Funk—which are far more plentiful than the words of Jesus in the Gospels—how would they fare? Some of his volumes were on the cutting edge of biblical scholarship while others were at least provocative, but what he said in these volumes was not echoed in other works of his. He often dealt with one issue in a book, abandoning the topic completely in later writings. Does this mean that he didn't really write those books and say these things?

In addition, like the criterion of dissimilarity, the criterion of multiple attestation is applied inconsistently by the Jesus Seminar. For example, consider the expression "I have come"/"the Son of Man has come," one of Jesus' pet phrases by which he introduced his mission. This is found in multiple sources. It is, in fact, found in *all four synoptic sources*—M, Mark, Q, and L (see Matt. 5:17; 11:19 [M]; Mark 2:17; 10:45 [Mark]; Matt. 10:34–35/Luke 12:49–51 [Q]; and Luke 19:10 [L]).[13] That he would speak of *his mission* (which "I have come" implies) obviously shows that he is more than a sage, a poet, or a peasant philosopher. Included in this mix of sayings is Mark 10:45 ("For even the Son of Man did not come to be served but to serve, and to give his life as a ransom for many"). One of the finest scholars on Luke's Gospel today, Darrell Bock, has observed the irony that

> the Jesus Seminar regards much of this famous line as "Mark's creation," printed in gray. Why do they reject it? The original saying in their view was about service, not redemption. The service concept belongs to Jesus, but not the redemptive idea. They argue that Luke's shorter version indicates that Mark made the change and supplied the more theological version of what originally was just a proverb, even though Mark, in this case, is recognized by all as the earlier Gospel![14]

Bock concludes by noting the inconsistency in the Jesus Seminar's methods:

> Again, the real criterion applied to this saying is not multiple attestation but the hidden Christological standard of the

Seminar that is applied even when the source evidence goes the other direction. In fact, one can suggest that Christology is the *real* issue in the debate over many sayings, much more so than history or the objective application of abstract criteria. In an almost circular kind of way, a saying is accepted because it reflects a certain circumscribed Christology formed on an impression not created by the consistent application of the criteria, but by the preconceived, limited Christology. This Christology is affirmed because Jesus was only, it is argued on the basis of the accepted sayings, a sage and teller of parables.[15]

CRITERION OF COHERENCE

Third is the criterion of *coherence.* This criterion argues that whatever else scholars discover about Jesus in the Gospels, it should conform to or *cohere* with the rest of the picture that scholars have painted of the real, or historical, Jesus. Of course, to the extent that they have painted an inaccurate picture of the real Jesus, this criterion will be invalid. Now the Jesus Seminar affirms only 18 percent of Jesus' words as authentic—as going back to Jesus either verbally or conceptually.[16] To the extent that that database is too small, the Jesus Seminar's Jesus is too small. Their inconsistencies in applying the other two criteria have already given them a skewed Jesus. The criterion of coherence is thus only valid when the first two criteria are applied properly.

CRITERION OF EMBARRASSMENT

A fourth criterion is that of *embarrassment.* This has to do with things in the Gospels that could be perceived to be an embarrassment to early Christians, to the disciples, or even to Jesus. The only reason to put such embarrassing sayings in the Gospels is that they were really uttered. It is hard to imagine the early Christians *inventing* embarrassments for themselves when they already had enough problems from persecution! Although this criterion is very important, like the others it is not used consistently by the Jesus Seminar.

For example, in Mark 13:32, Jesus declares, "But as for that day or hour no one knows it—neither the angels in heaven, nor the Son—except the Father." The early church came to see Jesus as more than a man—in fact, as deity in the flesh. So, such a statement would indeed cause them some embarrassment.[17] That Jesus identifies himself as "Son" here fits perfectly with his other self-descriptions. But the Jesus Seminar regards this saying as inauthentic. Why? "The Jesus Seminar was in general agreement that Jesus did not make chronological predictions about the end of history at all."[18] Here we plainly see a criterion against a high view of Jesus at work. But if the Jesus Seminar is against seeing Jesus as more than a man as an *a priori* assumption, wouldn't that unduly bias them in any assessment about who the real Jesus was? How can they honestly, openly assess the data if it is simply not possible for Jesus to predict the future?

There are other instances of the criterion of embarrassment in the Gospels. For example, the many negative statements in the Gospel of Mark about the first heroes of Christianity—the apostles—fits this criterion. Jesus' frequent rebukes of the disciples for their lack of faith, their apparent dullness in understanding his words, and their wrangling for positions of leadership all point to authenticity. It is hard to read the Gospel of Mark without getting a negative impression of the apostles, yet this is the earliest of the Gospels according to most scholars. Eyewitnesses would still be around, including some of the apostles. Negative statements are strong indications that these things were said. "The fact that the perplexing and offensive material . . . was preserved at all and reached Mark says much for the general reliability of the sources used by him."[19]

Another illustration of the criterion of embarrassment would be the first witnesses to the resurrection of Jesus. All four Gospels say that *women* were the first ones to the tomb, the first ones to learn that Jesus was alive (Matt. 28:1–10; Mark 16:1–8; Luke 24:1–11; John 20:1–14). Why should this cause embarrassment? Because women in Jewish society were not considered credible witnesses.[20] No wonder the disciples reacted as they did in Luke 24:11: "But these words [that the women spoke] seemed like pure nonsense to them, and they did not believe them."

By the criterion of embarrassment, the Jesus Seminar has fully agreed that Jesus was indeed baptized by John (especially since John's baptism was a baptism of repentance).[21] Why, then, do they reject the saying in Mark 13:32 or the testimony that Jesus had risen from the dead?

As Bock has noted, the Jesus Seminar has been inconsistent in the use of their own criteria, apparently because of a hidden agenda. Ironically, the Jesus Seminar warned readers about the "temptation . . . to create Jesus in our own image, to marshal the facts to support preconceived convictions."[22] They sum up all of their criteria as a single general rule: "Beware of finding a Jesus entirely congenial to you."[23] We couldn't agree more.

OTHER CONSIDERATIONS

One of the things missing in all these criteria is intersection with other parts of the New Testament. The rest of the New Testament, for example, places a high view on preserving the tradition, on keeping the fundamental truths about Jesus intact.

In Galatians 2, Paul expresses concern about the purity of his gospel. Paul had been preaching the gospel as he knew it for fourteen years. Then he came to Jerusalem to verify that his gospel was exactly the same as that of the rest of the apostles—those who had known Jesus in the flesh. He says, "But I did so only in a private meeting with the influential people, to make sure that I was not running—or had not run—in vain" (v. 2). He says that "those influential leaders added nothing to my message" (v. 6). Here we see, in an indisputable letter from the apostle Paul, that the gospel that Paul had been preaching for years was the same gospel that the rest of the apostles preached.

In Galatians 1, Paul says that about three years after his conversion, the church in Jerusalem had heard that he was preaching "the faith he once tried to destroy" (v. 23). What is significant here is the continuity between the apostles' gospel *prior to Paul's conversion* and Paul's gospel shortly thereafter. There is no hint of collusion, no sense that the gospel had changed over the years. From the very beginning, the good news about Jesus Christ always had the same key elements. There is a large gap left in scholars' use of the criteria of authenticity when they fail to consider the independent confirmation from Paul that *the gospel from the beginning was the same gospel.* Although such confirmation does not deal with many particulars in the life of Jesus,[24] the reasons for Jesus' death, the belief in his resurrection, the title *Messiah,* and by implication his performing of miracles, are all part of this independent confirmation. To reduce Jesus to a mere sage, as some skeptics want to do, simply does not handle the historical data adequately. Apart from the fact that such a minimalist view of Jesus cannot explain why he died on a cross as a criminal, to categorically deny that Jesus was called Messiah by his disciples or that he performed miracles is to ignore the available confirmatory data.

CONCLUSION

We have argued in this section that the period between Jesus and the writing of the Gospels was anything but dormant. The gospel spread, and the narratives about Jesus' life and teachings were repeated hundreds or thousands of times by reliable eyewitnesses. We also have noted that the Jewish culture of the first century A.D. was a memorizing culture. This, coupled with eyewitness testimony and the confirmation of memory in community rather than merely by individuals, argues strongly that the oral tradition behind the written Gospels was a stable, reliable source of information. We also have noted that the criteria of authenticity that scholars employ to determine what Jesus said and did can only make positive assessments, not negative ones. Otherwise, the Jesus portrayed is an eccentric Jesus who learned nothing from his own culture and made no impact on his followers.

After critiquing various critical reconstructions of the life of Jesus, Scot McKnight addresses the basic issue of historical cause-and-effect: "My fundamental disagreement with each of them is that *such a Jesus would never have been crucified, would never have drawn the fire that he did, would never have commanded the following that he did, and would never have created a movement that still shakes the world.*"[25]

In sum, it is hard to avoid James D. G. Dunn's conclusion about oral tradition: "What we today are confronted with in the Gospels is not the top layer (last edition) of a series of increasingly impenetrable layers, but the living tradition of Christian celebration which takes us with surprising immediacy to the heart of the first memories of Jesus."[26]

PART 2

POLITICALLY CORRUPT?

*The Tainting of Ancient
New Testament Texts*

Chapter 4

CAN WE TRUST THE NEW TESTAMENT?

The Quantity and Quality of Textual Variants

Even careful copyists make mistakes, as every proofreader knows. So we will never be able to claim certain knowledge of exactly what the original text of any biblical writing was.

—ROBERT W. FUNK, ROY W. HOOVER, AND
THE JESUS SEMINAR, *The Five Gospels*, 6

We have traced the oral tradition behind the Gospels to the written texts and have seen that the Gospels are at least generally reliable as witnesses to the person and work of Jesus Christ. But what if the copies of those Gospels were corrupted? And what if the New Testament books were copied so poorly that we can't possibly recover the original text? After all, hasn't the Bible been copied and recopied and translated and retranslated so many times that the original wording must have been lost long ago? In short, is what we have now what they wrote then?

In this section we will take a bird's-eye view of the issues involved in the transmission of the New Testament down through the centuries. There is a vast amount of literature on this topic. Our objective is to acquaint you with the general discipline known as *textual criticism*.

Myths and silly notions abound when it comes to this subject, but by
the end of this section you should understand the basic facts about
the text of the New Testament.

THE GOAL OF NEW TESTAMENT TEXTUAL CRITICISM

Textual criticism in general is the study of the copies of any written document whose original is unknown or nonexistent in order
to determine the exact wording of the original. Such a task is necessary for an extensive amount of literature, especially that which was
written prior to the invention of the movable-type printing press in
the mid-fifteenth century. And the New Testament is no exception
to this rule.[1] Textual criticism is needed for the New Testament for
two reasons: (1) the original documents (known as autographs) no
longer exist, and (2) no two copies agree completely. In fact, among
even the most closely related copies from the first millennium A.D.,
there are as many as ten differences per chapter. If the originals were
still with us, there would, of course, be no need for this discipline.
Since the remaining (or extant) copies disagree, however, some criteria are needed to determine the wording of the autographs.

THE QUANTITY AND QUALITY
OF THE TEXTUAL VARIANTS

The Greek New Testament, as we know it today, has approximately
one hundred thirty-eight thousand words. There are thousands
upon thousands of textual variants. A textual variant is any place
among the manuscripts of the New Testament where there is not
uniformity of wording. The best estimate is that there are between
three hundred thousand and four hundred thousand textual variants
among the manuscripts. That means that on average for every word
in the Greek New Testament there are at least two variants. If this
were the only piece of data we had, it would discourage anyone from
attempting to recover the wording of the original.

One way to measure the impact of these variants is a comparison of the Greek New Testament that the King James Version (1611) translators used and the Greek New Testament that most scholars today use. The Greek text behind the KJV was based essentially on about half a dozen manuscripts, none of which were earlier than the tenth century. The Greek New Testament used today is based on thousands of manuscripts, some of which even date back to the second century. We will discuss this point later, but what we should note here is this: Most modern scholars view the Greek manuscripts that stand behind the KJV to be inferior because, in part, the copyists *added* words to Scripture. But how much they added can be overstated. Over a period of many centuries, only about twenty-five hundred words were added to the original text. The New Testament grew in size from the earliest copies to the latest copies—fourteen hundred years later—by about 2 percent. That is a remarkably stable transmissional process. Thus, although the New Testament has grown over time, it has grown very little. Since the earliest texts that we have agree substantially with the later ones, if we were to project backward to the original, the changes from the original text to the earliest copies would be miniscule. One might be pardoned if he or she thinks that this remarkably stable transmission implies something about the providence of God in preserving the Scriptures.[2]

Nevertheless, even twenty-five hundred words is not an insignificant amount. Furthermore, these represent only the *additions*. There are also hundreds of substitutions that do not add to the length of the New Testament but are nevertheless differences between the earlier manuscripts and later ones. And what happened to all those hundreds of thousands of variants? They may not show up in the King James Version, but they need to be reckoned with.

We cannot consider the quantity of the variants without also looking at their quality. How many of them affect the meaning of the text? How many of them are "viable"—that is, they are found in manuscripts with a sufficient pedigree that they have some likelihood of reflecting the original wording? The variants can be broken down into the following categories:

- spelling differences and nonsense errors;
- minor differences that do not affect translation or that involve synonyms;
- differences that affect the meaning of the text but are not viable; and
- differences that both affect the meaning of the text and are viable.

Spelling Differences and Nonsense Errors

Of the hundreds of thousands of textual variants, the majority are spelling differences that have no impact on the meaning of the text. For example, the name for John is spelled in Greek two different ways, either *Iōannēs* or *Iōanēs*. The same person is in view either way; the only difference is whether the name has two *n*'s or one. One of the most common textual variants involves what is called a movable *nu*. The Greek letter *nu* (n) can occur at the end of certain words when they precede a word that starts with a vowel. This is similar to the two forms of the indefinite article in English: *a* or *an*. But whether the *nu* appears in these words or not, there is absolutely no difference in meaning. It is so insignificant that most textual critics simply ignore the variants involving a movable *nu* when transcribing the words of a manuscript.[3] It affects nothing.

Some of the spelling differences are nonsense readings. These come about when a scribe is fatigued, inattentive, or perhaps does not know Greek very well. Now, you might think that scribes who made such errors could have a serious impact on the copies of the text. In reality, nonsense readings are almost never repeated by the next scribe. Further, nonsense readings tell scholars a great deal about *how* a scribe went about his work. For example, an early manuscript of Luke and John, known as Papyrus 75, or P[75], has some interesting nonsense readings. Each reading involves one or two letters, suggesting that the scribe copied the text one or two letters at a time.[4] Indeed, this scribe was very careful. He (or she)[5] was a detail person!

Another early manuscript, Codex Washingtonianus, or Codex W

(so-called because it is in the Smithsonian Institution in Washington, D.C.), contains all four Gospels. In one place, the scribe wrote the word *and* when he should have written the word *Lord*. In Greek, the two words look somewhat similar *(kai* and *kurios),* thus creating the occasion for the mental lapse. But using the "and" makes no sense in the context. There is evidence that the error came at the end of the scribe's shift, when fatigue had set in.[6] In such cases, the wording that the scribe bungled is easy to reconstruct.

Differences That Do Not Affect Translation or That Involve Synonyms

The next largest category of variants consists of readings that do not affect translation or that involve synonyms. These are variants other than spelling and nonsense readings but nevertheless do not alter the way the text is translated—or at least understood.

We will begin with those variants that do not affect translation. For example, Greek sometimes uses the definite article with proper names, while English does not. The Greek New Testament will speak of "Mary" or "the Mary," "Jesus" or "the Jesus," "Paul" or "the Paul." Scholars debate the significance of the article with proper names, and no definitive principles have developed.[7] One of the reasons scholars do not see much significance in this is simply that the manuscripts vary on the presence of the article. But in English no translational difference occurs. Thus, for example, in Luke 2:16 we read, "So they hurried off and located Mary and Joseph, and found the baby lying in a manger," while the Greek text speaks of "the Mary" and "the Joseph."

Another frequent variant of this sort is known as *transposition.* Unlike English, the meaning of the sentence in Greek is more dependent on the inflection of the words than on word order. That is because Greek is a highly inflected language—one that has a myriad of suffixes on nouns and verbs, as well as prefixes and infixes on verbs. The forms of the words change to fit the syntax of the sentence. In English, a sentence comprised of the three words *God, loves,* and

Paul can mean two quite different things depending on the word order. But in Greek, since there is one form for *God* when it is the subject of the verb and another form for *God* when it is the direct object, word order is much more flexible. Because syntax resides in the forms rather than in the order, Greek can use a construction like the English words "God loves Paul" in any of several ways, even the order "Paul loves God" if the word endings mean "God loves Paul":

- "God loves Paul."
- "Paul loves God."
- "Loves God Paul."
- "Loves Paul God."
- "God Paul loves."
- "Paul God loves."

As long as "God" is in the nominative case and "Paul" is in the accusative case, all of the above sentences mean "God loves Paul." The difference in word order indicates emphasis, not basic meaning.

How does this relate to textual criticism? Word order changes are frequent in the manuscripts, yet these transpositions do not affect the basic syntax of what is being said.[8]

Then there are the variants that involve synonyms. The translation may be affected by these variants, but the meaning is not. We can understand how these variants arose when we consider the "growth" of the New Testament over time. One of the principal reasons why the New Testament grew over the centuries was due to its liturgical use. Specifically, manuscripts known as lectionaries contributed heavily to the expansion of the New Testament.

Lectionaries are manuscripts that have assigned Scripture readings for various days of the week. The assigned reading for a particular day could not very well begin with, "Now, when he was teaching by the seashore." Who is the *he?* The lectionaries added clarification to the text precisely because they pulled passages out of their larger contexts—passages that often used only pronouns to identify the main characters. The scribes knew the Scriptures well, especially because of constant use and memorization of the lectionaries. They would often import the added words from the lectionaries into the biblical text. For example, in the heart of Mark's Gospel, for the space of eighty-nine verses (Mark 6:31–8:26), Jesus is *never* identified by name or title. He is not called "Jesus," "the Lord," "teacher," or "rabbi." The pronouns[9] are the only indications to go on that tell who is in view. Because of the influence from the lectionaries, most manuscripts add nouns here and there to identify the person in view. In these eighty-nine verses in Mark, for example, the majority of later manuscripts add "Jesus" in 6:34; 7:27; 8:1, and 17. These variants certainly affect the translation, but the referent (Jesus) is still the same either way.

Meaningful Variants That Are Not Viable

The next largest category consists of variants that impact the meaning of the text but are not viable. They are variants found in a single manuscript or group of manuscripts that, by themselves, have little likelihood of going back to the wording of the original text. For example, in 1 Thessalonians 2:9, instead of "the gospel of God" (which is found in almost all manuscripts), a late medieval manuscript has "the gospel of Christ." This is meaningful, but it is not viable. There is little chance that one late manuscript could contain the original wording when the textual tradition is uniformly on the side of another reading.

The many harmonizations in the Gospel manuscripts offer other examples of meaningful variants that are not viable. Scribes had a tendency to harmonize parallel passages in Mark, Matthew, and Luke. Two groups of manuscripts, known as the Western text and the Byzantine text, especially did this kind of thing. Indeed, one of the ways that scholars can tell whether a particular variant is authentic is to see if it harmonizes. Since it is a known scribal practice to harmonize the wording between two Gospels,[10] the reading that does not harmonize is typically considered to be authentic. Especially when such *non*-harmonizations are found in earlier manuscripts, the evidence that there is no harmonization is convincing that these readings are authentic. An example of harmonization in the Gospel manuscripts can be found on any page of the Gospels. One will have to suffice for our purposes.

In Matthew 9, Jesus is eating with some unsavory people. (This story is also found in Mark 2 and Luke 5.) This offends the Pharisees. In verse 11 they ask Jesus' disciples, "Why does your teacher eat with tax collectors and sinners?" A handful of Greek manuscripts and other early versions add "and drink" after "eat" to conform the wording to what is found in Luke 5:30. Meanwhile, in Mark 2:16, the wording is similar to Matthew's, but here the *majority* of later manuscripts add the words "and drink." As for Luke 5:30, there is only one known manuscript that omits "and drink," thus bringing it into conformity with the wording in Matthew and Mark.

This textual problem illustrates a couple of things. First, scribes were prone to harmonize the Gospel accounts, even when there was no real discrepancy between them. Second, when it came to harmonization, the scribes tended to add material to one Gospel rather than take away material from another.

Meaningful and Viable Variants

The final—and by far the smallest—category consists of variants that are both meaningful and viable. Only about 1 percent of all textual variants fit this category. But even here the situation can be overstated. By "meaningful" we mean that the variant changes the meaning of the text *to some degree.* It may not be terribly significant, but if the variant affects our understanding of the passage, then it is meaningful. To argue for large-scale skepticism because we cannot be certain about a very small portion of the text is a careless overstatement, yet this is just the impression given by Funk, Hoover, and the Jesus Seminar.[11] We have seen that the vast bulk of textual variants are inconsequential. To be sure, whether John's name was spelled in Greek with one *nu* or two may remain a mystery. But the point is that John's name is not spelled *Mary.* The issues that textual critics face are, frankly, of such small importance to most other New Testament scholars that the latter often assume that there is nothing left to do in the discipline. The reality is that, although most of the text of the New Testament is not in dispute, some passages are. We will discuss in a later chapter what is at stake, but for now we wish simply to illustrate this last category of usage, the meaningful and viable variants.[12]

A notorious textual problem is found in Romans 5:1. Does Paul say, "We *have* peace" *(echomen)* or *"let us have* peace" *(echōmen)?* The difference between the indicative and subjunctive mood is a single letter. The similar sounding omicron (o) and omega (ω) were most likely pronounced alike in Hellenistic Greek (as they are in later Greek), making the decision even more difficult. Indeed, scholars are split on this textual problem.[13] But the point here is this: Is either variant a contradiction of the teaching of Scripture? Hardly. If Paul is saying that Christians have peace (indicative mood), he is speaking about their positional status with God the Father. If Paul is urging Christians to have peace with God (subjunctive mood), he is urging them to grab hold of the "indicatives of the faith"—the foundational truths on which the Christian life is based—and live them out in their daily lives.

In 1 Thessalonians 2:7, Paul describes himself and his colleagues either as "gentle" or "little children." The difference between the variants in Greek is just one letter—*ēpioi* versus *nēpioi*. If "little children" is the correct reading, then Paul has mixed his metaphors (though he is prone to do this from time to time[14]), for he follows this up by declaring that he has loved the Christians in Thessalonica "like a nursing mother."[15]

One of the most common variants involves the use of the first person plural pronoun and the second person plural pronoun. There is only one letter difference between the two in Greek. A significant place where this textual problem occurs is in 1 John 1:4. The verse says either, "Thus we are writing these things so that *our* joy may be complete," or "Thus we are writing these things so that *your* joy may be complete." The meaning is affected, and both readings have ancient testimony. At the same time, neither variant necessarily cancels out the other. Whether the author is speaking of his joy or the readers' joy, the obvious point of this verse is that the writing of this letter brings joy.[16] It's not much of a stretch to see one party as becoming the joy for the other.

Scholars look at a combination of factors in determining the wording of the original text. One of these of course is the manuscripts and ancient versions—known collectively as external evidence. But another, equally important factor, is internal evidence. We will discuss both of these issues in chapter 7. Suffice it to say here that what scribes were likely to do (such as harmonize passages) and what the author was likely to do constitute internal evidence. External evidence and internal evidence are normally on the same side—that is, both of them usually point to the *same* reading as authentic. Thus, they become a twofold cord, one that is not easily broken.

On rare occasions, the external evidence and the internal evidence are at odds with each other. For example, Philippians 1:14 says, "Most of the brothers and sisters . . . dare to speak the word fearlessly." The question naturally arises, *What* word? Paul doesn't say. Scribes predictably added "of God," clarifying what word is in view. Surprisingly, it is the early, better manuscripts that add "of God," while the majority of later manuscripts leave this out. Here is a classic example of the internal evidence and the external evidence disagreeing with one another. In such cases, scholars have to choose the reading that seems to give rise to the other. In this case, the shorter reading is deemed by most to be authentic. Nevertheless, there is no doctrine at stake and no great historical argument that rests with either variant.

As a last example of meaningful and viable variants, we will consider the largest textual variant in the New Testament. It involves a dozen verses.[17] In the last chapter of Mark's Gospel (chap. 16), the earliest and best manuscripts end the book at verse 8: "Then they went out and ran from the tomb, for terror and bewilderment had seized them. And they said nothing to anyone, because they were afraid." This is an awfully abrupt ending to a Gospel. The women who were afraid had been told by the angel that Jesus Christ had risen from the dead and that they were to announce this to the disciples. The vast majority of manuscripts have twelve more verses after this, but the earliest and best manuscripts stop here.

Scholars have debated whether Mark intended to end his Gospel at this point, whether he wrote more but his real ending was lost, or whether the twelve verses found in the majority of manuscripts are the original ending to the Gospel.[18] For our purposes, we simply want to point out that whether these verses are authentic or not, no fundamental truth is gained or lost by them. To be sure, the textual decision will affect how one views the Gospel of Mark as a whole, but it does not affect any cardinal doctrine. We will come back to the issue of what teachings of Scripture are influenced by viable textual variants in chapter 8. For now, we need only to note that this textual variant does not affect any cardinal doctrine.

Although the quantity of textual variants among the New Testament manuscripts numbers in the hundreds of thousands, the *quality* of these variants as changes in meaning pales in comparison. Only about 1 percent of the variants are both meaningful and viable. And, as we will see in our final chapter in this section, these do not affect foundational beliefs. We can visually represent the kinds of variants we have in the New Testament in a pie chart. Notice again how very few actually are significant.

Quality of Variants Among New Testament Manuscripts

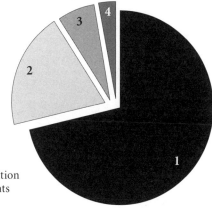

1=spelling errors
2=variants that do not affect translation
3=meaningful, but not viable variants
4=meaningful and viable variants

Chapter 5

MYTHS ABOUT MANUSCRIPTS

Even if we had more extensive copies of the Gospels from within a couple of generations of their writing, this would not establish the state of the originals, nor how much evolution they had undergone within those first two or three generations. It is precisely at the earliest phase of a sect's development that the greatest mutation of ideas takes place, and with it the state of the writings which reflect the mutation. . . . We have nothing in the Gospels which casts a clear light on that early evolution or provides us with a guarantee that the surviving texts are a reliable picture of the beginnings of the faith.

—EARL DOHERTY, *Challenging the Verdict*, 39

The temporal gap that separates Jesus from the first surviving copies of the gospels—about one hundred and seventy-five years—corresponds to the lapse in time from 1776—the writing of the Declaration of Independence—to 1950. What if the oldest copies of the founding document dated only from 1950?

—ROBERT W. FUNK, ROY W. HOOVER, AND THE
JESUS SEMINAR, *The Five Gospels*, 6

Our task in this chapter is to discuss a couple of attitudes that are held by some today. On the one hand, some skeptics make the situation look much worse than it really is. Although it is true that we do not know exactly, in every instance, what the wording of the original New Testament was, this does not mean that we should abandon all hope of grasping the New Testament's basic contents. Much more can be said, and much more will in the next chapter. On the other hand, some Christians have replaced a quest for truth with a quest for certainty. In so doing, any hint of doubt is anathema to them. But that, too, is an unreasonable position.

Myths and Attitudes

There are two attitudes to avoid when it comes to the text of the New Testament: absolute certainty and total despair. Essentially only one group claims to have absolute certainty, the "King James only" folks. For them, having certainty about the text is a *sine qua non* of the Christian faith. We won't spend much time on this viewpoint, but we do want to touch on it. As for absolute despair, only the most radical liberals embrace this—and with relish! To be skeptical about the text of the New Testament is essential to a postmodern agenda, in which all things are possible but nothing is probable. The only certainty of postmodernism is uncertainty itself. Concomitant with this is an intellectual pride—pride that one "knows" enough to be skeptical about all positions.

The Myth of Absolute Certainty

There is a popular myth that we are getting further from the original text of the New Testament as time passes. Since the King James Version was published four hundred years ago, this viewpoint argues, it must surely be closer to the original text than modern translations. Indeed, it must be four hundred years closer. But in order for this view to be true, three assumptions must be demonstrated: (1) We have lost all data about the manuscripts that were used in producing the KJV New Testament, (2) no earlier manuscripts have been discovered in the past four hundred years, and (3) all modern translations are based on earlier translations exclusively rather than on an examination of the manuscript data.

The Myth About Modern Translations:
"As time goes on, translations get further removed from the original."

CENTURY: II • IV • VI • VIII • X • XII • XIV • XVI • XVIII • XX

All three of these assumptions are demonstrably false. First, we still have almost all of the manuscripts that were used in producing the KJV. And of those manuscripts used in the King James Version that are no longer known to exist, their wording is found in the early printed Greek New Testaments of the sixteenth century. Erasmus's third edition of his *Novum Instrumentum* (1522) stands squarely behind the KJV, though through the route of several other editions of the Greek New Testament. Erasmus used about half a dozen manuscripts for the majority of his work, the earliest from the tenth century. The KJV, therefore, was based on manuscripts only six hundred to seven hundred years older than the translation itself.

Second, the number of Greek manuscripts known today is nearly one hundred times greater than the number used in producing the KJV. Not only this, but the principal manuscripts on which modern translations are based are significantly earlier than those that stand behind the KJV. Our earliest manuscripts date to the second century, and the major manuscripts are from the fourth and fifth centuries. Altogether, over four hundred manuscripts are known today that predate the earliest ones used by Erasmus.[1]

Third, although modern translations of the New Testament are produced by a comparison with former translations (and some of them are consciously in the tradition of earlier works[2]), the newer translations are also based on a detailed examination of the best critical editions of the Greek manuscripts.

Finally, since modern translations follow the eminently reasonable principle of being based on the earliest manuscripts unless there are good reasons to prefer later copies, we must admit to some doubt about the original wording. As the centuries passed, there was, in fact, greater uniformity among the Greek manuscripts of the New Testament.[3]

Modern translations are based on earlier and more numerous manuscripts than the KJV. The manuscripts that stand behind the KJV are not forgotten; rather, better and earlier witnesses have displaced them.

**The Manuscripts
Behind the Modern Translations**

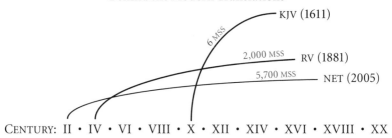

CENTURY: II · IV · VI · VIII · X · XII · XIV · XVI · XVIII · XX

The Myth of Total Despair

Earl Doherty's response to Lee Strobel's *The Case for Christ*[4] sets up an imaginary courtroom scene. In his third chapter, "Manuscripts and the Canon," he cross-examines Bruce Metzger, the preeminent New Testament textual critic from Princeton Seminary. He first tries to dismiss Metzger's credentials by asking whether Strobel's accolade of Metzger as "on the cutting edge of New Testament scholarship" leaves room "for true radicals like John Dominic Crossan and Burton Mack, or moderate liberals like Helmut Koester."[5] This sort of tactic mixes apples and oranges. Crossan, Mack, and Koester are well-known liberal New Testament scholars, but not one of them is a textual critic. Yet Doherty uses this sleight of hand to cast aspersions on Metzger's credentials.

He then argues that the wealth of New Testament manuscripts we have today gives us no indication of what the original New Testament text looked like.

> Even if we had more extensive copies of the Gospels from within a couple of generations of their writing, this would not establish the state of the originals, nor how much evolution they had undergone within those first two or three generations. It is precisely at the earliest phase of a sect's development that the greatest mutation of ideas takes place, and with it the state of the writings which reflect the mutation. . . . We have nothing in the Gospels which casts a clear light on that early evolution or provides us with a guarantee that the surviving texts are a reliable picture of the beginnings of the faith.[6]

This sort of skepticism is unwarranted. Although it is true that the textual transmission of the early decades after the New Testament was written are shrouded in mystery, it is inconceivable that the manuscripts, ancient translations, and patristic quotations that emerge shortly thereafter all got it wrong.

Similarly, the statement in *The Five Gospels* by Funk, Hoover, and the Jesus Seminar is also unwarranted: "The temporal gap that separates Jesus from the first surviving copies of the Gospels—about one hundred and seventy-five years—corresponds to the lapse in time from 1776—the writing of the Declaration of Independence— to 1950. What if the oldest copies of the founding document dated only from 1950?"[7] What is wrong with this statement?

First, the facts are wrong. Three pages later, *The Five Gospels* says that the earliest Gospel fragment "can be dated to approximately 125 C.E. or earlier." This would mean that this fragment comes from within one hundred years of the life of Jesus. And although it is but a small fragment, it agrees almost exactly with the earliest Gospel copies.

Second, if we applied this analogy to other ancient literature, we would *still* be waiting for hundreds of years before any text of Herodotus or Livy or Homer were to show up! No one thinks that a copy of these documents that came even hundreds of years later is created out of nothing. To be sure, it may not be exactly like the original, but the increase in early, diverse manuscripts from all over the Mediterranean world ensures that scholars have the tools to reconstruct substantially what the original text said.

Third, to argue the way the Jesus Seminar has—without reference to the copies of other ancient literature—is to ignore the relevant comparative data. Ironically, this is very much against a true liberal spirit of intellectual inquiry that pursues the truth at all costs.

As we look at the materials and methods of textual criticism in the succeeding chapters, we will see that there are solid reasons for regarding the manuscripts of the New Testament as substantially correct in representing the original text. The rest of this chapter will show why total despair is totally wrong. But we wish to begin by comparing the manuscripts of the New Testament with those of other ancient writings.

One often hears the line, "We really don't know what the New Testament originally said, since we no longer possess the originals *and* since there could have been tremendous tampering with the text before our existing copies were produced." Is this an accurate assessment of the data? Is that kind of skepticism true to the facts? Not exactly.

If this supposition is true, then we must deny that most facts of ancient history can be recovered, because whatever doubts we cast on the text of the New Testament must be cast a hundredfold on virtually any other ancient text. The New Testament manuscripts stand closer to the original and are more plentiful than virtually any other ancient literature. The New Testament is far and away the best-attested work of Greek or Latin literature in the ancient world.

Comparison of Extant Historical Documents[8]

HISTORIES	OLDEST MSS	NUMBER SURVIVING
Livy 59 B.C.–A.D. 17	4th Century	27
Tacitus A.D. 56–120	9th Century	3
Suetonius A.D. 69–140	9th Century	200+
Thucydides 460–400 B.C.	1st Century A.D.[9]	20
Herodotus 484–425 B.C.	1st Century A.D.	75
NEW TESTAMENT	c. 100–150	c. 5,700 (only counting Greek manuscripts) (plus more than 10,000 in Latin, c. more than 1 million quotations from church fathers, etc.)

We will discuss the New Testament manuscript evidence in the next chapter in more detail. But for now, we wish to make more comparisons with other ancient writings.

As noted above, approximately fifty-seven hundred full or partial New Testament manuscripts are known to exist at this writing. The number of sources is growing. Every decade and virtually every year new manuscripts are discovered. Meanwhile, the average classical author's writings are found in about twenty extant manuscripts.[10] The New Testament—in the Greek manuscripts *alone*—exceeds this by almost three hundred times. Besides the Greek manuscripts, there are Latin, Coptic, Syriac, Armenian, Gothic, Georgian, Arabic, and many other versions of the New Testament. The Latin manuscripts number over ten thousand. All told, the New Testament is represented by approximately one thousand times as many manuscripts as the average classical author's writings. Even the well-known authors—such as Homer or Herodotus—simply can't compare to the quantity of copies that the New Testament enjoys. Homer, in fact, is a distant second in terms of manuscripts, yet there are fewer than twenty-five hundred copies of Homer extant today.[11]

How do skeptics react to this sort of information? Doherty argues:

> Considering that the survival of ancient manuscripts was dependent upon Christian copyists, and that many ancient works were deliberately burned by the Christians, that disparity hardly proves anything. It is not surprising that the textual witness of many ancient works of literature survives by the merest thread. But I will suggest that it is not multiplicity per se which is the important factor here, or even any comparison at all with other ancient writings[;] it is how closely we can arrive at the original text of these Christian documents.[12]

Again, Doherty has mixed categories. It is true that "many ancient works were deliberately burned by the Christians," but these were *heretical* books. This is not to excuse the early Christians for doing such a thing, but it is to note that none of these books are the books in the comparison above. They were not the writings of the classical authors.

Doherty also fails to mention that Christianity was outlawed until the fourth century. Further, the worst pogrom against this new religion was conducted by Diocletian in 303–311—"the last war of annihilation waged by paganism against Christianity."[13] The persecution of Christians included wholesale destruction of their sacred Scriptures.[14] So successful was this campaign that after reversing Diocletian's edict and legalizing Christianity, Constantine felt the need in 331 to order the production of fifty Bibles.[15] When it comes to manuscript production and preservation from the first three centuries, the Christian documents were at a decided disadvantage because the political cards were stacked against them.[16] Yet, remarkably, the New Testament manuscripts are more plentiful during this era than are copies of any other ancient literature.

Finally, in the same sentence Doherty admits that "the survival of ancient manuscripts was dependent upon Christian copyists." Which ancient manuscripts is he *now* talking about? These would include classical Greek and Latin literature—including works in the chart above.[17] The argument that the plentiful and early evidence of New Testament manuscripts is really no evidence at all is an argument hardly worth considering. And given the early persecution of Christians and the preservation by Christian scribes of even classical writings, the claim is utterly falsified.[18]

MYTHS, ATTITUDES, AND REASON

We have seen that the attitudes of absolute certainty and total despair are inappropriate starting points for examining the New Testament text. Although we cannot be certain about every detail in the text, we can be certain about most. It is naïve to think that the KJV represents the original text better than do most modern translations. However, it is an overstatement to say that because we can't be sure about everything we can't be sure about anything. As we saw in the previous chapter, only a very small percentage of the New Testament text is in doubt. What is at stake in this small percentage of texts will be taken up later.

Chapter 6

AN EMBARRASSMENT OF RICHES

*Recovering the Wording of the
Original New Testament Text,
Part 1*

*Worse yet, for each book [of the New Testament] there exist different
families of [manuscript] types, often of approximately equal antiquity, but differing from each other in characteristic ways.*

—FRANK ZINDLER, "The *Real* Bible: Who's Got It?"

We have seen that most of the variation among the New Testament manuscripts involves mere spelling differences. The
smallest amount (about 1 percent) deals with meaningful and viable
alternative wording. But even here, the vast bulk of variants affect
only minor issues related to meaning.

Predictably, some folks are so skeptical of the early manuscripts
going back substantially to the original text that they end up making mountains out of molehills. These skeptics fall into two groups:
radical liberals and "King James only" fundamentalists. The radical
liberals want us to believe that we can have no assurances about anything regarding the wording of the original text. Nothing is probable; everything is only possible. Nothing can be affirmed. The "KJV

only" crowd wants us to believe that the early manuscripts are all corrupt and that we should trust the later, more uniform majority. Ironically, both approaches start with the result that they are seeking to prove, then deal only with the evidence that supports it. The results drive the method, rather than vice versa. This is hardly an honest pursuit of truth.[1]

Our task in this chapter is to discuss what textual critics have to work with in order to determine the wording of the original New Testament text. It is sometimes alleged that because the manuscripts can be grouped into families, we have no idea how to get back to the original wording. The reality is that these very families help determine the original wording. If the manuscripts were unrelated to each other, we would have few clues about which manuscripts faithfully reproduce the original. But with families of manuscripts, a genealogical tree can be constructed to show which groups of manuscripts are derived from which. Not only this, but a family presupposes a common ancestor. And although that common ancestor has to be reconstructed, textual critics have many tools at their disposal to find when and even where such a common ancestor would have existed.

We will discuss these genealogical relationships more in the next chapter to show that, rather than hamstringing our attempts to recover the original wording, groups of manuscripts facilitate it.

The fundamental problem of New Testament textual criticism is this: Since the originals no longer exist and since there are disagreements among all the remaining copies, how are we to determine the wording of the original? Two things must be discussed: materials and method. This chapter will explore the former.

It is an understatement to say that the materials used for determining the wording of the Greek New Testament are overwhelming. What adjectives can truly describe the situation? While scholars of other ancient literature suffer from a lack of data, those who work with New Testament manuscripts suffer from an embarrassment of riches. These have three subcategories: Greek manuscripts; ancient translations (or versions) of the New Testament into other languages; and quotations from the New Testament in the writings of the church fathers.

GREEK MANUSCRIPTS

The Greek manuscripts are the principal documents used to determine the wording of the New Testament. They can be broken down into groups denoting papyri, uncials, minuscules, and lectionaries. The first group—papyri—consists of manuscripts identified by the material that they are made of. The second and third groups—uncials and minuscules—refer to the writing style (either capital letters or cursive) of the manuscripts. The last group—lectionaries—refers to manuscripts that do not contain continuous texts from the Gospels, or Epistles, but rather are texts arranged for daily study and meditation.

New Testament manuscripts are primarily transcribed on vellum or parchment, with the exception of the papyri and some of the latest manuscripts, which were written on paper. Generally speaking, the papyri are the earliest of these four groups of manuscripts, and certainly the rarest (owing to the fragile writing material), while the uncials are next, followed by the minuscules and lectionaries.

As of January 2006, the statistics on the Greek manuscripts of the New Testament are as follows:[2]

Papyri	Uncials	Minuscules	Lectionaries	Total
118	317	2,877	2,433	5,745

Most of these manuscripts date from the second to the sixteenth centuries.[3] The earliest fragment is most likely from the first half of the second century (100–150), known as Papyrus 52 or P[52].[4] In recent years, a cache of several papyri was discovered at Oxford University, bringing the number to ten to fifteen that are as early as the second century.[5] Two of these papyri are substantial. Beginning in the third century, there is a steady stream of witnesses to the text of the New Testament.

By the fourth century, the great uncial manuscripts were produced, including what is now the earliest complete New Testament, Codex Sinaiticus, and Codex Vaticanus, a manuscript that is probably from the early fourth century. Sinaiticus (designated in manuscript shorthand by the Hebrew letter *aleph* [א]) and Vaticanus (designated B) both belong to what is called the Alexandrian text-type. (Text-types will be discussed in the next chapter.) These two manuscripts are closely related to each other. However, they are not as closely related as some might think. There are thousands of differences between them. Yet both are fourth-century manuscripts. Many scholars believe that since both manuscripts belong to the same text-type yet have so many differences, their common ancestor must have been copied several generations before. This is similar, to some degree, to relatives at a family reunion. Some members may be tall, thin, blue-eyed, and blond, while others are short, fat, brown-eyed, and have black hair. Others are somewhere in between. Those that look substantially like each other could well be more closely related.[6] Following this analogy, א and B are distant cousins from long after their common ancestor, which itself must go back several generations. Indeed, when they agree, their common reading usually is from the early second century.

Some of the later manuscripts show evidence of being copied from a much earlier source. For example, manuscript 1739, a tenth-century minuscule manuscript, was most likely copied directly from a late-fourth-century manuscript.[7] Even some of the early manuscripts show compelling evidence of being copies of a much earlier source. Consider again Codex Vaticanus, whose text is very much like that of P^{75} (B and P^{75} are much closer to each other than B is to א). Yet the papyrus is at least a century older than Vaticanus. When P^{75} was discovered in the 1950s, some entertained the possibility that Vaticanus could have been a copy of P^{75}, but this view is no longer acceptable since the wording of Vaticanus is certainly more primitive than that of P^{75} in several places.[8] They both must go back to a still earlier common ancestor, probably one that is from the early second century. In combination with א, this is a powerful witness to the earliest form of the text.

Many other examples could be given of early manuscripts that are from the same text-type and what their agreement means for the date of the reading. We will discuss these issues in the next chapter.

VERSIONS

The second most important witnesses to the New Testament text are known as versions. A version is technically a translation. The value of a version depends on its date, the translation technique and care, and the quality of the text it is translated from. But the textual basis and technique are not always easy to determine, hampering scholars' assessment of various versions. For example, Latin has no definite article, while Greek has a highly developed use of the definite article. Latin simply cannot adequately represent the Greek in places where the textual problem involves the article. However, *major* differences in the text can easily be detected (such as adding or dropping whole phrases). Also, by comparing the text-forms of the various versions with New Testament quotations in patristic writers (or church fathers), it is possible to determine when the various versions came into existence. Except in rare and controlled instances, once a version was completed it did not interact with the Greek manuscripts again. This means that when a particular version consistently has one reading in its remaining copies, one may usually regard that reading as going back to that version's origin.[9] The three most important versions are the Latin, Coptic, and Syriac. Other versions of relative value are the Gothic and Armenian, followed by the Georgian and Ethiopic.

Latin

Through a rich and complex history, the Latin manuscripts of the New Testament have come to predominate this field—in quantity. There are roughly twice as many Latin manuscripts of the New Testament as there are Greek, more than ten thousand, compared to about fifty-seven hundred.[10] They date from the third century to the sixteenth, but their origins may go back deep into the second century. This can be confirmed by an examination of the text-form used by certain church fathers: Irenaeus, Tertullian, Justin Martyr, and others all seemed to use the form of text (known as the Western text-type) that is found in the oldest Latin manuscripts.[11]

Coptic

The Coptic language is based on the old Egyptian hieroglyphic language. Essentially, Coptic is hieroglyphics in Greek dress (with a few new letters added). The most important dialects are the Sahidic and the Bohairic. The origin of the Sahidic New Testament reaches back to the beginning of the third century. Hundreds of manuscripts exist, perhaps even thousands, but only a few hundred have been catalogued. Probably at least a thousand Coptic manuscripts exist, representatives of the Alexandrian text-type.

Syriac

The Syriac church finds its origins in the second century. Although no extant Syriac New Testament manuscripts are that early, it is certain that the New Testament was translated into Syriac no later than the early third century.[12] The earliest form, the Old Syriac, is a representative of the Western text. The surviving copies of Syriac New Testament manuscripts number in the hundreds, perhaps thousands.

Other Versions

Besides the Syriac, Latin, and Coptic, other ancient versions should be noted. The Gothic originally was translated in the fourth century, as was the Ethiopic, and the Armenian probably from the fifth. Well over two thousand manuscripts represent these versions today.

All told, probably between fifteen and twenty thousand texts of the ancient versions of the New Testament remain. There are no exact numbers because not all the manuscripts have been carefully catalogued.

CHURCH FATHERS

"Besides textual evidence derived from New Testament Greek manuscripts and from early versions, the textual critic compares numerous scriptural quotations used in commentaries, sermons, and other treatises written by early church fathers. Indeed, so extensive are these citations that if all other sources for our knowledge of the text of the New Testament were destroyed, they would be sufficient alone for the reconstruction of practically the entire New Testament."[13]

The quotations by the church fathers of the New Testament number well over one million—and counting![14] The Fathers are as early as the late first century, with a steady stream through the thirteenth, making their value for determining the wording of the New Testament text extraordinary.

However, there are problems in citing the Fathers. First, their writings are found only in copies, not originals. Consequently, the Fathers' texts need to be reconstructed. Second, some are notorious for quoting the same passage in different ways. These differences are usually due to lapses in memory, integration of Scripture into the warp and woof of the father's sentence structure, or the use of different biblical manuscripts.

In many cases there are ways to determine with a great deal of certainty what form of the New Testament text a particular father was quoting. In particular, when a father is quoting from a long passage, it is likely that he is not quoting from memory but is transcribing from a manuscript. There are other ways to gain certainty about a father's text of the New Testament.[15] In addition, sometimes a father discusses textual variants, noting manuscripts that have one wording or another.[16] "When properly evaluated . . . , patristic evidence is of primary importance . . . : in contrast to the early Greek MSS, the Fathers have the potential of offering datable and geographically certain evidence."[17]

CONCLUSION

The wealth of material that is available for determining the wording of the original New Testament is staggering: more than fifty-seven hundred Greek New Testament manuscripts, as many as twenty thousand versions, and more than one million quotations by patristic writers. In comparison with the average ancient Greek author, the New Testament copies are well over a thousand times more plentiful. If the average-sized manuscript were two and one-half inches thick, all the copies of the works of an average Greek author would stack up four feet high, while the copies of the New Testament would stack up to over a *mile* high! This is indeed an embarrassment of riches.

As we saw in a previous chapter, these thousands of manuscripts, versions, and patristic quotations have produced hundreds of thousands of textual variants. We also noted that the New Testament text is remarkably stable over the many centuries of its transmission and that only about 1 percent of the variants are both meaningful and viable. These two considerations—the number of manuscripts and the number of variants—lead to our next issue: How do scholars sift through all this material? What methods do they use to determine exactly the original wording of the New Testament?

Chapter 7

THE METHODS OF TEXTUAL CRITICISM

*Recovering the Wording of the
Original New Testament Text,
Part 2*

*There is a stray manuscript (Old Latin manuscript b) that omits
Mary's question in Luke 1:34, "How shall this be, since I know not
a man?" . . .*

*Note that without this verse there is nothing in Luke that even
implies a supernatural conception or birth.*

—ROBERT M. PRICE,
The Incredible Shrinking Son of Man, 70

With this great wealth of material at their disposal, how do textual critics go about determining the wording of the original New Testament? After all, the manuscripts disagree with each other significantly, which means that some method must be employed to cut through the Gordian knot. In short, how do scholars know which variants are authentic?

For the vast majority of the textual variants, there is simply no difficulty determining the original wording. But for a small percentage of the variants, a combination of approaches is the key to making a determination. First, scholars examine the external evidence—the manuscripts, versions, and biblical quotations by the Fathers. There are ways to tell from the external data how early a particular reading is. Second, they examine the internal evidence—the habits and writing styles of the authors, as well as the habits and even mistakes of scribes. These two approaches are handled separately, then the results are compared. The governing principle of the whole endeavor is this: *The reading that gives rise to the other readings is most likely the original reading.* When the external and internal evidence point in the same direction, textual critics have great confidence that they have the wording of the original. We will look briefly at the process and conclude with one or two illustrations to show concretely how it works.

EXTERNAL EVIDENCE

There are three external criteria used to judge which variant is more likely to be the wording of the original: date and character; genealogical solidarity; and geographical distribution.

Date and Character

The preferred variant or reading normally is the one found in the earliest manuscripts. Less time has elapsed between those manuscripts and the originals and fewer intermediary copies have introduced errors. The more direct pipeline a manuscript has to the original, the better are its chances of getting the wording right. Also, the manuscripts that elsewhere prove to be the most reliable are given preference. Thus, a meticulous scribe working on a fifth-century manuscript may produce a more reliable text than a third-century scribe who is more interested in getting the job done quickly.

As for character, it is usually considered more important to see if a given manuscript is a good witness to its text-form rather than to the original text, because the route to the wording of the original text is through the various text-types. This is an important distinction, but one that must be maintained in doing textual criticism.

Thus, the *date* of the manuscripts is a significant factor in determining the value of a given reading, and the general *character* of said manuscript, at least in relation to its text-form, is also an important factor.

Genealogical Solidarity

Most of the manuscripts were written in locales in which certain traditional variants were copied repeatedly. That is to say, most manuscripts find their roots in a local ancestor (or what we might call a regional archetype) that influenced the various descendants in this area. Thus, geographical patterns of readings emerged, giving each locale a distinctive type of text. When all or almost all of the manuscripts that are identified as belonging to a certain text-type agree on a certain reading, one can conclude that the local ancestor of that text-type probably contained that reading.

What exactly is a text-type? English-language Christian culture provides a modern analogy. Often, when people in church hear a preacher read from the Bible, they can figure out which of the numerous English translations is used—even when a copy of the translation is not in front of them. This is because translations take on a stylistic pattern of language use. Thus, the KJV sounds archaic but elegant; the NIV sounds almost conversational; *The Message* sounds lively.

Now, suppose that the printing press had not yet been invented and each pastor had to spend the first year of his seminary training writing out his own copy of the Scriptures. At each seminary, a different version of the Scriptures is used, and the students are expected to learn that version well. Students in Chicago might write out a copy of the NIV; those in Los Angeles the NASB; those in Dallas the NET. None of the handwritten copies of the various versions would be exactly like the "local original." But they would be close, and a comparison of them to each other would help one to see what the original archetype looked like.

Now, suppose that hundreds of years have gone by and all that remains of the NIV, NASB, or NET are a dozen or so copies of each "text-type." But one of the NIV copies was found in Dallas, and it has several NET-like readings in it. One would say that that manuscript had mixture. And even if it was early, the mixture would make it less important than a purer NIV copy that came later. It would be less important because it would not be as reliable a witness to its text-type. This is how the "character" of a manuscript can be assessed: Is it close to the wording of the local original, or does it have a lot of mixture from other text-types? The former is better than the latter for the purposes of trying to get back to wording of the local archetype.

The text of the New Testament is similar to this. There are three major text-types: the Alexandrian, the Western, and the Byzantine. The Alexandrian was produced especially in Egypt, the Western in Rome and the West (though also elsewhere), and the Byzantine mostly in the East. Most scholars agree that the Alexandrian text-type began in the second century, as did the Western. The Byzantine text, however, was a later development, based largely on Western and Alexandrian manuscripts.[1] The best Alexandrian manuscripts are those that do not have mixture from Western or Byzantine readings. And when one looks at all the Alexandrian manuscripts, a pattern emerges for a given reading. When the better Alexandrian manuscripts have the same reading, then scholars can be relatively assured that the Alexandrian local original had that reading. This is true even though that local original no longer exists. It is a simple deduction from the available evidence. Thus, by genealogical solidarity, one can push back the date of a reading *within* a text-type to its local original. This is similar to the deduction one would make if he were to meet an extended family of fifty blue-eyed Swedes: the ancestors also most likely had blue eyes. Since the Alexandrian and Western texts have roots in the second century (which can be confirmed by patristic quotations from certain locations in the second century), when each of these text-types has genealogical solidarity, their readings are said to be second-century readings.

Consider two families whose ancestors immigrated to the United

States in the early 1800s. In the Dodd family, the story of where they came from, what year they arrived, and where they landed is consistent: Wales, 1833, New York. Virtually all the sources agree, whether those sources are living voices or diaries and letters from previous generations. To be sure, some later sources have different information, but there is very little disagreement. One letter, written by a twelve-year-old, says that her ancestors arrived in 1883; the diary of a person who married into the family said that they came from England. Thus, although not all the records agree entirely, the best witnesses agree and the deviating ones don't deviate too much. Further, the deviations can be explained. In one case, the difference is due to accident (1883 vs. 1833), while in the other case it may be due to the tendency to replace the less familiar with the more familiar.

The Wallace family has a less-certain history. Some say that the ancestors came to the United States in 1819, while others say it was 1847; some say the ancestors came from Scotland, while others say they came from Germany;[2] some say the ancestors landed in Boston, but others say it was Rhode Island. When there are discrepancies of this sort, there is no genealogical solidarity. The truth needs to be determined by some other means. However, the Dodd family has a consistent story, and genealogical solidarity suggests that this story reaches all the way back to 1833. By itself, genealogical solidarity is not enough to prove that a reading is authentic, but it does demonstrate that it is older than any of the remaining manuscripts of that text-type.

Even when the manuscripts of the Alexandrian text-type are not completely solid, one can often suggest a date for *two streams* of tradition that predate the extant witnesses. This is because the Alexandrian text most likely had two branches—a primary Alexandrian and a secondary Alexandrian. Both of these are ancient streams of transmission, with the primary Alexandrian being more carefully produced. Thus, even though the original copies of various regional archetypes have disappeared, it is possible to suggest a date for a variant that predates any of the manuscripts in which it is found.

Geographical Distribution

The variant that is found in geographically widespread locations in the first few centuries of the Christian era is more likely to be original than the one that is found in only one location. Collusion of witnesses is much less probable when these witnesses are distributed in Rome and Alexandria and Caesarea than when they are all in Jerusalem or Antioch. Thus, if a third-century manuscript in Egypt, a third-century version in Rome, and a third-century father in Gaul all agreed on the wording of a passage, chances are that they all are reproducing an earlier source. The geographical spread of sources that agree with each other is a very important factor in determining the wording of the original text.

Not only does this demonstrate that the particular reading was not produced by some sort of collaboration, but it also shows that the reading is much earlier than any of the extant sources. By this method, scholars can legitimately "push back" the date of a reading to a time that predates the sources that attest it.

Consider again our analogy with the Dodd and Wallace families. If another family, unrelated to either of these families, were to confirm some of the statements in the family records of the Dodds or Wallaces, that would be similar to geographical distribution. There is no relation between this other family and the Dodds or Wallaces, yet they offer an independent witness that confirms the truth of events recorded in the Dodd or Wallace family records. This kind of "multiple attestation" strengthens the likelihood that the event really happened. By itself, this evidence is not proof, for there could be independent reasons for both sets of records to say the same thing, as we will see below. Though not infallible, geographical distribution is an important factor in determining the wording of the original New Testament.

It should be noted that after the first four centuries, geographical distribution is no longer nearly as helpful since by this time there would be extensive cross-pollination (mixture) among the manuscripts, due to the freedom of exchange of information once Christianity became a legal religion.

Geographical distribution also can be imperfectly illustrated by a variation of the "telephone game." This game involves a line of people, with the first one whispering some statement into the ear of the second. As this message is repeated down the line, it gets garbled. The whole point of the telephone game, in fact, is to see how garbled the original message can become. There is no motivation to "get it right." Now suppose that instead of one line we used three lines and the last person in the line is not the only one who tells what has become of the message. We can learn how it was understood at various points along the way. One may well be able to construct much of the original utterance by comparing the three lines and finding the things they had in common. This is geographical distribution.

Taking this one step further, suppose it was determined that one of the lines was far more accurate than the other two in conveying the utterance. This could be tested by hearing what someone "up the stream" said compared with someone farther down the line. If there were very little change from person to person, that line would be deemed superior to the other lines. But to solve the riddle, internal evidence would need to be brought in.

Date and character, genealogical solidarity, and geographical distribution are three indications in external data that help us decide which reading is the earliest—the reading from which the rest originated. But external evidence is not the whole approach. For example, in places where the early manuscripts disagree, or there is minimal geographical distribution, or one of the readings is just the kind of wording a scribe would be likely to create, internal evidence may be far more important.

INTERNAL EVIDENCE

Internal evidence is an examination of the *wording* of the variants to determine which reading gave rise to the other(s) and is, therefore, probably original.

The Canons of Internal Evidence

The basic guideline of internal criticism is: Choose the reading that best explains the rise of the other(s). This is the same rule for all of textual criticism, external or internal. Same principle, different (but complementary) methods. Judging internal evidence is sometimes quite subjective, sometimes very objective. Everyone practices this sort of textual criticism every day. David Parker ingeniously illustrates this in *The Living Text of the Gospels*:

> Everybody who reads the newspaper is expert in textual
> criticism, in coping with those distctive errors of omssion and
> displaced lines, and jumbling of letrset. This sophisticated process
> of recognizing nonsense and picking up the sense is so natural to us
> the classical scholars of ancient Alexandria or the Benedictines of
> that we perform it without thinking, unaware of our kinship
> with St Maur. Textual criticism is not an arcane science. It belongs to
> all human communication.[3]

Although some of the errors in the above paragraph may take a little while to figure out, you should be able to establish exactly what they are. You need no other manuscripts to compare the statement to; you can determine what the author meant to say simply by examining the wording and eliminating known errors. This is internal evidence.

Although there are numerous guidelines under the broad umbrella of choosing the reading that best explains the rise of the other(s), two of these rules stand out: The harder reading is preferred, and the shorter reading is preferred.[4]

The Harder Reading Is to Be Preferred

The harder reading is the reading that is more awkward, more ambiguous, more cumbersome. Harder readings also use rarer words or involve wording that could be perceived as a discrepancy. This canon is important because scribes tended to smooth out difficulties in the text rather than create difficulties. In chapter 4, we noted that Mark described Jesus only with the use of pronouns through eighty-nine consecutive verses. (Actually, the pronouns themselves are often absent, since Greek uses the verb endings to indicate the person and number of the subject.) Scribes would naturally want to add the name of Jesus to clarify who is in view. In such instances, the original reading is both shorter and harder.

Or consider a textual problem in John 4. This is in the narrative of Jesus' encounter with the woman at the well in Samaria. After a brief exchange, Jesus instructs the woman to go home and bring her husband back: "Go, call your husband, and come here" (v. 16). The woman responds, "I don't have a husband" (v. 17). To this Jesus responds, "Correctly you have said, 'A husband I don't have'" (v. 17). Now, at this stage some scribes had a problem. Jesus has quoted the woman's words, but he has reversed the order, as our translation above shows. To some, it may have looked like he misquoted her. So what do they do? They don't change the order of Jesus' words— rather, they change the order of the woman's words! To these scribes Jesus didn't quote the woman incorrectly; she said it wrong in the first place! So they conformed the order of her words to his quotation of her words. Only a few (though ancient) manuscripts do this, but they obviously create the smoother reading.

This sort of thing often happens with Gospel parallels. A smoother reading is introduced to harmonize the wording of one Gospel to another. Scribes smoothed out grammar, style, and even theology— yes, theology. Over time, scribes would change the wording of a text to make it conform more explicitly to their theological convictions. This does not mean that the original text was not orthodox; rather, it is not always as *explicitly* orthodox as the scribes would like, or its orthodoxy is slightly different from what the scribes believed.

Perhaps an analogy regarding the rough texture of the original text is in order. For those acquainted with J. R. R. Tolkien's *The Lord of the Rings*, this analogy will make good sense. When the beleaguered hobbits meet the dark stranger, Strider, at the Prancing Pony

Inn, they are relieved to learn that he is on their side. He announces that he is Aragorn, and that if he had been their enemy, he could have killed them easily.

> There was a long silence. At last Frodo spoke with hesitation, "I believed that you were a friend before the letter came," he said, "or at least I wished to. You have frightened me several times tonight, but never in the way that servants of the Enemy would, or so I imagine. I think one of his spies would—well, seem fairer and feel fouler, if you understand."[5]

Likewise, the original text has a stubborn way of making Christians nervous, but in the end it is something that we can both discern and trust.

An illustration of moving the text into conformity with orthodoxy is found in 1 Timothy 3:16, a verse we discussed in chapter 6 (see note 9). The wording "God was revealed in the flesh" is an explicit affirmation of the deity of Christ, while "who was revealed in the flesh" is only implicit.[6] Although there are plenty of texts that affirm the deity of Christ, orthodox scribes occasionally changed other texts to make them say this too. The harder reading, in this instance, is "who."

The Shorter Reading Is to Be Preferred

Scribes had a strong tendency to add words or phrases rather than omit them. The text tended to grow over time rather than shrink, although, it grew only 2 percent over fourteen hundred years. Scribes almost never *intentionally* omitted anything.[7] Thus, as long as an unintentional omission is not likely, the shorter reading is usually to be preferred. We have already discussed the addition of the name *Jesus* in several places in the Gospels where it was not originally used.

At the end of every book of the New Testament, the word *amen* appears in at least some of the manuscripts. Such a conclusion is routinely added by scribes to New Testament books because a few of these books originally had such an ending (Rom. 16:27; Gal. 6:18; Jude 25). A majority of Greek witnesses have the concluding "amen" in every New Testament book except Acts, James, and 3 John (and even in these books, "amen" is found in some manuscripts). It is thus a predictable variant and a longer reading.

Scribes also made more substantial additions. For example, in Romans 8:1, the external evidence points conclusively to the wording, "There is therefore now no condemnation for those who are in Christ Jesus." Two variants compete with this wording. Some manuscripts add "who do not walk according to the flesh." Still later manuscripts add "but who walk according to the Spirit." Scribes had a tendency to add to grace, to qualify absolute statements. In this instance it is obvious that the third reading originated from the second. If it arose without the second reading in place, the verse would make no sense at all: "There is therefore now no condemnation for those who are in Christ Jesus, but who walk according to the Spirit." In this instance, the shortest reading gave rise to the intermediate reading, which then gave rise to the longest reading.

These two rules are very helpful in determining the wording of the original text. At the same time, they must not be applied in isolation from other considerations. Some manuscripts, especially of the Western text, were prone to omit whole verses. Although the Western text is early, it is also somewhat careless. Here is where external evidence weighs in and exercises some quality control over internal evidence.

The Divisions of Internal Evidence

Transcriptional Probability

Transcriptional probability has to do with what a *scribe* (copyist) would be likely to do. There are two types of changes to the text that scribes made—intentional and unintentional.

Often scribes intentionally altered the text for grammatical, theological, or explanatory reasons as noted above. It is here especially that the two canons of shorter and harder reading are helpful. (See discussion above for illustrations.)

Many scribal changes were unintentional. Due to problems of sight, hearing, fatigue, or judgment, scribes often changed the text unwittingly. Some of these instances were discussed in a previous chapter. We can add here that a common mistake of the scribes was to write once what should have been written twice. This is called haplography. It occurred especially when a scribe's eye skipped a second word that ended the same way as the word before it. But it also occurred when two lines ended the same way. For example, in 1 John 2:23 we read, "Everyone who denies the Son does not have the Father either. The person who confesses the Son has the Father also." In Greek these two clauses both end with "has the Father." A literal rendering would be, "Everyone who denies the Son neither has the Father; everyone who confesses the Son also has the Father." Now, if this were written in sense-lines, the parallels would be even more striking:

> Everyone who denies the Son neither *has the Father*;
> everyone who confesses the Son also *has the Father*.

The Byzantine text-type lacks the second clause of this verse. Although shorter readings are usually preferred, this rule doesn't apply if an unintentional error is likely. This is a classic example of such an unintentional omission: The "has the Father" of the preceding clause occasioned the haplography.

Intrinsic Probability

This examines what the biblical *author* was likely to have written. Although there are others, two key issues are involved—context and style.

Which variant best fits the context? For example, in John 14, Jesus is speaking to his disciples on the night before he was crucified. In verse 17 he tells them about the Holy Spirit: "But you know him, because he resides with you and will be in you." There is a textual variant here; instead of "will be," some early and fairly reliable manuscripts have "is." The difference is between a future tense and a present tense verb. When one considers what the author would have written, the future is on much stronger ground. The immediate context in 14:16 and in the chapter as a whole points to the future, and John's Gospel overall regards the advent of the Spirit as a decidedly future event. The future tense thus has better credentials in terms of the context.[8]

Which variant better fits the author's style? Here the question concerns what an author normally does, how he normally expresses himself, what his motifs and language usually involve. For example, one of the reasons that most scholars do not regard Mark 16:9–20 to be authentic is that the vocabulary and grammar in these verses are quite unlike what is found in the rest of the Gospel of Mark. When this observation is coupled with the strong likelihood that scribes would want to finish Mark's Gospel with more than "they were afraid," and with the fact that the earliest and best manuscripts lack these twelve verses, the evidence is overwhelming that Mark 16:9–20 was added later.

Stylistic considerations even weigh in when the variant involves only one word. Thus, in John 4:1, the manuscripts vary between "Now when *Jesus* knew that the Pharisees had heard that he was winning and baptizing more disciples than John" and "Now when *the Lord* knew that the Pharisees had heard that he was winning and baptizing more disciples than John. . . ." Indeed, many of the better and earlier manuscripts have "the Lord" here instead of "Jesus." However, the narrative of John calls Jesus "Lord" at most only twice prior to the Resurrection (6:23; 11:2). Meanwhile, "Jesus" is used scores of times. Thus, the stylistic consideration is in support of "Jesus" instead of "the Lord."

CONCLUSIONS

When external evidence and internal evidence are compared, scholars come to a conclusion as to which reading is the original.

The textual variant that has the greater claim to authenticity will be found in the earliest, best, and most geographically widespread witnesses. It will fit the context and author's style, and will be the obvious originator of its rival readings on a literary level. Ninety-nine percent of all textual problems are easily resolved by comparing the external and internal evidence. And even a good portion of the remaining 1 percent that are meaningful and viable can be resolved with a great deal of confidence by a careful comparison of the external and internal evidence.

However, there are many occasions in which the external evidence seems to point one way, while the internal evidence points another. How do scholars decide in such instances? This is the kind of conundrum that fills theological journals! In the next chapter we will wrestle with exactly what is at stake in such situations. But here, we need to stress one very important thing: if a particular variant is found only in non-Greek manuscripts or is found only in a few late manuscripts, even if its internal credentials are excellent, it must be rejected. When we are dealing with as many thousands of manuscripts as we are, unpredictable accidents and unknowable motives may be the cause of a stray reading here or there that internally may have good credentials. On the other hand, on a rare occasion the external evidence is very solidly on the side of one reading, but there are sufficiently important manuscripts for an alternate reading, and the internal evidence is completely on the side of the second reading. In such instances, the second reading is most likely original.

In Philippians 1:14, the NET Bible has "and most of the brothers and sisters, having confidence in the Lord because of my imprisonment, now more than ever dare to speak the word fearlessly." But *what* word do they speak fearlessly? This kind of ambiguity left the scribes in a quandary. Some sort of clarification just begged to be added. A predictable variant arose: "of God." This particular variant is found in some of the best and earliest manuscripts, especially of the Alexandrian text-type. Some manuscripts of the Western text-type have "of the Lord." It is not easy to see why "of God" or "of the Lord" would have dropped out of the text. No intentional or unintentional reason on the part of the scribes can be discerned. This, coupled with the fact that Paul is often a bit ambiguous, means that the internal evidence—both the transcriptional and intrinsic—are on the side of the shorter, harder reading. Internally, it seems clear that Paul wrote "speak the word fearlessly" rather than "speak the word of God [or of the Lord] fearlessly," and scribes added an explanatory phrase to make the meaning clearer.

Turning to the external evidence, the shorter reading is supported by the majority of later manuscripts (those that belong to the Byzantine text-type). However, it is also supported by the earliest witness to Philippians, P[46] (dated to about 200). In addition, other non-Byzantine manuscripts have the shorter reading (most notably, Codex 1739, which we discussed in chapter 6). Although the external evidence is not compelling for the shorter reading, one can easily see how the original reading could be found in these manuscripts without the support of the rest of the early witnesses. Most of the usually better manuscripts in this instance have added a predictable variant, one that could have arisen in several places *independently* of other manuscripts. What is crucial to understand is that if a scholar thinks that the original reading is found in inferior manuscripts, he has to have some plausible explanation for how these manuscripts ended up with the right reading while better manuscripts did not. He has to explain *history*. In this case, the fact that Paul's wording is often ambiguous, the fact that *both* "of God" *and* "of the Lord" are variants that some manuscripts add, and the fact that the shorter reading has at least some excellent and early manuscripts on its side is sufficient grounds for seeing "speak the word fearlessly" as the authentic reading. The external evidence for the shorter reading is not strong, but it is adequate, and the internal evidence on its behalf is overwhelming. These two combine to indicate that "speak the word fearlessly" is what Paul wrote.

Now consider another textual problem. This is the one we started the chapter with, the textual problem in Luke 1:34. Listen again to Robert Price on this verse:

There is a stray manuscript (Old Latin manuscript b) that omits Mary's question in Luke 1:34, "How shall this be, since I know not a man?" . . .

Note that without this verse there is nothing in Luke that even implies a supernatural conception or birth. . . . It makes a lot of sense [to see this verse as added by later scribes], but the evidence is too meager for us ever to be able to settle the question.[9]

Robert Price was a fellow of the Jesus Seminar. He is a New Testament scholar. But is he treating the evidence fairly? Let's examine his evidence in light of the standard principles of textual criticism.

We will address the internal evidence first. Price tries to argue his case mostly on internal evidence: "Verse 34 makes Mary counter the angel with a skeptical objection *precisely parallel* to Zechariah's in 1:18, 'How shall I know this? For I am an old man, and my wife is advanced in years.' Gabriel strikes him deaf and mute until the child John is born, in punishment for daring to doubt his word. Would Luke so easily attribute the same incredulity to Mary, and if he did, would he let her off with no angelic reprisal?"[10]

Price assumes that the internal evidence is all on the side of the omission of this verse, largely because the parallel between Mary's and Zechariah's responses to the angel elicit a different response from Gabriel. But are Zechariah's and Mary's responses "precisely parallel" as Price alleges? Zechariah asks, "How shall I know this?" He is asking for a sign that the angel is telling the truth. But Mary's response is, "How will this be?" As Darrell Bock notes, "She does not doubt the announcement, for she does not ask for a sign as Zechariah did. Rather she is puzzled as to how . . . this birth can occur, a question that causes the angel to elaborate (1:35)."[11] The internal evidence thus is very much on the side of inclusion.

Not only this, but a characteristic feature of Luke is to use doublets to develop his argument. In this case, he is showing by Mary's different response that she is more righteous than Zechariah. He is also showing, by the parallel accounts, that Jesus' birth is more miraculous than John the Baptist's. Furthermore, if her conception were by natural means, why does the angel say, "The Holy Spirit will come upon you, and the power of the Most High will overshadow you. Therefore the child to be born will be holy; he will be called the Son of God" (v. 35)? This is the angel's response to Mary's query; it would be a most curious thing to have the angel respond to a question that was not asked. The intrinsic evidence, then (Luke's style as well as the context), is entirely on the side of the inclusion of verse 34.

Perhaps the external evidence is stronger for the omission. If so, it would have to be nearly unanimous in order to overcome such strong opposition from the internal evidence. But Price acknowledges that external evidence is terribly weak—one Latin manuscript! Basically, there is no external evidence to support his claim. One fifth-century *Latin* manuscript involves no geographical distribution, no genealogical solidarity, and only minimal date and character credentials. The rest of the Latin manuscripts have this verse, as well as all the Greek manuscripts. And patristic writers have commented on this verse from early times.

Price is entirely too generous in his assessment of the omission when he gives it equal billing with the inclusion. His conclusion that "the evidence is too meager for us ever to be able to settle the question"[12] sounds as if we need to suspend judgment because the evidence is so evenly balanced. Rather, the evidence for the omission is too meager to take Price's suggestion seriously. Remarkably, earlier in the book he invoked the name of F. C. Baur as a model of good biblical scholarship:

> We must ever keep in mind the dictum of Ferdinand Christian Baur that anything is *possible*, but that we must ask what is *probable*. This is important because of the very widespread tendency of conventional Bible students, even of otherwise sophisticated scholars, to weigh arguments for critical positions and then toss them aside as "unproven." . . . But scholarly judgments can never properly be a matter of "the will

to believe." Rather, the historian's maxim must always be Kant's: "Dare to know."[13]

It seems that Price has not taken his own advice in following this dictum of Baur (who also did not always take his own advice!). Further, we can reverse this: Scholarly judgments also can never properly be a matter of the will to disbelieve. The evidence for the lack of Luke 1:34 is so palpably weak that it is not even entertained by any serious New Testament scholar. How is it possible for one lone Latin manuscript to have gotten the wording right when all the other thousands of manuscripts—many of which are significantly earlier and with far better credentials than this one manuscript—let it slip through their nets? Price offers no plausible way in which the transmission of the text could have occurred so that the true text somehow was missed through more than four hundred years of copying but was caught by this one scribe. A good historian must at least offer some plausible explanation for such a unique anomaly. And he should also give evidence that, elsewhere in the text, a versional manuscript—or even a group of versional manuscripts—can contain the original wording when all the others produce an error.

It is instructive that Price enlists Baur and Immanuel Kant in defense of his destructive view of the text. Baur applied a method learned from philosophy (Hegelian dialectic) to the New Testament. Though his views were all the rage in the middle of the nineteenth century, they have since been proven false by *historical* evidence. Kant, of course, was a philosopher. But for Price to put "historian" and Kant in the same sentence gives the impression that Kant was primarily a historian. Philosophical presuppositions and historical evidence are not always good friends. It has often been said regarding new ideas in New Testament scholarship that "the Germans create it, the British correct it, and the Americans corrupt it." Price has started with a presupposition and sought to find any scrap of evidence that will support it. This is a method driven by the results one wants to find.

Nevertheless, if at all possible, it would be helpful to explain how this lone manuscript—Old Latin b—left out Mary's response in Luke 1:34. The most likely explanation is that the scribe made an error known as *haplography*—that is, writing once what should have been written twice. Both v. 34 and v. 38 begin exactly the same way: "And Mary said." In Latin, this is written *dixit autem Maria*. The scribe's eye skipped to v. 38 when reading *dixit autem Maria*. After he wrote the response from v. 38, his eye went back up to v. 35. (Anyone who has copied texts knows how easy it is make this sort of mistake.) Then when he got to v. 38, he recognized that he had written this text already and so he omitted the entire response in this location. The reading of Old Latin b in v. 38 is simply "and the angel departed from her." Thus, Mary's response in v. 38 has been removed and placed in v. 34.

But if Price is right, not only would a lone Latin manuscript contain the correct wording in v. 34, but the same lone manuscript would contain the correct wording in v. 38. All other witnesses—Greek, Latin, Coptic, Syriac, etc.—would have gotten wrong the wording in *both* places. The likelihood that Price's assessment of the data is correct is infinitesimally small.[14]

In other words, non-Greek witnesses are secondary in importance, and even whole versions (not just isolated manuscripts within a version), by themselves, cannot point to the wording of the original text.

Price's basis, then, is rather paltry. It seems that his philosophical presuppositions are driving his decisions. How then can he say, "The evidence is too meager for us ever to be able to settle the question"? The evidence, on the contrary, is absolutely solid that the Gospel of Luke never lacked 1:34. As William Lane was fond of saying, "An ounce of evidence is worth a pound of presumption."

In this case, we have a pound of evidence versus an ounce of presumption. Even scholars who deny the Virgin Birth know that the texts that speak of it are not in question. It is a mere grasping at straws to seriously entertain the possibility that this is not the case, and it unmasks a wholesale agenda of destroying the faith of Christians by playing fast and loose with historical data.

Chapter 8

IS WHAT WE HAVE NOW
WHAT THEY WROTE THEN?

When Constantine commissioned new versions of these documents, it enabled the custodians of orthodoxy to revise, edit, and rewrite their material as they saw fit, in accordance with their tenets. It was at this point that most of the crucial alterations in the New Testament were probably made and Jesus assumed the unique status he has enjoyed ever since. The importance of Constantine's commission must not be underestimated. Of the five thousand extant early manuscript versions of the New Testament, not one predates the fourth century. The New Testament as it exists today is essentially a product of fourth-century editors and writers—custodians of orthodoxy, "adherents of the message," with vested interests to protect.

—MICHAEL BAIGENT, RICHARD LEIGH,
AND HENRY LINCOLN,
Holy Blood, Holy Grail, 368–69

Pop culture promotes bizarre myths about the Bible. These urban legends are then fueled by self-proclaimed authorities on the Internet or in novels that make it on the best-seller lists. Meanwhile, biblical scholars tend to ignore these childish antics, since they know that there is no substance to them. This leaves the layperson without a clue as to what's really going on.

As an illustration of the sort of unfounded myth we're talking about, the comments of Sir Leigh Teabing, a character in Dan Brown's *The Da Vinci Code*, readily come to mind. He pontificates, "The Bible is a product of *man*, my dear. Not of God. The Bible did not fall magically from the clouds. Man created it as a historical record of tumultuous times, and it has evolved through countless translations, additions, and revisions. History has never had a definitive version of the book."[1] There is of course a grain of truth in all this. The Bible did not fall magically from the clouds, and the Bible had human authors. But to say that the Bible has evolved through translations, additions, and revisions, with the implication that the original is no longer detectable, is just plain silly. We discussed these issues in our first chapter on textual criticism, noting that this kind of myth involves unwarranted assumptions that are easily disproved by the manuscripts themselves. It plays on the experiences of everyone who has passed on information *without recourse to the earlier sources* (such as in the telephone game). But in the case of the New Testament, this is not valid. As time goes on, we are getting closer and closer to the wording of the original text because of the vast number of manuscripts—many of which are quite early—that scholars continue to uncover.

But what about the claim that Jesus' divinity was not to be found in the New Testament manuscripts—that Constantine essentially invented this doctrine? We will address that specific issue toward the end of this chapter with concrete evidence that again shows how this kind of language is patently false and misleading.

What is *really* at stake when it comes to the accuracy of the copies of the New Testament text? We have already noted four kinds of textual problems relevant to this issue:

1. The largest number of textual variants (well over half) involve spelling differences and nonsense readings that are easily detectable. These affect nothing of significance in the text.

2. Next in number are those variants that do not affect translation or, if they do, involve synonyms. Variants such as "Christ Jesus" versus "Jesus Christ" may entail a slightly different emphasis, but nothing of great consequence is involved.
3. Other, more meaningful variants are not viable. They simply have no plausibility when it comes to reflecting the wording of the original because the manuscripts in which they are found have a poor pedigree. This issue involves careful historical investigation and requires the scholar to take the transmission of the text seriously. We saw that Robert Price's attempt to excise Luke 1:34 from the Bible belonged to the category of "meaningful but not viable." In his case, there was absolutely no manuscript evidence on his side, only wishful thinking.
4. The smallest category, about 1 percent of all textual problems, involves those variants that are both meaningful and viable. Most New Testament scholars would say that there are far fewer textual problems in this category than even 1 percent of the total. But even assuming the more generous amount (by expanding the scope of both "meaningful" and "viable"), not much of a *theological* nature is affected.

Our objective in this chapter is to discuss this fourth kind of variant in more detail to see whether the deity of Christ (as well as other cardinal beliefs) is affected by these variants. We will first look at the possibility of "conjectural emendation"—variants that have *no* manuscripts in support of them. How many are there, and how do scholars deal with them? Then, we will discuss which doctrines are affected by the variants. Finally, we will examine some of the early manuscripts to see what they have to say about the deity of Jesus Christ.

CONJECTURAL EMENDATION

We have noted throughout this section that New Testament textual criticism suffers from an "embarrassment of riches" unparalleled by

any other piece of ancient literature. The manuscript copies of the
New Testament are far more plentiful and earlier than any other
Greek or Latin texts. In terms of manuscript data, any skepticism
about the Jesus of the Gospels should be multiplied many times for
any other historical figure. We have more and earlier manuscript
evidence about the person of Jesus Christ than we do anyone else
in the ancient world—including Julius Caesar and Alexander the
Great.

But let's quantify that more specifically. How many gaps are in
the New Testament that need to be filled in—places where no manuscripts exist and scholars simply must guess at what was originally
written?

It might be good to get a frame of reference. Is there a need for
conjectural emendation for other ancient literature and, if so, how
great is this need? For many important authors, we only have partial
works. Thus, of the ancient historian Livy's 142-volume work on
the history of Rome, copies of only thirty-five volumes survive. Of
Tacitus's *Histories*, fewer than five of the original fourteen books
can be found in any copies.[2] Hundreds of books from antiquity are
known to us only by name; no manuscripts remain. And even in some
of the better-preserved writings, there are many significant gaps.
For example, in his *Patristic Textual Criticism*, Miroslav Marcovich
complains that the surviving copies of some of the early patristic
writers are "lacunose [filled with gaps], corrupt, dislocated and
interpolated."[3] He then proceeds to lay out principles of conjectural
emendation that he must follow in order to reconstruct the original
wording.[4]

The situation with New Testament textual criticism is entirely
different: Virtually no conjectural emendation is required because
of the great wealth, diversity, and age of the materials we have.[5] Most
New Testament scholars would say that there are absolutely no places
where conjecture is necessary. Again, this is because the manuscripts
are so plentiful and so early that in almost every instance the original
New Testament can be reconstructed from the available evidence.

For example, Kurt and Barbara Aland, the first two directors of the Institute for New Testament Textual Research in Münster, Germany (Institut für neutestamentliche Textforschung or INTF), wrote a standard textbook on New Testament textual criticism. At the INTF, over 90 percent of all Greek New Testament manuscripts are on microfilm. For the past forty-five years, the institute has been more influential than any individual, school, or group of scholars anywhere else in the world for determining the exact wording of the original New Testament. In short, they know their stuff. "Every reading ever occurring in the New Testament textual tradition is stubbornly preserved, even if the result is nonsense . . . any reading ever occurring in the New Testament textual tradition, from the original reading onward, *has been preserved* in the tradition and needs only to be identified."[6]

The Alands go so far as to say that if a reading is found in just one manuscript, it is almost surely not authentic: "The principle that the original reading may be found in any single manuscript or version when it stands alone or nearly alone is only a theoretical possibility."[7] Further, "textual difficulties should not be solved by conjecture, or by positing glosses or interpolations, etc., where the textual tradition itself shows no break; such attempts amount to capitulation before the difficulties and are themselves violations of the text."[8] Their opinion in these matters should be considered as that of expert witnesses. Most in the discipline share their views.[9]

The "non-need" to guess about the wording of the original New Testament means that in virtually every instance the original reading is to be found *somewhere* in the manuscripts. That "somewhere" can be narrowed down by the methods we discussed in the last chapter. Further, since the original reading need not be guessed at, we have an actual database—the pool of variants found in the manuscripts—that can be tested for theological deviations.

An illustration is in order here. Suppose conjectural emendation were needed for Abraham Lincoln's Gettysburg Address. In the opening sentence, a comparison of the manuscripts might show something like this:[10]

Manuscript A: Four score and seven _____ ago our _____ ____ brought forth, upon this continent, a new nation, conceived in _____dom, and dedicated to the proposition that "all _____ are created equal."

Manuscript B: Four score and _____ _____ ago our ___ _____s brought forth, upon this continent, a new nation, _____ in lib_____, and dedicated to the proposition that "all _____ are created _____."

Comparing these two manuscripts, we notice that there are gaps. Perhaps there is a wormhole in one manuscript and water damage on the other. Fortunately, some of the gaps are filled in by the other manuscript, but not all. Putting the data together from both manuscripts, we can get the following:

Four score and seven _____ ago our _____s brought forth, upon this continent, a new nation, conceived in {lib_____/_____dom?}, and dedicated to the proposition that "all _____ are created equal."

In such an instance, would Lincoln scholars have the right to put *anything they wish* in the gaps? Of course not. There are a finite number of options. For example, since we know the date of the Gettysburg Address, the "four score and seven" cannot refer to days or months. It must refer to *years*. Also, if one variant has "lib____" while the other has "____dom," scholars may guess that something like either *liberty* or *freedom* belonged here. Perhaps they cannot decide between these two, but they do not have the right to think that *libations* or *Christendom* was the appropriate word. Common sense has to prevail when doing conjectural emendation. As to who brought forth the new nation, scholars might suppose that something like *fathers, forefathers,* or *leaders* would be appropriate. Nothing of substance is at stake here, of course, except for the exact wording. But again, only a finite number of options are really possible. Finally, the last statement—that "all

_____ are created equal"—might require something like *people* or *men*. But *people* would hardly do in 1863, since *men* was the generic term used at that time when all people were in view.

Finally, to make their argument, Lincoln scholars would have to find other speeches by the president, as well as his writings, to get a sense as to what he might have said. Manners and customs of the day would be examined, and the conjectures would have to make sense. All in all, even in a text such as this, there would be a finite number of options, and no reasonable person would consider all conceivable options as equally possible.

The situation for the New Testament is hardly as bleak as this! Of the 138,000 words of the original text, only one or two might have no manuscript support. And in the places where conjecture may be necessary, this does not mean that we have no idea what the original text said. Instead, precisely because almost all the possible variants are already to be found in the manuscripts, scholars have a rather limited number of options with which to contend. Now, suppose that when faced with variants, textual critics simply picked readings at random without any genuine scholarly method, like chimps taking a multiple-choice exam. But even if this were the case, virtually all of the answers would make sense, and most of them are very close to the wording of the others. Furthermore, almost never is there the option, "None of the above." Of course, as we saw in the previous chapter, New Testament textual criticism is a very exacting discipline, with several checks and balances. It is not a bunch of chimps randomly picking from a list of options. Frankly, when skeptics try to make the claim that we simply have no clue what the original New Testament text said, one has to wonder what drives their dogmatic skepticism, because it certainly isn't the evidence.[11]

WHAT THEOLOGICAL TRUTHS ARE AT STAKE?

The short answer to the question of what theological truths are at stake in these variants is—none. Most New Testament scholars are of the opinion that no doctrine, no teaching of the New Testament, is jeopardized by textual variants. The view goes back to J. A. Bengel (1687–1752), who came to this conclusion after examining thirty thousand variants.[12] Since his day, many others have argued the same thing—that no doctrine is jeopardized by textual variants.[13]

Some scholars, however, have argued that doctrines—even cardinal, foundational affirmations—are affected by the variants. Kenneth W. Clark, for example, attempted to show that a particular New Testament teaching was *suppressed* in some manuscripts.[14] Of course, even if true, this does not demonstrate that the doctrine is eradicated or truly jeopardized. Still, the wording in Acts 1:11, for example, differs among the manuscripts. One manuscript group known as the Western text lacks "into heaven" in the clause: "this Jesus who was taken up from you into heaven. . . ." Thus, some claim that the Western text undercuts the New Testament affirmation of the ascension of Christ because of this verse. However, to maintain that view, the Western text must lack *all* references to the ascension. Yet Acts 1:11 reads, "Men of Galilee, why do you stand here looking up into the sky? This same Jesus who has been taken up from you into heaven will come back in the same way you saw him go into heaven." The "into the sky" and the second "into heaven" in this verse are untouched in the Western text. And most other ascension texts are not altered either. It may be that the Western scribes were trying to trim words and phrases for stylistic reasons, but it is extremely doubtful that they were attempting to eradicate any reference to the ascension of Christ. If that had been their motive, they were singularly incompetent in their attempt.[15]

More recently, Bart Ehrman, a leading textual critic, has written a book for a popular readership titled *Misquoting Jesus*. Ehrman is well known for his indefatigable scholarship and provocative opinions.[16] This work, which, according to Ehrman, is the first book written on New Testament textual criticism for a lay audience,[17] concludes that

It would be wrong . . . to say—as people sometimes do— that the changes in our text have no real bearing on what the texts mean or on the theological conclusions that one draws from them. We have seen, in fact, that just the opposite is the case.[18]

Some of the chief examples of theological differences among the variants that Ehrman discusses are a passage in which Jesus is said to be angry (Mark 1:41), an explicit statement about the Trinity (1 John 5:7–8), and a text in which "even the Son of God himself does not know when the end will come" (Matt. 24:36 NIV).[19] But Ehrman's argument is overstated in each instance. For example, although certain ancient manuscripts speak of Jesus as being angry in Mark 1:41 while others speak of him as having compassion, the fact is that in Mark 3:5 Jesus is said to be angry—wording that is indisputably in the original text of Mark. So it is hardly something that changes the interpretation or theology of Mark's Gospel to see Jesus as angry in 1:41. As for the explicit Trinitarian passage, see our discussion below.

Regarding Matthew 24:36, many manuscripts record Jesus as speaking of his own prophetic ignorance ("But as for that day and hour no one knows it—neither the angels in heaven, *nor the Son*—except the Father alone"), but many others lack the words "nor the Son."[20] Whether "nor the Son" is authentic or not is disputed, but what is not disputed is the wording in the parallel in Mark 13:32: "But as for that day or hour no one knows it—neither the angels in heaven, nor the Son—except the Father." Thus, there can be no doubt that Jesus spoke of his own prophetic ignorance in the Olivet discourse. Consequently, what doctrinal issues are really at stake in Matthew 24:36?

Curiously, in his six discussions of Matthew 24:36, *not once* does Ehrman mention this parallel passage. Instead, he insists that scribes struggled over the wording, even altering the text because of their theological convictions. (He also does not mention that even if "neither the Son" is not explicitly stated in Matthew, the idea of the Son's ignorance is implicitly seen in the final phrase of verse 36: "except the Father *alone*.") Why, then, did these same scribes simply skip over Mark 13:32, leaving the wording untouched? The notion that Jesus confessed prophetic ignorance is solidly attested in the Scriptures. There is no new revelation here. The only issue is whether Matthew represents the words of Christ the same way that Mark does. But since the early church obviously knew of such a text in Mark and left it unaltered, this tells us that the theology taught in Mark 13:32 hardly caused a ripple[21] (since only a handful of late manuscripts deleted the words) and that therefore the reasons for its omission or addition in Matthew 24:36 must be accounted for on other grounds.[22] One simply cannot maintain that the wording in verse 36 changes one's basic theological convictions about Jesus since the same sentiment is already implied in Matthew and explicitly stated in Mark.

The idea that the variants in the New Testament manuscripts alter the theology of the New Testament is overstated, at best.[23] Quite a bit more nuance is required to see what the real trouble areas are. Unfortunately, as careful a scholar as Ehrman is, his treatment of major theological changes in the text of the New Testament tends to fall under one of two criticisms. Either his textual decisions are suspect or his interpretations are suspect. These criticisms were made of his earlier major work, *Orthodox Corruption of Scripture*, from which *Misquoting Jesus* has drawn extensively. Yet, the conclusions that he put forth there are still stated here without a recognition of some of the severe criticisms of his work the first go-around.[24] For a book geared toward a lay audience, one would think that he would want to nuance his discussion a bit more, especially with all the theological weight that he says is on the line. Significant textual variants that alter core doctrines of the New Testament have not yet been produced.

A little perspective is in order here. Two groups of people tend to claim that the early manuscripts of the New Testament are badly corrupted, radical liberals and "KJV only" advocates (and advocates of the Greek New Testament that the KJV is translated from, the *Textus Receptus* or *TR*).

The "KJV only" pamphleteers have waged a holy war on all who would use any modern version of the New Testament, or any Greek text based on the few ancient manuscripts rather than on the many late ones.[25] Jasper James Ray is a highly influential representative of this approach.[26] In his book, *God Wrote Only One Bible*,[27] Ray says that no modern version may properly be called the Bible, that salvation and spiritual growth can only come through versions based on the *TR*, and that Satan is the prime mover behind all translations based on the more ancient manuscripts.[28] David Otis Fuller calls the modern translations "bastard Bibles,"[29] and argues that anyone who uses them has been duped by Satan.[30]

When it comes to the details, however, the "KJV only" folks get a little fuzzy. New Testament scholar Dr. Greg Herrick relates the story of a conversation he had with a "KJV only" man recently:

> When this fellow told me that all modern translations were based on corrupt manuscripts, and that they were filled with heresy, I began to ask some questions:
>
> "Do you believe in the deity of Christ?" I asked.
>
> "Yes, of course!" the KJV man said.
>
> "Do you believe in the Virgin Birth of Christ?" I inquired.
>
> "Yes, I do!" he responded.
>
> "What about the bodily resurrection of Christ, the Trinity, salvation by grace?" I asked.
>
> "Yes, I believe in all these things."
>
> "Whew! I'm relieved to hear that, because I got all those doctrines from my modern translation."[31]

It is not only the "KJV only" advocates, however, who think that the ancient manuscripts are terribly corrupt. Frank Zindler, an outspoken atheist and critic of Christianity, discusses the famous *Comma Johanneum*, a passage found in 1 John 5 in the KJV but not in modern translations. This text says, "For there are three that bear record in heaven, the Father, the Word, and the Holy Ghost: and these three are one" (1 John 5:7 KJV). Zindler correctly notes that this verse was added to an early edition of the Greek New Testament, published in 1522, because of pressure from church hierarchy. He also notes that the wording was not found in any Greek manuscripts prior to the fifteenth century. But then he stumbles:

> The discovery that the oldest Bibles omit 1 John 5:7 leaves Christians without biblical "proof of the Trinity." While there are still other verses that are compatible with trinitarian doctrine, none are proof of it. Unless Christian apologists consider the Trinity trivial, they must admit that the differences in MSS are important![32]

Is the Trinity truly a trivial doctrine? Is it something that cannot be demonstrated by the oldest manuscripts? If so, how is it possible that the Council of Constantinople in 381 explicitly affirmed the Trinity? How could they do this without the benefit of a verse that didn't get into the Greek New Testament for another millennium? Further, Constantinople's statement was not written in a vacuum: the early church put together in a theological formulation what they saw in the New Testament. Zindler does not answer the historical question; rather, he simply wants to cast doubt on the orthodoxy of the early manuscripts. His logic is flawed because it doesn't square with history. As we have said before, an ounce of evidence is worth a pound of presumption.

An important distinction needs to be made here. If a particular verse does not teach the deity of Christ in some of the manuscripts, does this mean that that doctrine is suspect? It would only be suspect if all the verses that affirm Christ's deity are textually suspect. And even then the variants would have to be plausible. It is well known that later manuscripts did add words here and there that conformed to orthodoxy.[33] But this hardly means that all the verses that affirm a particular doctrine are affected.

If major teachings of the New Testament are not impacted by viable variants, what about *minor* doctrines? By minor doctrines we mean some noncentral belief or practice. Yes, some of those seem to be affected. But these are quite rare.[34] Thus it is better to say that no viable variant affects any cardinal truth of the New Testament. The key words here are *viable* and *cardinal.* Many New Testament scholars, however, would say that that is too cautious a statement.[35]

The Early Manuscripts and the Deity of Christ

In their 1982 best-seller, *Holy Blood, Holy Grail*, authors Michael Baigent, Richard Leigh, and Henry Lincoln suggest that Constantine changed the text of the New Testament in the fourth century:

> In A.D[.] 303, a quarter of a century earlier, the pagan emperor Diocletian had undertaken to destroy all Christian writings that could be found. As a result Christian documents—especially in Rome—all but vanished. When Constantine commissioned new versions of these documents, it enabled the custodians of orthodoxy to revise, edit, and rewrite their material as they saw fit, in accordance with their tenets. It was at this point that most of the crucial alterations in the New Testament were probably made and Jesus assumed the unique status he has enjoyed ever since. The importance of Constantine's commission must not be underestimated. Of the five thousand extant early manuscript versions of the New Testament, not one predates the fourth century. The New Testament as it exists today is essentially a product of fourth-century editors and writers—custodians of orthodoxy, "adherents of the message," with vested interests to protect.[36]

As we have argued throughout this section, the factual errors in this sort of statement are legion. The authors set the reader up for their shocking assertion by claiming that there are "five thousand extant early manuscript versions of the New Testament." Although nothing in ancient Greek or Latin literature compares to the New Testament in terms of the surviving documents, it is hardly accurate to say that there are five thousand *early* manuscripts of the New Testament. There are several hundred from the first millennium; the rest are from 1000 or later. The implication that *Holy Blood, Holy Grail* seems to make is that with thousands of *early* manuscripts, and none before the fourth century, a conspiracy is afoot. And Constantine is the culprit. This, of course, makes for titillating reading, but it bears no resemblance to historical fact.

We will focus on a single point here (see the later section "The Divinity of Jesus: Early Tradition or Late Superstition?" for evidence of belief in the divinity of Christ prior to Constantine): Is it true that no New Testament manuscripts predate the fourth century, thus allowing for the possibility that Constantine invented the doctrine of the deity of Christ? Hardly. The reality is that there are at least *forty-eight* Greek New Testament manuscripts that predate the fourth century.[37] Now, to be sure, all of these are fragmentary, but many of them include very large fragments (such as most of Paul's letters or almost the entirety of two Gospels). Altogether, they cover about half of the New Testament.

Let's look at some of the verses in pre-fourth-century manuscripts that speak explicitly of Christ's deity. We are restricting our discussion to those verses in which Jesus is called "God." Beyond these, there are dozens of other passages that affirm his deity implicitly (some of which we will discuss in the section "The Divinity of Jesus"). But here we want to show that it is quite impossible for Constantine to have invented the deity of Christ when that doctrine is already found in manuscripts that predate him by a century or more.

Explicit References to Christ's Deity in
New Testament Manuscripts Before the Fourth Century

	John 1:1	John 20:28	Romans 9:5	Hebrews 1:8
P^{46} (A.D. 200)			X	X
P^{66} (A.D. 175–225)	X	X		
P^{75} (early 3d century A.D.)	X			

It is important to note that these three papyri are among our most important manuscripts of the New Testament. P[46] includes eight of Paul's letters and the letter to the Hebrews. P[66] covers most of John's Gospel. P[75] includes most of Luke and part of John. The later manuscripts from the fourth century—the manuscripts that Constantine allegedly corrupted—are very much in agreement with these manuscripts. Indeed, the manuscript that modern translations rely on as much as any other is Vaticanus, a fourth-century codex that has about three-fourths of the New Testament. The agreement between Codex Vaticanus and P[75] is as great as any two ancient manuscripts.[38] Not only this, but in all the passages listed above, *there are no significant variants from any manuscripts of any age.*[39] They all tell the same story: Jesus is true deity.

We have argued two basic points in this chapter. First, there is virtually no need for conjecture about the original wording. That is, the wording of the original text is almost always to be found in the extant (remaining) copies. Second, any uncertainty over the wording of the original New Testament does not have an impact on major teachings of the New Testament. The deity of Christ certainly is not affected by this.

There is simply no room for uncertainty about what the New Testament originally taught. Whether one chooses to believe it is a different matter, and that is taken up in other chapters. Our concern here is simply to show that the fundamental teachings of the New Testament are undisturbed by viable textual variants.

PART 3

DID THE EARLY CHURCH MUZZLE THE CANON?

Chapter 9

THE RANGE OF THE CANON

Eventually, four Gospels and twenty-three other texts were canonized (declared to be the Holy Scriptures) into a Bible. This did not occur, however, until the sixth century.

—DAN BURSTEIN,
Secrets of the Code, 116

So far we have argued that the Gospel writers basically got the story of Jesus right. We discussed the deeply rooted oral tradition in the Jewish culture and noted that the story of Jesus would have been passed on faithfully from teacher to student in the first few decades of the Christian faith. When the Gospel writers put pen to papyrus, each one certainly had his own take on things. Each selected what to put in and what to emphasize, shaping the material for his particular readers.

But shaping what was already found in the story of Jesus and *inventing*—out of nothing—a life of Christ are two very different things. The fact that the Gospels have several differences shows that they were not produced in collusion with one another. And even though Matthew and Luke used Mark's Gospel as a template, this in no way means that they gullibly copied his narratives without verifying the truth of the story. Just the opposite seems to be the case: If they used Mark, then they approved of Mark in his essential affirmations. We can't have our cake and eat it too. That is, we can't, on the one hand, affirm that Luke and Matthew gullibly copied Mark but, on the other hand, claim that they strayed from Mark because of their own creativity. Frequently, when they stray from Mark, the story gets blander and shorter, clearer, or stated more accurately. This kind of editing can hardly be due to the imagination of the authors! The oral tradition, coupled with the way in which Matthew and Luke used Mark, argues that all three Synoptic Gospels got the essentials of the life of Jesus right.

We also have seen that the rest of the New Testament was copied in such a way that we can recover most of the original wording. The suggestion that the scribes went wild on the text, that there were no controls, and that scholars cannot determine the wording of the original because of such chaos is nonsense. Even though we may not know exactly, in every instance, what the original wording is, that's a far cry from saying that we don't know *anything* about the original wording. Further, no cardinal doctrine depends on any plausible variant. Although we cannot have absolute certainty about the wording of the original, there is no need for total despair. The lack of one does not necessarily produce the other, even though alarmists on both the left and the right argue that this must be so. Neither dogmatic certitude nor dogmatic skepticism is warranted when it comes to the text of the New Testament. In sum, we can have a high degree of confidence regarding the authentic wording behind the great majority of *variants* in the New Testament.

INTRODUCTION

But how do we know which *books* should be included in the New Testament? How did the early church decide what was Scripture and what was not? What were the criteria? In particular, how do we know that our four Gospels should be there rather than, say, the Gospel of Thomas or some other work? Some radical scholars today are arguing, in fact, that the Gospel of Thomas should find its place next to the other four Gospels, or even replace the Gospel of John in our New Testaments.[1] Are their claims justified?

Discerning which books belong in the Bible and how we can tell is called *canonization*. This process involves a long and complicated history. A book accepted as Scripture is said to be *canonical* or to have the status of *canonicity*. Some of the issues include when the New Testament books were considered as Scripture; what criteria were used to determine which books were in and which books were out (we will look at only a couple of these criteria); how the New Testament canon relates to the Old Testament canon; why Protestants have a different list of Old Testament books than do Roman Catholics; and whether the canon is truly closed in that no more books can be added. Thinking Christians wrestle with these topics. But as important as they are, they are not central to what occupies us here. Our goal is simply to highlight a few major issues that ultimately relate to the person of Christ. In the back of the book we list some helpful works on this subject that you can consult for more information.

In this section, we want to explore three key questions: (1) *When* and *why* were the books of the New Testament accepted into the canon, and, especially, which were accepted early on and without dispute? (2) What did the ancient church think of forgeries? (3) Was there a conspiracy against the "lost books of the Bible"? Before we begin, it might be helpful to offer a definition of "canon."

DEFINITION OF CANON

What does it mean to say that the New Testament is canon? "Canon" is a transliteration of the Greek word *kanōn*, which means "rule" or "standard." When applied to the New Testament, two similar, though different, answers are given to the question: either the New Testament is "a collection of authoritative books or an authoritative collection of books."[2] That is, either the twenty-seven books of the New Testament were *discovered* to be authoritative because of their intrinsic worth, "ring of truth," and obvious authority (thus, a collection of authoritative books), or those books were *determined* to be authoritative by some *other* authority (thus, an authoritative collection).

William Barclay said, "It is the simple truth to say that the New Testament books became canonical because no one could stop them doing so."[3] Bruce Metzger concurs: "The Church did not create the canon, but came to recognize, accept, affirm, and confirm the self-authenticating quality of certain documents that imposed themselves as such upon the Church."[4] This implies that their authority was intrinsic and only needed to be discovered by the early church. Thus, the canon is a list of authoritative books.

A CANON WITHIN THE CANON?

Many discussions about the canon of the New Testament focus on the books that struggled for acceptance, as though this told the whole story. For example, Dan Burstein suggests that the entire process was long and drawn out: "Eventually, four Gospels and twenty-three other texts were canonized (declared to be the Holy Scriptures) into a Bible. This did not occur, however, until the sixth century."[5] Such a statement has a grain of truth in it. It is true that in *one* branch of the ancient church (the Syrian), *some* books were not considered canonical until the sixth century.[6] But the Syrian church was the exception to the rule. By the end of the fourth century, the church in the West had accepted all twenty-seven books as canonical. The church in the East, to some degree, wrestled with a few of the books much longer.[7] But the majority of the New Testament books were accepted centuries earlier by all branches of Christianity.

The problem with a statement such as Burstein's is that it gives the impression that all the books were up for grabs until the sixth century. It is akin to saying that World War I did not end until June 1921 because that is when the United States signed a peace treaty with Germany (the U.S. Senate never ratified the Treaty of Versailles). But even though the war was not *officially* over until 1921, hostilities ceased on November 11, 1918.

Should a major conflict be considered terminated only when it is officially terminated or when the fighting stops? If we argue that it's not over until some official document says it is, then World War I went on for two and one-half years after the cessation of hostilities. But in World War II, just the opposite happened: The war officially ended on September 2, 1945, but the hostilities continued for decades. Many know the story of Hiroo Onoda, the Japanese soldier on the Philippine island of Lubang, who hid out in the jungles for twenty-nine years. But many do not know that thousands of Japanese soldiers did not lay down their arms on September 2, 1945. By January 1948, nearly five hundred more Japanese soldiers had surrendered, not realizing that the war had been over for more than two years. Later in 1948, as many as twenty thousand soldiers in the mountains of Manchuria surrendered. Between 1949 and 1973, more than thirty other Japanese soldiers surrendered. Hiroo Onada was not the last holdout. Captain Fumio Nakahira surrendered on Mindoro Island in the Philippines in 1980. No one today would claim that World War II lasted for forty years beyond 1945—even though it did not end that year for thousands of soldiers.

When it comes to the canon of the New Testament, no official churchwide creed ever pronounced the canon closed.[8] Even during the Protestant Reformation, some of the Reformers as well as Catholics expressed serious doubts about books on the fringes of the canon. As recently as 1968, several clergy argued that Martin Luther King Jr.'s "Letter from a Birmingham Jail" should be included in the New Testament![9] On the other hand, the majority of New Testament books were accepted as authoritative very early. And by the fourth century, the canon was unofficially closed in the West. Further, in the East several lists, beginning in the fourth century, gave the same twenty-seven books as the New Testament canon. Thus, apart from a few stragglers (both churches and books), the canon was *practically*, though not officially, closed in the fourth century. It's a misrepresentation of the facts to claim that the books of the New Testament were not considered canonical until the sixth century, just because a few were still doubted by one segment of the church.

Three key criteria were used to assess the authority of these books—apostolicity, orthodoxy, and catholicity. Was a book written by an apostle or an associate of an apostle (apostolicity)? Did it conform to the teachings of other books known to be by apostles (orthodoxy)? Was it accepted early and by a majority of churches (catholicity)? Although the ancient church wrestled with a few of the books in light of these criteria, a substantial core was accepted quickly and without dispute.

At first, Christians did not have a New Testament canon. The proclamation of the gospel was by word of mouth. Even Paul's letters, though obviously viewed as weighty and authoritative, were most likely not perceived to be Scripture as soon as they were penned. Further, to circulate the books of an illegal religion in the ancient world was not an easy task. Prior to the second century, they could not even be collected into one volume because the modern book form, the codex, had not been invented yet, and scrolls could hold only so much information. The largest usable scroll, in fact, could hold little more than one of the Gospels.

But it is one thing to say that the early church did not recognize the New Testament books as Scripture immediately, and another to say that they did not recognize them as authoritative in some sense. Our question in this chapter has to do especially with the collection and formal recognition of these books that would later be labeled *Scripture.*

The first canon list we are aware of was written by Marcion in about 140. Marcion was a Docetist—that is, he believed that Jesus Christ only appeared to be human. He was also anti-Semitic, denying, among other things, that the Old Testament was Scripture. He denied that Jesus was the son of the Old Testament God, which he called a demiurge;[10] rather, Jesus was the son of the good God of the New Testament. Consequently, Marcion's canon excluded Matthew, Mark, and John. Of the Gospels, the list included only a heavily edited copy of Luke. Marcion's canon included ten of Paul's letters, also edited. Marcion was influenced by the radical dualism common in Greek philosophy, which saw spirit as good and material as evil.[11]

Two important facts relate to Marcion's list. First, since he was a heretic, Marcion's list gave the early church impetus "to publish more comprehensive and less idiosyncratic lists."[12] Several books were already circulating in collections, such as Paul's letters and the Gospels, but no formal list had been drawn up. Marcion's canon prompted the church to do just this.

Second, even though Marcion was a heretic whose views were largely compatible with Gnostic teaching,[13] which was gaining a foothold at this time, he *only* included parts of our *New Testament* in his list. To be sure, he edited these books heavily to suit his own purposes, but why didn't he include such works as the Gospel of Thomas or the Gospel of Mary or the Acts of Peter? Marcion was certainly exposed to Gnostic ideas,[14] so why didn't he include *any* Gnostic writings in his list? The most likely inference is that they did not yet exist. And even if some of them did exist, they would not have been regarded as authentic because of their obviously recent vintage. Marcion easily could have edited any Gnostic work for his own purposes, just as he did the New Testament books. Indeed, his job would have been considerably easier, since he would not have had to cut out nearly as much material! The fact that he used only New Testament books for his truncated canon, and mutilated those copies, suggests that even a radical heretic like Marcion knew that these books were already highly regarded.[15]

After Marcion, other canon lists started to appear. The Muratorian Canon was composed in the latter part of the second century,[16] most likely in Rome. Although the copies of the Muratorian Canon are all fragmentary,[17] most of it can be made out. The list includes the four Gospels, Acts, Paul's thirteen letters, Jude, Revelation, 1 John, and either 2 John or 3 John or both.[18] Thus, at least twenty-one or twenty-two books are listed as authoritative before the end of the second century.

The anonymous author of the Muratorian Canon also comments on other books, which fall into three categories: disputed books, edifying but not authoritative books, and books that were to be rejected as heretical. The one disputed book was the Apocalypse of Peter:

"We receive only the apocalypses of John and Peter, though some of us are not willing that the latter be read in church."[19] One book that was judged to be edifying but not authoritative was The Shepherd of Hermas. It was recognized as a recent work and thus could be read privately. Finally, several other works are mentioned as both recent productions and heretical and therefore not acceptable at all.[20]

It is important to note that the age of a work was a determining factor in canonicity. A book that was perceived to have been written after the time of the apostles was categorically rejected. As time went on, and as memories of the age of certain books died out, canonical claims were made for some of the second-century documents. But in the earliest canon lists, these books were absent (in Marcion's list) or were explicitly rejected (in the Muratorian Canon) as being recent works and therefore nonapostolic.

Other writers began to explicitly discuss the canon. Over the following decades, some of the books "sitting on the fence" of the canon were disputed, but the core remained largely the same. In some places, various noncanonical books were looked on favorably, even receiving temporary and localized canonical status. But over all, the same books showed up on each list as undisputed authoritative books on which the faith and practice of the church were built.

As New Testament scholar Bruce Metzger notes:

> What is really remarkable . . . is that, though the fringes of the New Testament canon remained unsettled for centuries, a high degree of unanimity concerning the greater part of the New Testament was attained within the first two centuries among the very diverse and scattered congregations not only throughout the Mediterranean world but also over an area extending from Britain to Mesopotamia.[21]

So what did the ancient church recognize as the "greater part of the New Testament" or the "canon within the canon"? The four Gospels (Matthew, Mark, Luke, John) and Paul's thirteen letters were almost always on the lists, as well as the book of Acts. Only on rare occasions was any doubt expressed about any of these. As well, 1 Peter and 1 John were usually included. In the East, Hebrews was considered canonical and placed with Paul's letters. Revelation was considered canonical in many circles. Thus, twenty to twenty-two of the twenty-seven books of the New Testament were consistently regarded as Scripture as early as that label was applied to the New Testament.

THE CLOSING OF THE CANON?

By the fourth century, Christians were coming to terms with even some disputed books. The early fourth-century church historian Eusebius of Caesarea (c. 260–340) has a lengthy discussion of the canon of the New Testament as it was perceived in the East. But his discussion reflects the attitudes of still earlier fathers, Clement and Origen:

> At this point it seems reasonable to summarize the writings of the New Testament which have been quoted. In the first place should be put the holy tetrad of the Gospels. To them follows the writing of the Acts of the Apostles. After this should be reckoned the Epistles of Paul. Following them the Epistle of John called the first, and in the same way should be recognized the Epistle of Peter. In addition to these should be put, if it seem desirable, the Revelation of John, the arguments concerning which we will expound at the proper time. These belong to the Recognized Books [homolegoumena]. Of the Disputed Books [antilegomena] which are nevertheless known to most are the Epistle called of James, that of Jude, the second Epistle of Peter, and the so-called second and third Epistles of John which may be the work of the evangelist or of some other with the same name.[22]

Eusebius recognizes twenty-two of the twenty-seven books of the New Testament as undisputed (though he later vacillates on Revelation), and the rest as disputed but widely read and recognized. He includes Hebrews among the letters of Paul, even though elsewhere he is aware that some do not regard it as Pauline. By the early fourth century, then, all twenty-seven books of the New Testament were tentatively considered canonical, with twenty-two of them definitely so. We will come back to Eusebius in the next chapter to see what he has to say about some other writings. But for now, we simply wish to stress that the majority of the books of the New Testament had been accepted from early times, and about half a dozen books still on the fringes of canonicity were nevertheless recognized as ancient and orthodox. As D. A. Carson and Douglas J. Moo observe concerning Eusebius's statement, "The Gospels, Acts, the thirteen Paulines, 1 Peter and 1 John are universally accepted very early; most of the remaining contours of the New Testament canon are already established by the time of Eusebius."[23]

In the West, a flurry of unofficial canon lists were composed by leading church fathers, and during the fourth century, the core books were always included. By 393, the canon was effectively closed when Augustine weighed in on the matter. Jerome added icing on the cake by discussing at some length the disputed books. Further, he included the twenty-seven New Testament books in his translation of the Bible (known as the Vulgate). Since that time, the Catholic Church (except in rare instances) has never questioned which books were in and which were not.

The situation in the East was not quite as decisive. There was greater sensitivity in the East to works of value even if apostles did not write them. Hence, the Eastern lists often included those books that were definitely canonical, those that were possibly canonical, and those that were good sources of spiritual truth but not canonical.

In 367, Athanasius, in his Thirty-ninth Festal Letter, pronounced without reservation the twenty-seven books of the New Testament as canonical. Not all in the East agreed with Athanasius on this list. Gregory of Nazianzus (d. 389) agreed with him except on the book of Revelation. Amphilochius (c. after 394) accepted all except 2 Peter, 2 and 3 John, Jude, and Revelation. Didymus the Blind (d. c. 398) accepted all except, apparently, 2 and 3 John. Chrysostom, Theodore of Mopsuestia, and Theodoret, all from the East and writing in the late fourth or early fifth century, all included at least twenty-two of the twenty-seven books. Thus, even though Eusebius and Athanasius argued for a canon of twenty-seven books, later Eastern fathers restricted the list.

It is important to note, however, that none of them *added* any other gospels or letters or apocalypses to the New Testament canon. Furthermore, the books they rejected had been disputed from the beginning—the shorter letters (2 and 3 John and Jude), 2 Peter (because it differed in style from 1 Peter), and Revelation (because it differed in style from John's Gospel and because of its apparent eschatological viewpoint). But the twenty-two core books remained solidly confirmed.

CONCLUSION

The canon of the New Testament was a list of authoritative books "that imposed themselves as such"[24] upon the early church. As early as the label *Scripture* was applied to any books of the New Testament, the four Gospels and Paul's thirteen letters were included. As well, Acts, 1 Peter, and 1 John were generally undisputed. The same can be said for the most part for Hebrews and Revelation. By the end of the fourth century, the canon was effectively, though not officially, closed in the West. In the East, certain influential voices argued for a canon of twenty-seven books, but some writers dissented. It is important to realize that their dissent did not move in the direction of a larger canon but a smaller one. Only a few books on the edges of the canon were disputed. These same writers rejected outright the heretical books, if they discussed them at all.

What are we to make of the fact that in the East the canon remained an open question for a long time? This belongs to the larger question of why no official churchwide council or no ancient creed made a pronouncement on the canon. We can draw at least three implications from this fact.

First, there was never any great pressure within the church to accept certain books as canonical.[25] This makes it all the more im-
pressive that the church came to such firm conclusions about the
majority of the books early on, and the rest in due time.

Second, because there was no pronouncement, some books naturally were debated, at least in a part of the church. The debates always
related to apostolicity, catholicity, and orthodoxy. On this score, the
shorter letters came up short on catholicity because their very brevity
made them easy to overlook, 2 Peter was suspect because its apostolic
authorship was questioned, and Revelation was doubted for reasons
of orthodoxy. But Paul's letters and the Gospels were always the core
on all three fronts. The very lack of a council's decree allowed the
ancient church to wrestle with the legitimacy of these books. And on
this score, the most important books were never doubted.

Third, that no decree ever announced what books were canonical
also tells us implicitly that the canon was a list of authoritative books
rather than an authoritative list of books. Those books that belong in
the canon belong there because of their intrinsic worth and authenticity as witnesses to Jesus Christ, not because some church council
declared them to be authoritative. As Metzger notes:

> Neither religious nor artistic works really gain anything by
> having an official stamp put on them. If, for example, all the
> academies of music in the world were to unite in declaring
> Bach and Beethoven to be great musicians, we should reply,
> "Thank you for nothing; we knew that already." And what
> the musical public can recognize unaided, those with spiri-
> tual discernment in the early Church were able to recognize
> in the case of their sacred writings through what Calvin
> called the interior witness of the Holy Spirit. This *testimo-
> nium Spiritus Sancti internum*, however, does not create the
> authority of Scripture (which exists already in its own right),
> but is the means by which believers come to acknowledge
> that authority. It is the correlative to the self-authentication
> (*autopistia*) of Scripture, and neither the Fathers nor Calvin

attempted to resolve differences over the delineation of the canon by a simple appeal to the Holy Spirit's dictates.[26]

We wish to conclude this chapter by coming back to our original question: Did the early church get it right when it came to which books should be included in the canon? Let us suppose, for sake of argument, that only Eusebius's "recognized books" *(homolegoumena)* should be in the canon. What is lost? Five books comprising eleven chapters of material. It is not accidental that some of the shortest books of the New Testament were on the disputed list. They simply would not have been quoted as often as the longer works and could have flown under the radar of the early church fathers' affirmation. To require notice of them would be akin to requiring notice of *every chapter* in Paul's letters, since three of these books are merely one chapter long. None of these books are primary witnesses to the historicity of Jesus Christ, though they certainly make a contribution to understanding who he is and what the early church believed about him.

Of course, we are not suggesting that they should be removed from the New Testament. But even if they were removed, *the portrait of Jesus would be essentially the same.* To suggest that because the canon was still open in the fourth century means that we have a right to replace the four Gospels with any others, or that we can throw out Paul's letters, is a ridiculous notion. It simply does not stand up to the facts of history. Rather than seeing the ancient church as involved in some sort of cover-up, we might question the motives of those who make such claims. They are so selective and cavalier in how they remember the past that historical facts seem to be trivial things that just get in the way of a good story. Just as Marcion cut up his copy of Luke, so these historical revisionists have carved up the data of history and have told only that part of the story that supports their claims.

Chapter 10

WHAT DID THE ANCIENT CHURCH THINK OF FORGERIES?

It is a remarkable fact that although nearly all modern forms of Christianity do not question the texts included in the New Testament, in the first four centuries every single document was at some time or other branded as either heretical or forged!

—Timothy Freke and Peter Gandy,
The Jesus Mysteries, 224

Many Christians seem to think that any particular New Testament book belongs in the Bible just because it claims to be written by an apostle. When Paul tells the Thessalonian church that the letter is from him, that's enough to settle the issue in their minds. It might surprise them to learn that a large number of other ancient books claimed to be written by apostles or other well-known New Testament figures. Why aren't these books part of our New Testament if they make the claim of apostolic authorship? After all, if they make the claim of apostolic authorship, they belong in the New Testament, right? Not necessarily. Should such books as the Gospel of Peter, the Gospel of Thomas, the Gospel of Mary, the Acts of John, the Acts of Paul, and the Apocalypse of Peter be in the New Testament? What about the Epistle of Barnabas or Paul's Letter to the Laodiceans? Did the ancient church get rid of books that belong in the New Testament and keep some that don't? Did the ancient church muzzle the canon?

Dozens of books allegedly written by apostles or other leading figures in the New Testament didn't make it into the New Testament. What criteria did the early church use? If apostolic authorship was one of them, didn't the church fail since so many other books also claimed to be by apostles? Further, aren't some of the books in the New Testament *pseudonymous* written by someone other than the purported author?

The next two chapters discuss how the ancient church dealt with the issue of forgeries. This chapter will focus on *method*: What criteria did the church use to sniff out a fake? The next will focus on *content*: What did the books that are not in the New Testament have to say? This chapter also will focus on what books are in the New Testament, while the next chapter will focus on which books are not. Finally, this chapter will examine four New Testament books—one Gospel, two letters, and one apocalypse—that offer insights into the process of canonization, while the next chapter will focus especially on the gospels that didn't make the cut.

THE IMPULSE OF APOSTOLIC AUTHORITY

The New Testament states clearly and forcefully that the apostles held a special place in the establishment of the church. Ephesians 2:20 goes so far as to claim that the church has "been built on the foundation of the apostles and prophets, with Christ Jesus himself as the cornerstone."

The immediate successors of the apostles recognized that the authority the Lord had given the apostles was unique. The Apostolic Fathers (church leaders in the generations immediately following the apostles) recognized a definitive break in authority between the apostles and themselves. Ignatius, bishop of Antioch (d. c. 110), acknowledged that the apostles belonged to a clearly marked era that was now completed. He tells one church, "Be eager, therefore, to be firmly grounded in the precepts of the Lord and the apostles."[1] He is viewing what the apostles taught as the standard by which all other Christian teachings should be measured. On the way to his execution, he writes to another church, "I did not think myself qualified for this, that I, a convict, should give you orders as though I were an apostle."[2] The apostles were eyewitnesses to the person and work of Jesus Christ. As such, their testimony naturally became the standard by which other teaching was measured.

The authority of the apostles regarding the truth of the gospel was obvious to anyone acquainted with Christianity in its early centuries. This explains why dozens of pseudepigraphical gospels, epistles, and apocalypses (books written in someone else's name) were produced: It was an easy route to claim authority for some document that otherwise would have none. The motive thus seems clear.[3]

The clear demarcation in the early patristic period between the authority of the apostles and that of the current church leaders must have created a strong impulse to attribute apostolic authorship to various books. If the ploy worked, these books would gain instant credibility and an air of authority.[4] The question that we now turn to is whether this same motive existed for the New Testament books. That is, were some of the books falsely attributed to apostles?

We will look at four cases that have contributed to our understanding of the canonization process: the Gospel of Mark, the letter to the Hebrews, the book of Revelation, and 2 Peter.

The Gospel of Mark

The New Testament includes Matthew, Mark, Luke, and John as Gospels. We all know them by these names. What may be surprising is that originally they all were *anonymous* works.[5] The titles we know were attached to the writings very early and used consistently: two were by apostles (Matthew, John), one was by a close associate of

Paul (Luke), and one was by Mark. It is this last Gospel that interests us here.

The most ancient testimony about the authorship of the Gospel of Mark is by Papias, the bishop of Hierapolis until c. 130. Born most likely in the 60s A.D., Papias learned from first-generation Christians about the roots of the faith. His testimony about the authorship and composition of Mark's Gospel thus should be given much weight:

> And the Elder used to say this: "Mark, having become Peter's interpreter, wrote down accurately everything he remembered, though not in order, of the things either said or done by Christ. For he neither heard the Lord nor followed him, but afterward, as I said, followed Peter, who adapted his teachings as needed but had no intention of giving an ordered account of the Lord's sayings. Consequently Mark did nothing wrong in writing down some things as he remembered them, for he made it his one concern not to omit anything which he heard or to make any false statement in them."[6]

Papias is appealing to an earlier testimony, "the Elder," as his source. That elder is possibly John the apostle or, if not, at least a first-generation Christian in a position of some authority.

The testimony of the ancient church after Papias is consistent on two points about Mark's Gospel: first, Mark wrote it; second, Mark got his information from Peter. But this raises a serious question: If early Christians wanted to ascribe apostolic authorship for their sacred books, why didn't they do so for *this* Gospel? The ancient testimony always makes a distinction between Mark as the author and Peter as the source of information. Further, Irenaeus, writing several decades after Papias, disagrees with Papias on one key point. He believes that Mark wrote the Gospel *after* Peter had died. Here is where we see the impulse toward apostolic authorship come into play: Irenaeus wanted the *first* Gospel to be written by an apostle (in this case, Matthew), so he disagreed with Papias on *when* Mark wrote. But Irenaeus's chronology of events is doubtful.[7] What is important for us to see is that even Irenaeus—whose motives in making Matthew earlier than Mark are questionable—does not say that Mark's Gospel was really written by Peter. The patristic writers were notorious for getting chronological facts mixed up, but when it came to authorship, they fared better. The ancient writers, even those who succumbed (to a degree) to the temptation of apostolic authority, never completely yielded to this temptation.[8]

The treatment of the Gospel of Mark in the ancient church ought to serve as a bold reminder that the early Christians took seriously the question of authorship. Especially when a particular book was *anonymous*, it allowed any influential person to fill in the blank with his favorite apostle. But this was not done with the Gospel of Mark. Surely the impulse to claim that one of the Gospels was written by Peter was especially strong. That the church refrained from this, claiming only that Mark got his Gospel from Peter, shows remarkable restraint. In fact, the claim has all the earmarks of authenticity.

If the early church refused to call this Gospel "The Gospel according to Peter," would they capitulate when it came to less important works? Many today question the authenticity of Ephesians, 1 and 2 Timothy, Titus, and 2 Peter. But only one of these books was ever questioned in the ancient church. Perhaps the church fathers had more savvy than modern scholarship gives them credit for. Should we not give these ancient authors the benefit of the doubt when there was *no* dissent about authorship?

We can apply this question to another Gospel. Many scholars deny that Matthew wrote Matthew because they believe the church fathers wanted to ascribe apostolic authorship to the Gospel. Yet the same fathers do not give in to that temptation with Mark. Further, Matthew, like Mark, received unanimous testimony in the early church as to its authorship, even though it too was originally an anonymous work. Finally, if the impulse to ascribe authorship to an apostle could overcome conscience, this still doesn't explain why *Matthew's* name is always assigned to the first Gospel. After all, he was not a major disciple. Why, then, is his name—and only his name—

associated with the Gospel that stands first in the New Testament? Unless we want to be totally selective, picking and choosing from the Fathers what we like and don't like, we might want to give them the benefit of the doubt in these matters.

The Letter to the Hebrews

The letter to the Hebrews is another anonymous work. One author says, "Scholarly comments on the New Testament document sometimes called the Letter of Paul to Hebrews usually contain the quite valid observation that the document is not a letter, is not by Paul, and is not written to Hebrews."[9] It is true that no author's name is on this book. And it is also true that it looks more like a homily than a letter, although it does have *some* resemblance to ancient letters. But even letters often had ascriptions of authorship.[10] One very plausible suggestion as to why no name appears on the document is that it originally was written on a scroll. Scrolls dispatched in the ancient world often had the addressee and author's name on the outside of the scroll (much as we have on envelopes today), and these may have worn off before copies of the document were made.

Regardless of the reason for the anonymous nature of Hebrews, this letter soon became associated with Paul. In part, this was no doubt due to the mention of Timothy in Hebrews 13:23 ("You should know that our brother Timothy has been released. If he comes soon, he will be with me when I see you"). As well, the letter has similarities with Paul's way of thinking and seems to be clearly indebted to Paul's ideas.[11]

The first author to cite this epistle was Clement (c. 96), though he does not say who wrote the book. Hebrews is omitted from both Marcion's canon and the Muratorian Canon. From the earliest times in church history, there was much dispute as to its authorship. Unlike the Gospel of Mark, a number of different authors were proposed, though Paul headed the list (so Clement of Alexandria and others). Yet Pauline authorship was explicitly denied by Origen, the successor to Clement, who uttered his famous agnostic confession: "Whoever wrote the epistle, God only knows for sure."

Why did the ancient church ultimately reject Pauline authorship of Hebrews, and what were the consequences? Although the Revised Version (1881) uses the title, "The Epistle of Paul the Apostle to the Hebrews" (following in the footsteps of the King James Bible), almost no one today argues that Paul wrote this book.[12] There are simply too many differences between Hebrews and Paul's letters. These differences were noticed by readers in the ancient church as well.

If Paul did not write Hebrews, then who did? Since the letter did not pass the test of apostolicity, could it be regarded as authoritative, as Scripture? The fact that Hebrews displayed an obvious literary and theological depth, was quoted frequently (beginning in the late first century), and agreed with the known apostolic writings ultimately assured its place in the canon.

The debates regarding the authorship of Hebrews that eventually resulted in the church recognizing its anonymous character (i.e., that it was *not* written by Paul) tell a remarkable story of ecclesiastical integrity. The temptation to call this letter apostolic (because to do otherwise might exclude it from the canon) was overcome. As important as this letter was—and as loved as it was, for it bore the ring of truth—the church did not capitulate to false advertising regarding its authorship. The fact that dozens of names of possible authors have been offered over the centuries shows the keen interest and fascination that Christians have had with this letter. That no consensus has been reached shows that its canonical status is firmly based *on other grounds*. Hebrews is a mirror on the entire canonical process. As William Barclay noted, "It is the simple truth to say that the New Testament books became canonical because no one could stop them doing so."[13]

The Book of Revelation

In the last book of the New Testament, the book of Revelation, the author identifies himself only as "John" (Rev. 1:1, 4, 9; 22:8). He does not call himself "John the apostle" or "John the elder" but simply "John." Unlike other ancient apocalypses that used pseudonyms of well-known figures of the past, this author apparently had no intention to deceive, for "John" doesn't really narrow down the field much!

Revelation's struggle for canonical status is related to this question. It is neither anonymous nor pseudonymous. But the question as to the identity of this John prompted doubts about its inclusion in the New Testament.

The earliest testimony about Revelation seems to assume that John the apostle wrote the book (so Melito, Justin Martyr, Irenaeus, the Muratorian Canon, and possibly Papias). Not only this, but two of these writers, Irenaeus and Melito, were from two of the cities addressed in Revelation, Sardis and Smyrna respectively. They thus "could well be reporting firsthand evidence."[14]

But not all agreed that John the apostle wrote this book. Marcion rejected apostolic authorship, as did Dionysus, a third-century bishop from Alexandria. Lively debates about the authorship ensued. To see this author as other than the apostle John took some mental gymnastics. As D. A. Carson and Douglas J. Moo note,

> We might question whether a John who is never mentioned in the abundant sources for first-century Asian church life would have had sufficient stature to write a book of this sort, so different from anything else in the New Testament, simply under his own name. Particularly does this seem unlikely when we recall that there was a John [the apostle] who was well known in this area at just this period.[15]

Even with significant evidence that the John of this book was the apostle John, the church balked. Early Christians did not naïvely accept this book as authentic because it had the name John in it. Further, everyone who accepted it as canonical in the ancient church recognized that the author was really *someone* named John. It was no forgery.

Whether John the apostle wrote Revelation ultimately is not what decided the issue of this book's canonicity. Today, many conservative scholars question apostolic authorship but still regard the book as Scripture. Other tests besides apostolic authorship obviously were in play in making decisions about the canon in the early church,[16] although apostolic authorship was an important factor. Thus, as strong as the evidence was for John the apostle as the author, there were and are some doubts. The very fact that the church accepted this book as canonical without necessarily affirming apostolic authorship speaks highly of the church's integrity. To argue that John the apostle wrote it would have been a great temptation to those who embraced its theology. That they did not succumb to this temptation gives us a window on their method.

Second Peter

The shorter letters of John, Jude, and James were often disputed. So was Revelation. But the most disputed book of the New Testament, in terms of authorship, is 2 Peter. Unlike the Gospel of Mark and the letter to the Hebrews, it is not an anonymous work. The author claims to be Simon Peter (1:1), the apostle. This letter is not quoted or alluded to very often in the second century[17]—some would say not at all—and this raised suspicions about its authorship early on.

We will not delve deeply into why the early church disputed the authorship of this letter, but we need to note two things: There were doubts about its authenticity because there were doubts about its antiquity; the style of writing in 2 Peter was perceived to be markedly different from the style of writing in 1 Peter. Jerome notes that the stylistic differences between 1 Peter and 2 Peter are substantial, though he believed they could be explained by Peter's use of different secretaries who contributed their own stylistic touches.[18] Eusebius, who doubted the authenticity of the letter, argued that it was not mentioned by name by the most ancient church fathers.[19] These still are two of the most prominent reasons scholars give in arguments that the apostle could not have written this letter.

Without entering into the debate about the authorship of 2 Peter, we simply wish to make two observations. First, *the letter was not accepted without a struggle.* The combination of lack of ancient citations and stylistic differences from 1 Peter was almost a fatal blow to 2 Peter's placement in the canon. Second, since this letter *claimed* to be by Peter, *the early church could not accept it if it were deemed a forgery.* They would either reject it as non-Petrine or accept it as authentic. There was no middle ground; there was no sense of a "benign forgery."

Whether the church was ultimately correct in their assessment of the authorship of this letter is a very important question. But it is not the most important. More significant is that most of the books of the New Testament were never questioned as to authorship precisely because they were used, quoted, and loved from the very beginning. And no book was ever accepted if it was thought to be a forgery.

These debates over authorship are a window into the ancient church's struggles over the canon of the New Testament: The early Christian writers were fully engaged in thinking about the authenticity of various documents. They were not willing to accept even purported apostolic documents at face value but evaluated those claims on two bases. First, they examined the external historical evidence, asking whether the testimony to a particular book was ancient and plentiful. Second, they compared the internal consistency with the undisputed works that were regarded as having divine authority.

Furthermore, the early Christians ultimately resisted the urge to grant instant authority to an anonymous document by ascribing apostolic authorship to it. Contrary to the notion that the ancient church rushed to put an apostle's name on an anonymous work, they carefully worked out their understanding of authorship. The very fact that several books of the New Testament were originally anonymous or insufficiently labeled to make a positive identification of the author (e.g., "John" for Revelation, "Jude" for his letter) shows that the craving for authority that was exhibited regarding so many later heretical works did not seem to be a major factor for the New Testament books. Paul's letters are an exception to this; that is, in many of his letters apostolic authority is consciously defended. But this was due to his opponents questioning his authority and apostleship.

FORGERIES AND FORGERS IN THE CHURCH

We have seen, then, that the early church was very much engaged in thinking about which books were authoritative and canonical. They simply did not rubber-stamp books as "sacred." This brings us to the final question of this chapter: How did the church react to forgeries?

Many scholars today see pseudepigraphy (the writing of a document in someone else's name) as a practice accepted in the ancient church. The topic of forgery actually was discussed at some length in the early church. We wish to make three brief observations.

First, there are examples of forgeries coming to light in the ancient church, and the church's response to them is illuminating. For example, 3 Corinthians, a document that circulated both by itself and as part of the Acts of Paul, was discovered to be a forgery. The author, an elder who wrote the work because of his love for Paul, was defrocked by Tertullian for this fabrication. In about 200, when Serapion, bishop of Antioch, learned that the Gospel of Peter was not written by the apostle, he declared, "For our part, brethren, we receive both Peter and the other apostles as Christ, but the writings which falsely bear their names we reject, as men of experience, knowing that such were not handed down to us."[20]

In the second century, the Muratorian Canon condemned both the letter to the Laodiceans and the letter to the Alexandrians because both were "forged in Paul's name."[21] One of the proofs of forgery was a lack of early attestation. In fact, if a work was found to be of recent origin, even if its authorship was not in doubt, it was not considered to be canonical. For example, the Muratorian Canon rejected the Shepherd of Hermas because, though it was edifying literature, it was composed "very recently, in our times, in the city of Rome." Lack of antiquity was the sole reason for its rejection, for this document was written after the time of the apostles.[22]

Eusebius echoes this sentiment. In the first quarter of the fourth century, he spoke about the New Testament canon at length. In chapter 9, we quoted the first part of Eusebius's remarks to show that at least twenty of the twenty-seven New Testament books were already accepted by his time and that the rest were tentatively accepted. It is worthwhile to see all of his reasoning and why some books were to be rejected outright:

> At this point it seems reasonable to summarize the writings of the New Testament which have been quoted. In the first place should be put the holy tetrad of the Gospels. To them follows the writing of the Acts of the Apostles. After this should be reckoned the Epistles of Paul. Following them the Epistle of John called the first, and in the same way should be recognized the Epistle of Peter. In addition to these should be put, if it seem desirable, the Revelation of John, the arguments concerning which we will expound at the proper time. These belong to the Recognized Books [homolegoumena]. Of the Disputed Books [antilegomena] which are nevertheless known to most are the Epistle called of James, that of Jude, the second Epistle of Peter, and the so-called second and third Epistles of John which may be the work of the evangelist or of some other with the same name. Among the books which are not genuine must be reckoned the Acts of Paul, the work entitled the Shepherd, the Apocalypse of Peter, and in addition to them the letter called of Barnabas and the so-called Teachings of the Apostles. And in addition, as I said, the Revelation of John, if this view prevail. For, as I said, some reject it, but others count it among the Recognized Books. Some have also counted the Gospel according to the Hebrews in which those of the Hebrews who have accepted Christ take a special pleasure. These would all belong to the disputed books, but we have nevertheless been obliged to make a list of them, distinguishing between those writings which, according to the tradition of the Church, are true, genuine, and recognized, and those which differ from them in that they are not canonical but disputed, yet nevertheless are known to most of the writers of the Church,

in order that we might know them and the writings which are put forward by heretics under the name of the apostles containing gospels such as those of Peter, and Thomas, and Matthias, and some others besides, or Acts such as those of Andrew and John and the other apostles. To none of these has any who belonged to the succession of the orthodox ever thought it right to refer in his writings. Moreover, the type of phraseology differs from apostolic style, and the opinion and tendency of their contents is widely dissonant from true orthodoxy and clearly shows that they are the forgeries of heretics. They ought, therefore, to be reckoned not even among spurious books but shunned as altogether wicked and impious.[23]

Beyond the twenty or more books Eusebius considered undisputed, some books were disputed because of doubts about authorship or antiquity. But if they were sufficiently early and widely read, they were considered as possible candidates for the canon. Finally, other books were rejected outright because they were of recent vintage or plainly taught error. Thus, forty years before the first definitive canon list of twenty-seven books was composed by Athanasius in 367, the church already had been wrestling seriously with the criteria of canonicity: apostolicity, catholicity, and orthodoxy. The heretical books failed all three tests.

Second, the heretical gospels were products of the second and later centuries. We will consider this point more in the next chapter. One piece of evidence that supports this is found in the very first canon list, produced by the heretic Marcion in about 140. Marcion lists only Luke and ten of Paul's letters in his canon. As noted previously, Marcion was a Docetist, whose views would be largely compatible with Gnostic teaching. Why then did he include parts of *only* our New Testament in his list? Why didn't he include such Gnostic works as the Gospel of Thomas or the Gospel of Mary or the Acts of Peter? The most likely inference is that these books did not yet exist, or they were too new to be regarded as authentic.

Third, as Carson and Moo note, "So far as the evidence of the Fathers goes, when they explicitly evaluated a work for its authenticity, canonicity and pseudonymity proved mutually exclusive."[24] Even though scholars today often argue that the ancient church was soft on issues of authorship, if these Christians were convinced that a book was bogus, it got the boot.

In his important work, *The Making of the New Testament Documents*, E. Earle Ellis discusses the possibility of benign forgeries, or "'Innocent' Apostolic Pseudepigrapha." He concludes:

> In the patristic church apostolic pseudepigrapha, when discovered, were excluded from the church's canon. This applied whether or not the pseudepigrapha were orthodox or heretical.
>
> The hypothesis of innocent apostolic pseudepigrapha appears to be designed to defend the canonicity of certain New Testament writings that are, at the same time, regarded as pseudepigrapha. It is a modern invention that has no evident basis in the attitude or writings of the apostolic and patristic church . . .[25]

CONCLUSION

Was the early church totally naïve about which books belonged in the canon and which did not? Hardly. As we noted in chapter 9, the majority of the New Testament books were accepted as authentic from the very beginning. The notion that all the books were disputed is a gross exaggeration. Although it is likely that someone could dig up a stray quotation here or there to this effect, it hardly represents the facts.[26]

We have seen that the ancient church did not instantly and uncritically assign apostolic authorship to anonymous books, even though that would have been a temptation. Even when a book had an apostle's name on it, the church could be very skeptical. Ultimately, they questioned whether the book was cited from the earliest era of the church, was accepted widely, and was orthodox. Most New Testament books made the cut without much ado—but *precisely* because they obviously met all three criteria. Others struggled for acceptance. This very struggle should put an end to the question of whether the early Christians were terribly gullible about their sacred books.

On the other hand, some unworthy books were accepted as Scripture in parts of the church for a limited time. But these books could not pull the wool over the church's eyes for long.[27]

Eventually, three kinds of literature were decisively rejected as noncanonical: (1) those that were obvious forgeries; (2) those that were late productions (i.e., second century or later); and (3) those that did not conform to the orthodoxy of the core books *already known* to be authentic. That this method is not an antiquarian peculiarity—a curiosity from the past—is seen in the fact that the same three criteria are used by scholars today. One has to wonder, then, why some modern writers simply refuse to give the ancient Christian writers the benefit of the doubt. Indeed, one has to wonder who really is being naïve about the canon.

Chapter 11

WHAT DID THE ANCIENT
FORGERS THINK OF CHRIST?

More than eighty gospels were considered for the New Testament, and yet only a relative few were chosen for inclusion—Matthew, Mark, Luke, and John among them.

—DAN BROWN, *The Da Vinci Code*, 231

The early church needed to convince the world that the mortal prophet Jesus was a divine being. Therefore, any gospels that described earthly aspects of Jesus' life had to be omitted from the Bible.

—DAN BROWN, *The Da Vinci Code*, 244

In chapter 10 we discussed the criteria that the early church used to determine whether a book was worthy of being included in the canon. There were essentially three criteria: (1) apostolicity (or antiquity); (2) catholicity; and (3) orthodoxy. Was a book old enough to be considered authentic? Was it widely read in churches all over the Mediterranean region? And was it in line with the books that had unimpeachable credentials on the first two criteria? The records from the ancient church show no evidence of tolerating pseudepigrapha (works written by one person in someone else's name). But even

151

if they did, since the Gospels themselves were all originally anonymous, this pretty much rules out the motive of forgery on the part
of the authors!

In this chapter we want to see what all the fuss is about. What
were these *other* gospels really like, and why didn't they make the
cut? Specifically, how many other gospels were there, when were they
written, and what did they have to say about Jesus?

THE PURPOSE OF OTHER GOSPELS

Gospels not accepted into the canon are called *apocryphal gospels*. The ancient Greek word *apocrypha* means "hidden things." It
described a variety of Jewish and Christian books and, because of
its elastic meaning, could be used in two quite different ways. Those
who approved of such books saw them as hidden in the sense that
they "were withdrawn from common use because they were regarded as containing mysterious or esoteric lore, too profound to be
communicated to any except the initiated."[1] But other ancient writers said that these books were apocryphal because they deserved to
be hidden! That is, they were heretical in their teaching and should
not be read in public.[2] We will refer to these apocryphal gospels as
gospels (spelled with a lowercase "g") that did not make it into the
New Testament. These are distinguished from the canonical Gospels
(spelled with an uppercase "G").

We know of several apocryphal gospels that floated around in
the early centuries of the church. Some of them we know only by
name, since no remnants exist today. We have fragments of others
and whole documents of still others. In general, all of these gospels
intended to accomplish one of two things: "to supplement [or] . . . to
supplant the four Gospels received by the Great Church."[3] Some of
them, it seems, wanted to do a little of both. The apocryphal gospels
focused on two tantalizing gaps in the life of Jesus as recorded in the
Gospels: his childhood and the three days between his death and
resurrection.[4] In the following section, we will look at some of the
gospels that deal with these aspects of the life of Jesus.

Among those who wrote to supplement the four canonical Gospels, the desire sometimes may have been only to entertain the growing population of Christians. After all, books were *the* medium of communicating creative ideas among the literate who could gain access to them and share their words with others. Christians craved more information, especially about the infancy of Jesus. Thus, the motive could have been, in some cases, no more than that of benign entertainment, of capturing the imagination of the reader. No harm was meant; no deep theological agendas were involved. Likewise, no one took these gospels seriously (or, at least, no one should have!). Sometimes, of course, even a work meant to entertain has a point to make. For example, sci-fi thrillers entertain, but often they intend more. From *The Boys from Brazil* to *Jurassic Park*, cloning as a science fiction theme uncovers its dark side. Whether this was the main point of the authors and screenwriters is hard to assess. Likewise, it is not always possible to determine for certain the agenda of the apocryphal gospels.

Another, more pernicious, motive of the apocryphal gospels was to offer a different Jesus. Again, just as some movies today are intended to alter the public's perception of an individual, so many of the apocryphal gospels intended to promote a Jesus who didn't look like the one in the Gospels.

What kind of Jesus do the majority of these gospels present? One who was *not really human*. It's almost as if this Jesus hovered three feet above the ground: He doesn't need to learn anything as a human being, speaks in intelligent sentences as an infant, and seems altogether otherworldly. The predominant heretical gospel envisioned Jesus as more than a man and other than a man.

Dan Brown speaks of *more than eighty gospels* being considered for inclusion in the New Testament. He says, "Any gospels that described *earthly* aspects of Jesus' life had to be omitted from the Bible."[5] But such statements are terribly misleading, having next to nothing to do with the evidence. For one thing, the vast majority of rejected gospels emphasized Jesus' divinity over his humanity, rather than the other way around.[6] This hardly supports Brown's argument! For another thing, these gospels came *later*—often centuries later—than the canonical Gospels. So how could they have been considered for the canon if they didn't even exist by the time the four Gospels were recognized as authoritative? Finally, we don't know where Brown got the number of *more than eighty* gospels. Any way we look at the historical data, the numbers don't seem to add up that high.

What do we really know about these apocryphal gospels? Actually, quite a bit. In the next section, we will look at some representative apocryphal gospels to see what they actually say about Jesus.

THE JESUS OF THE APOCRYPHAL GOSPELS

Dozens of apocryphal gospels did exist at one time or another. A few are known only by name; some are fragmentary; others survive in complete copies.[7] Some obviously were intended to supplement the canonical Gospels, others to supplant them with a Jesus who differed from the one in the four Gospels. We will look at examples of two kinds of gospels, infancy gospels and the so-called Gnostic gospels.

Infancy Gospels

Although we are distinguishing the infancy gospels from the "Gnostic" gospels, in many cases the former belong to the latter category. But the motives for writing an infancy gospel were broader than that of promoting a sectarian view of Jesus. Sensationalism or entertainment seems to have been a driving force. "These texts were the popular literature of the pious for many centuries."[8] Those that were influenced by Gnostic thought viewed Jesus as not really human and as someone fully mature as an infant. This child's deep wisdom permeated all his activities. He could perform miracles at will, even miracles of dubious value.[9]

The earliest infancy gospels are the Protevangelium of James and the Infancy Gospel of Thomas (not the same Gospel of Thomas that we will discuss later). Most scholars date these books to the second half of the second century. Some later infancy gospels are based on these first two, including the Gospel of Pseudo-Matthew, the Arabic Infancy Gospel, Arundel 404, and the History of Joseph the Carpenter.[10]

The Protevangelium of James is more about Mary, the mother of Jesus, than about Jesus. It is unashamedly a work intended to glorify her. As perhaps the earliest infancy gospel, it shows more restraint than later gospels. But there are still remarkable incidents in the life of Mary and Jesus that go beyond the conservative descriptions found in the canonical Gospels. For example, Mary is dedicated to the temple at a young age; she was "nurtured like a dove and received food from the hand of an angel" until she was twelve years old.[11] The Protevangelium of James expands on the infancy narratives in the Gospels of Matthew and Luke, filling in details with vivid imagination. It obviously is based on Matthew and Luke but adds much more entertaining material.

In the Infancy Gospel of Thomas, Jesus is seen as a spoiled child, an uncontrollable, monstrous prodigy. But other infancy gospels also portray Jesus in a ridiculous way. Consider the following statements about Jesus from these gospels:

- Infancy Gospel of Thomas 3.1–3: The boy Jesus (apparently when he was five years old) calls a playmate an "insolent, godless dunderhead" when the child stirs up some water that Jesus had somehow "gathered together." The boy shrivels up and dies on the spot at Jesus' command.[12]
- Infancy Gospel of Thomas 4.1–2: When a boy accidentally ran into Jesus, Jesus declared, "'You shall not go further on your way,' and the child immediately fell down and died." Some of the villagers complained to Joseph, asking him to take his family and leave: "Since you have such a child, you cannot dwell with us in the village; or else teach him to bless and not to curse. For he is slaying our children."[13]
- Infancy Gospel of Thomas 5.1–3: Joseph rebukes Jesus for doing these things. Then Jesus makes blind his accusers and rebukes Joseph, saying, "Do not vex me."[14]

- Infancy Gospel of Thomas 7.2: Again, when Jesus was five years old, Zacchaeus, his Greek teacher, claims that "this child is not earth-born; he can tame even fire. Perhaps he was begotten even before the creation of the world."[15] This statement by Zacchaeus was in response to Jesus' unfolding the mysteries of the Greek alphabet before his eyes. The Gospel of Thomas seems to have picked up where this Infancy Gospel of Thomas left off in seeing Jesus as a "mystery man."
- Infancy Gospel of Thomas 14.3: People feared the boy Jesus. At one point Joseph told Mary, "Do not let him go outside the door, for all those who provoke him die."
- In the Arabic Infancy Gospel, written in the fifth or sixth century, we read of the mischievous child Jesus. One day, he goes into a dyer's workshop and puts all the cloths into a cauldron that is full of indigo. This ruins the cloths. When the dyer finds out, he is distraught and says to Jesus, "What have you done to me, son of Mary? You have ruined my reputation in the eyes of all the people of the city; for everyone orders a suitable colour for himself, but you have come and spoiled everything." But the child Jesus responds, "I will change for you the colour of any cloth which you wish to be changed." When Jesus performs this miracle, the villagers are amazed and praise God.[16] Unlike any miracle in the Gospels, this is one that Jesus did to make up for the trouble he had caused.
- Elsewhere, in the same infancy gospel, Jesus turns his playmates into goats and then back into children! Apparently these children don't mind either way, because they "began to skip around him" while they were goats.[17]
- Pseudo-Matthew, an eighth-to-ninth-century work, had enormous influence on medieval art depicting Jesus and Mary. Like the Protevangelium of James, this infancy gospel glorifies Mary. It also portrays the child Jesus as fully mature in his thinking, able to perform miracles, and deeply concerned for his mother. The infant Jesus, while escaping to Egypt with Joseph and Mary, speaks as an adult and performs

several miracles, even while his mother carries him through the desert. For example, Joseph complains to Jesus about the unbearable heat. Jesus responds, "Do not fear, Joseph; I will shorten your journey: what you were intending to traverse in the space of thirty days, you will complete in one day."[18] The prophecy and miracle are then fulfilled.

Such absurd tales certainly do not do justice to the historical Jesus. Are these really the gospels that *competed* with the canonical Gospels for inclusion in the canon, as Brown alleges? The problem with seeing such gospels as in any way competing with the canonical Gospels is threefold: (1) They are late, sometimes many *centuries* later than the canonical Gospels. (2) Although some were popular among the masses, the patristic writers condemned them as unworthy descriptions of the real Jesus. They were seen to be hokey and palpably untrue. (3) They usually included docetic ideas—that is, that Christ only *appeared* to be human—or even Gnostic ideas.[19] As such, they did not see Jesus in any sense as a real human being who developed naturally, but as a supernatural being who was born already with powers of mature thought and the ability to do miracles, even malicious miracles.[20] Thus, these gospels were unorthodox in that they greatly diminished the *humanity* of Jesus while elevating his deity.

Brown argues that the shape of the canon was dictated by Constantine, who "commissioned and financed a new Bible, which omitted those gospels that spoke of Christ's *human* traits and embellished those gospels that made Him godlike. The earlier gospels were outlawed, gathered up, and burned."[21] Certainly he cannot be speaking about the infancy gospels! *They* embellished the accounts of the canonical Gospels, were later than the canonical Gospels, and emphasized the divinity of Jesus over his humanity. Indeed, the remarkable thing about the canonical Gospels, when compared to the infancy gospels, is their tremendous *restraint*.

Perhaps the second group of apocryphal gospels will fit Brown's description, because these gospels certainly don't.

So-called Gnostic Gospels

Several gospels have been identified as Gnostic gospels, proto-Gnostic gospels, or gospels that at least have Gnostic leanings.[22] The Gnostics were a knockoff pseudo-Christian group that came to be defined by (1) a "commitment to a radical anticosmic dualism in which all that is material—the world and the body—is seen as evil";[23] and (2) a view of spirituality that equated knowledge—especially *secret* knowledge—with salvation.[24]

Gnosticism seems to have been influenced by Docetism, a heresy that taught that Jesus was divine but not human. The biggest problem with defining Gnosticism has to do with the date of the material: the earlier it is, the less it has the so-called "defining characteristics." Nevertheless, asceticism (the extreme self-denial and austere lifestyle), the matter–spirit dualism, and the emphasis on secret knowledge as the path to salvation, all seem to be part of it from very early on. At the same time, it may be gratuitous to label a particular gospel as Gnostic. For our purposes, it does not matter whether these apocryphal gospels were Gnostic works or not.

Regardless of the label one puts on them, their deviation from orthodoxy, their late date, and their lack of acceptance in the ancient church rendered them unfit for inclusion in the canon. Today, some scholars still refer to the bulk of these gospels as Gnostic, while others dispute that term at every turn. For those gospels in doubt as to identification, we will use "Gnostic" in quotations.

"Although the Gnostics themselves called most of their writings 'gospels' and composed them to some extent as counterpoints to the Gospels of their opponents in the Great Church, these gospels are remarkably non-narrative."[25] The fundamental reason why "Gnostic" gospels typically lack narrative is that they have little regard for the humanity of Christ. Their view of spirit as good and matter as bad means that what they can extract from the life of Jesus are his *words* rather than his deeds.[26]

By far, the most notorious "Gnostic" gospel is the Gospel of Thomas. Although referred to in the writings of church fathers, no copy of the Gospel of Thomas was known to exist until 1945, when the Nag Hammadi manuscripts were discovered. The copy of Thomas found in Nag Hammadi is in Coptic, though it is probably based on an earlier Greek text. Most scholars date the original Thomas to about the mid-second century, though it is possible that it could be *somewhat* earlier.[27]

The Gospel of Thomas might be better characterized as "proto-Gnostic" rather than full-blown Gnostic in its teachings. "Although many of the sayings have a Gnosticizing tendency, the practical spirituality taught is not one that would have been untenable in catholic Christianity."[28]

Other gospels, such as the Gospels of Philip, Mary, Peter, and the Egyptians, are also Gnostic or proto-Gnostic, or Gnostic-like. None were written earlier than the second century. The tendency in these gospels toward asceticism produced a loathing of marriage, sexual intimacy, and the bearing of children. In such documents, Mary, Salome, and other women are elevated in their status as disciples of Jesus. (It was not just Mary who was the lead female disciple in these gospels. In the Gospel of the Egyptians, Salome gets top billing.[29]) Why would these women be featured prominently in these gospels? They were not elevated, as Brown and others allege, because of their intimacy with Jesus—especially *sexual* intimacy—but precisely because, as women, they modeled for the men what it meant to be a *celibate* and ascetically minded disciple. These very gospels that discourage marriage would hardly have promoted a picture of sexual intimacy between Jesus and *any* woman.[30]

For a time, a *few* of these apocryphal gospels were temporarily considered canonical in some corners of the church.[31] But when push came to shove, they were rejected.

What caused the early church to finally sift out such literature? The major catalyst was the persecution of Christians by Emperor Diocletian. One author describes Diocletian's eight-year attack on the church (303–311) as "the last war of annihilation waged by paganism against Christianity."[32] It was indeed a bloody campaign and included wholesale destruction of the church's sacred Scriptures.[33]

This surely must have had a powerful effect on Christians in thinking about what really belonged in the canon.

> When the imperial police knocked at the door and demanded of Christians that they surrender their sacred books, it became a matter of conscience in deciding whether one could hand over the Gospel of John as well as, say, the Gospel of Thomas without incurring the guilt of sacrilege. In such an existential moment most Christians would naturally be careful to determine on solid grounds precisely which were the books for adherence to which they were prepared to suffer. The persecution under Diocletian may almost be said to have given the touch by which previously somewhat unsettled elements of the canon were further crystallized and fixed.[34]

Thus, although some segments of the church had dabbled with a few apocryphal works, the purifying fires of persecution drew a line in the sand. After all, who wanted to be punished for owning a book that was not really Scripture? Significantly, "During the Diocletian persecution Mensurius, the bishop of Carthage, hid his copies of the Scriptures in a safe place, and in their stead handed over to the waiting magistrates writings of 'the new heretics.'"[35] Similar acts were no doubt played out over and over across the empire.

What was it that made these gospels obviously inferior? First, as we have mentioned repeatedly, they were recent productions. They did not bear the stamp of antiquity. "In general, these gospels show far less knowledge of Palestinian topography and customs than do the canonical Gospels—which is what one would expect from the circumstances and date of the composition of such books."[36]

Second, many, if not most, of them had Gnostic tendencies, and some may have been full-blown Gnostic documents. That is, they emphasized the deity of Christ while sacrificing his humanity. Further, they deviated from what was known about Jesus in many other respects. "Gnostic documents represent neither the earliest nor most authentic materials about Jesus and his followers. Indeed they represent a departure from early materials in various ways, including their theology of creation and redemption. Gnosticism was not only out of line with mainstream Christianity, it was also out of line with Judaism as well."[37]

Third, they were generally nonnarrative gospels, giving snippets of Jesus' teaching without a context. This made it all the more difficult to interpret them—or rather, easier to take Jesus' words any way one pleased, opening the door wide for all sorts of unorthodox views of Jesus.

Fourth, when they did give a narrative description, it was often an embellishment of the canonical Gospels and sometimes a bizarre one at that. Such embellishments show that the apocryphal gospels were later, because they were dependent on the four Gospels. As well, they simply didn't have the restraint, the ring of truth, the lack of forced apologetic that the canonical Gospels displayed.

Fifth, they tended to self-consciously promote their claim to authorship by an apostle. As we have seen, the canonical Gospels were all anonymous works to begin with. But many of the apocryphal gospels claim apostolic authorship. This marked difference suggests that they were trying to get on the fast track to acceptance by the church. Since they were not first-century documents, *something* had to be done to give them an edge. Claiming to be written by an apostle was just the ticket. But in due time, the church was able to sniff them out and declare them heretical or, at least, noncanonical.

Below are some examples of what these apocryphal gospels have to say. You can judge for yourself whether they bear the stamp of authenticity.

- The Gospel of Thomas consciously moves in the realm of nonverifiability, for it allegedly consists of *secret* sayings of Jesus given just to Thomas. The opening of this gospel says, "These are the secret words which the living Jesus spoke and Didymus Judas Thomas wrote down." That this is at least proto-Gnostic is seen in the first saying (or *logion*): "And

[Jesus] said, 'He who finds the interpretation of these sayings will not taste death.'"[38] Later, after the disciples compare Jesus to others, Thomas declares, "Master, my mouth is incapable of saying whom you are like." When Thomas said this, Jesus "took him and drew him aside and spoke three words to him. When Thomas returned to his companions they asked him, 'What did Jesus say to you?' Thomas said to them, 'If I tell you one of the words which he spoke to me, you will pick up stones and throw them at me. And fire will come from the stones and burn you up.'"[39] This is unlike the canonical Gospels, where Jesus' instruction is to multiple disciples.

- In Gospel of Thomas 22, Jesus speaks out against marriage: "When you make the two one, and when you make the inner as the outer and the outer as the inner and the upper as the lower, and when you make the male and the female into a single one, so that the male is not male and the female not female, when you make eyes in the place of any eye, and hand in place of a hand, and a foot in place of a foot, an image in place of an image, then you shall enter the kingdom."

- The Gospel of Thomas, like other nonnarrative gospels, includes several sayings of Jesus that are puzzling precisely because they are not placed in any context. For example, logion 105 reads: "Jesus said, 'He who knows father and mother will be called the son of a harlot.'" Logion 108 has: "Jesus said, 'He who drinks from my mouth will be as I am, and I shall be that person, and the hidden things will be revealed to him.'" Logion 74 says, "Lord, there are many standing around the drinking trough, but no one in the well." Such statements without a context enabled readers to twist their meaning into any shape they desired.

- Perhaps the most notorious saying in the Gospel of Thomas is the last saying, logion 114: "Simon Peter said to them, 'Let Mary leave us, because women are not worthy of life.' Jesus said, 'Look, I shall lead her so that I will make her male in order that she also may become a living spirit, resembling you males. For every woman who makes herself male will enter the kingdom of heaven.'" Here we see plainly the asceticism that found a home in Gnostic circles and an attitude toward women that is hardly compatible with the biblical portrait.

- The Gospel of Peter, probably written in the middle of the second century,[40] embellishes the resurrection narrative as follows: "When those soldiers saw this [the stone moving from the entrance of Jesus' sepulcher], they awakened the centurion and the elders, for they also were there to mount guard. And while they were narrating what they had seen, they saw three men come out from the sepulcher, two of them supporting the other and a cross following them and the heads of the two reaching to heaven, but that of him who was being led reached beyond the heavens."[41] This kind of bizarre embellishment nowhere occurs in the canonical Gospels.

- In another second-century "gospel," the Gospel of Mary, Jesus is clearly seen as more than a mere man. In this work, Jesus says that "the Son of Man is within you."[42] This is reminiscent of Paul's teaching that the *ascended* Christ would reside in believers, but it is not something that can be found in the earthly ministry of Jesus in the canonical Gospels.

- Very tellingly, we can see perhaps a more orthodox view of Mary in this Coptic document: "But Andrew answered and said to the brothers (and sisters), 'Tell me, what do you say about what she has spoken? I at least do not believe that the Saviour said this. For these teachings seem to be according to another train of thought.' Peter answered and spoke about these same things, he reflected about the Saviour: 'After all, he did not speak with a woman apart from us and not openly. Are we to turn and all listen to her? Has he chosen her above us?'" (17.10–22).[43] Of course, at this point, Peter is rebuked by both Mary and Levi, since he and Andrew are the orthodox antagonists who must be answered! But the secret knowledge that Jesus imparted to just a few of his disciples is in line with Gnostic tendencies.

- The gospels are not the only ones having fun at truth's expense. In the Acts of Paul, Paul is facing down the gaping jaw of a large lion in the Ephesian amphitheater. Unshaken, Paul approaches the beast and simply reminds the creature that he had baptized the lion (after the lion uttered his confession of faith, of course) some time before! The lion then helps Paul to escape.

- In the Acts of John, Jesus seems to be out of this world. John says, "Sometimes when I meant to touch him [Jesus] I met with a material and solid body; but at other times when I felt him, his substance was immaterial and incorporeal, as if it did not exist at all. . . . And I often wished, as I walked with him, to see his footprint, whether it appeared on the ground (for I saw him as it were raised up from the earth), and I never saw it."[44] Clearly, a divine Jesus—but not a human Jesus—is in view. Elsewhere, Jesus was "constantly changing shape, appearing sometimes as a small boy, sometimes as a beautiful man; sometimes bald-headed with a long beard, sometimes as a youth with a prepubescent beard (§§87–9)."[45]

These fanciful descriptions have nothing to do with biblical Christianity or historical Christianity. They are stories devised, at best, as bubblegum for the soul and, at worst, as propagandist devices to persuade the church to abandon its orthodox roots.

Obviously, fringe Christian groups had their own agenda, which had nothing to do with the biblical narratives.

What can be said about this myriad of apocryphal works? They are sensational, bizarre, secretive, and unorthodox. Many are pseudepigraphical, which means that the author of each work is pretending to be someone he is not in order to gain a hearing and credibility for his ideas. And they were universally rejected by the ancient church, at one time or another, as noncanonical works. Indeed, the closer we look at these gospels, the worse they look and the better the canonical Gospels look. Bruce Metzger summarizes the situation well:

One can appreciate the difference between the character of the canonical Gospels and the near banality of most of the gospels dating from the second and third centuries. Although some of these claimed apostolic authorship, whereas of the canonical four two were in fact not apostolically titled, yet it was these four, and these alone, which ultimately established themselves. The reason, apparently, is that these four came to be recognized as authentic—authentic both in the sense that the story they told was, in its essentials, adjudged sound by a remarkably unanimous consent, and also in the sense that their interpretation of its meaning was equally widely recognized as true to the apostles' faith and teaching. Even the *Gospel of Peter* and the *Gospel of Thomas*, both of which may preserve scraps of independent tradition, are obviously inferior theologically and historically to the four accounts that eventually came to be regarded as the only canonical Gospels.[46]

Criteria of Canonicity and the Apocryphal Gospels

We have seen in this chapter that the evidence for authenticity within these apocryphal books is disappointing at best. The material is secretive, the Jesus in view floats above the earth, and he discourages marriage as a valid lifestyle choice of a disciple. His relation to women is ascetic in the extreme, to the point that they need to be changed into men in order to become his disciples. None of the apocryphal works have credentials that would demand a first-century production. They are, in fact, all works from the second century or later. And as such, when they claim to be written by an apostle, they are already on thin ice because of the church's view of pseudepigrapha. Further, their acceptance was always short-lived—if they were accepted at all. They were never commended to the church universal. Finally, they had some unorthodox features that were known to go against the truth that had been revealed in the Scriptures. Thus they were rightly rejected as at least noncanonical and sometimes heretical. Brown's claim that such books emphasized the humanity of Christ and therefore were swept under the rug simply does not square with the facts. The vast majority of apocryphal works that were rejected were not rejected because they had too *low* a view of Jesus—a too human and earthly Jesus—but because the Jesus they envisioned could hardly be called human in any sense. His deity was so pronounced that even his footsteps made no marks in the sand! Such hyperembellishments of the canonical Christ cannot be reasonably believed to represent the real, historical Jesus.

By contrast, the canonical Gospels were accepted from the earliest periods, were not given to bizarre embellishments, and proclaimed Jesus of Nazareth as both man and more than a man. If Constantine had really picked the Gospels to go into the New Testament, wanting only those that elevated Jesus to the heavens, he must have been singularly incompetent because he left out all the juicy tales! The four Gospels, on the other hand, have the earmarks of authenticity due to their age, their use in the churches, and their conformity to the truth of the gospel as it was known, both in oral tradition and in the New Testament letters that were emerging when the Gospels began to be penned.

PART 4

THE DIVINITY OF JESUS

Early Tradition or Late Superstition?

DIVINE PORTRAITS

Jesus in the Gospels

Jesus' establishment as "the Son of God" was officially proposed and voted on by the Council of Nicaea.

—DAN BROWN,
The Da Vinci Code, 233

There is nothing recorded in the Gospels showing that Jesus clearly affirmed his own divinity.

—SHABIR ALLY, Muslim apologist on PAX's
Faith Under Fire program, November 27, 2004

Whatever trouble the modern mind has with the idea of God becoming a man,[1] this much is certain: Jesus' earliest followers viewed him as divine. Even scholars who do not personally embrace the divinity of Jesus readily recognize that the New Testament authors did. Somehow this fact escaped the attention of Leigh Teabing, the scholarly gadfly in Dan Brown's *The Da Vinci Code*. Speaking of the Council of Nicea, an ecumenical meeting of bishops that took place nearly *three hundred years* after the time of Jesus, Teabing declared, "Until *that* moment in history, Jesus was viewed by his followers as a mortal prophet . . . a great and powerful man, but a *man* nonetheless."[2] We have no argument with the fact that

Jesus was a man.[3] But, as we intend to show in the next few chapters, the notion that his divinity was invented at the Council of Nicea is nothing more than a novel speculation.

Throughout this section we'll see that the bishops at Nicea did not unveil new doctrine when they affirmed that Jesus was the Son of God. Rather, the council unpacked the significance of a belief rooted in centuries-old texts. We'll survey those texts in the next few chapters, beginning with the canonical Gospels.

THE HISTORICAL LANDSCAPE

In order to appreciate early Christian testimony about Jesus, it is vital to understand the Jewish context in which it emerged. First-century Jews were stubbornly monotheistic. To be monotheistic in a fiercely polytheistic Greco-Roman culture was to have an unflinching belief that dominated—and often endangered—one's life. At least twice each day, all faithful Jews recited the Shema, a text that begins: "Listen, Israel: The Lord is our God, the Lord is one" (Deut. 6:4). This passage not only affirms the uniqueness of God; it implies that he is the only one worthy of worship.

New Testament scholar Richard Bauckham cuts to the heart of this conviction when he asks, "What distinguished God as unique from all other reality, including beings worshiped as gods by Gentiles?"[4] Significantly, "the answer given again and again, in a wide variety of Second Temple Jewish literature, is that the only true God, YHWH, the God of Israel, is sole Creator of all things and sole Ruler of all things."[5] In other words, exclusive worship of YHWH was the defining feature of first-century Judaism.

Christianity not only arose in a Jewish monotheistic context; it also embraced the monotheistic convictions of Judaism. Indeed, Christianity shared Judaism's intolerance for devotion to any so-called god but the supreme God. In light of this fact, it would be remarkable to find any *hints* in early Christian writings that Jesus was treated as divine. Yet the Gospels and the larger New Testament supply such hints—and more.

Our focus in this chapter will be upon the Gospels. Much could be said about these documents and their diverse, yet unified portraits of Jesus.[6] Scores of commentaries and books include discussions of specific texts in the Gospels that implicitly point to the deity of Christ or explicitly equate him with God.[7] Rather than survey these texts that permeate Matthew, Mark, Luke, and John, we'll provide snapshots of prominent themes in each Evangelist and take a close look at two powerful scenes in the earliest Gospel.

How the Gospels Frame Their Portraits of Jesus

Biblical authors frequently use a literary technique known as *inclusio* to stress important themes in their writings. An *inclusio* "frames" a paragraph, chapter, or book by beginning and ending it with the same word, phrase, or concept. It is the author's way of identifying a theme and telling his readers that everything between the "frames" should be read in light of that theme. Interestingly, all four Gospels make use of the *inclusio* technique.

Consider Mark, which most scholars believe to be the earliest of the four Gospels, written no later than the 60s. (See chapter 1: "The Gospel Behind the Gospels" for a discussion of the dates of Matthew, Mark, and Luke.) Mark opens with the words, "The beginning of the gospel of Jesus Christ, the Son of God" (Mark 1:1)[8] and climaxes with the confession of the Roman centurion attending to Jesus' crucifixion: "Truly this man was God's Son!" (Mark 15:39).[9] The *inclusio* formed by references to Jesus as God's Son suggests that everything between is to be read in light of the belief that Jesus was no mere man. From beginning to end, Mark presents Jesus as the unique Son of God.

It's significant to note that, in spite of Mark's emphasis upon the divinity of Jesus, his Gospel reveals Jesus' *disciples* to be a bit slow in recognizing his true identity. In the least, this demonstrates that Mark was not trying to theologically embellish his Gospel. To the contrary, he seems genuinely constrained by actual history.

A poignant moment in the Gospel is when Jesus and his followers are on a boat in the Sea of Galilee. The winds and waves suddenly convulse, causing the disciples to panic. Jesus wakes from his nap and commands nature to quiet down. There is a buzz among the disciples: "Who then is this? Even the wind and the sea obey him!" (Mark 4:41b).

The question both reveals the disciples' perplexity about who Jesus is and hints that he is more than a man. At the same time, the question reflects the fact that the disciples did not *readily* or *uncritically* embrace the divinity of Jesus. The reason for this is plain to see: they were Jewish monotheists devoted to the one true God. To see a man as both on par with God and, indeed, as God himself was a radical paradigm shift that took some time to sink in. Yet Mark gives significant clues as to Jesus' true nature, even early on, and he invites the reader to go on the same journey of discovery that the first disciples did.

Like Mark, Luke probably was written no later than the 60s. And, like Mark, Luke stresses Jesus' identity as the unique Son of God. Though Jesus' role as Messiah is foremost in Luke's mind when he refers to Jesus as God's Son, Luke uses the "Son of God" *inclusio* to make clear that he views Jesus' sonship as one-of-a-kind.[10] In Luke 1:35, the angel declares to the Virgin Mary: "The Holy Spirit will come upon you, and the power of the Most High will overshadow you. Therefore the child to be born will be holy; he will be called the Son of God." Whatever can be said about the theological implications of the Virgin Birth, at least this must be acknowledged: Luke presents Jesus as a man with a supernatural origin.

Luke also presents Jesus as a man with a supernatural destiny. The Gospel's "Son of God" *inclusio* concludes with the words of Jesus' accusers at his trial: "'Are you the Son of God, *then*?' [Jesus] answered them, 'You say that I am'" (Luke 22:70, emphasis added). The word "then" looks back to Jesus' statement in the previous verse: "But from now on *the Son of Man will be seated at the right hand* of the power of God" (Luke 22:69). When Jesus' accusers ask him whether he is the Son of God, it is in the wake of Jesus' staggering claim that he will be uniquely exalted to God's right hand as one exercising God's universal rule. (See the discussion of "right hand" language later in this chapter.) In other words, once again, Jesus is referred to as God's Son in a way that underscores his one-of-a-kind role as God's stand-in. This is hardly appropriate imagery to describe, in the words of Dan Brown, "a mortal prophet"![11]

Mark and Luke, both penned before 70, declare Jesus to be the unique representative and Son of God. Surely this is enough to undercut Dan Brown's claim that Jesus was seen to be no more—though no less—than a great man by his early followers. But there's more. As the Gospels of Matthew and John make clear, Jesus' identity went beyond his divine *position* as God's Son. He also was viewed as a divine *person* who was God's equal.

Matthew moves in this direction through the use of a conceptual *inclusio* that emphasizes Jesus' divine presence. Composed as early as the 60s, this Gospel begins with the proclamation that Jesus' name means *"God with us"* (Matt. 1:23) and climaxes with Jesus' promise to his disciples then and now: *"I am with you* always, to the end of the age" (Matt. 28:20, emphasis added). If God is with Jesus, then God is with the disciples who are with Jesus. Matthew's *inclusio* forms a theological framework for his Gospel that stresses the intimacy Christians share with God through the *ever-living* Son.

According to the Gospel of John, which most scholars agree was written no later than the 90s,[12] Jesus is not only the *ever-living* Son but also the *eternal* Son. That is, the divine person of the Son—who took on human flesh at a specific moment in history and permanently conquered physical death through his resurrection—has always existed.

John wastes no time in making this plain: "In the beginning was the Word, and the Word was with God, and the Word was fully God.[13] . . . All things were created by him" (John 1:1, 3). To be sure his readers make no mistake, John identifies "the Word" for them: *"the Word became flesh* and took up residence among us. We saw his glory—the glory of the one and only, full of grace and truth. . . . For the law was given through Moses, but grace and truth came about through *Jesus Christ*" (1:14, 17, emphasis added). In short, the eternal Word became incarnate in the earthly Jesus. And since the Word is called "God," Jesus must be called "God," too.

John's opening salvo is like a theological two-by-four over the head. He boldly asserts that Jesus is fully God and sets out to authenticate his claim. That this is John's intent is clear from the *inclusio* he constructs between John 1:1 and another text in which Jesus is called "God." In John 20:24–28, Thomas refuses to believe that Jesus has risen from the dead, despite the testimony of the other disciples who have seen their master alive. But when doubting Thomas sees the living Jesus, he is persuaded of more than just the resurrection. Amazingly, he calls Jesus "My Lord and my God!" (20:28). This is an incredible response: not only does Thomas now believe that Jesus has been raised, but he also identifies him with the God of heaven. And so does John. The combination of John 1:1 with 20:28 is a one-two punch that levels any doubts about early belief in the divinity of Jesus.

As we conclude our brief look at portraits of Jesus in the Gospels, some readers may be wondering, *Why do the Gospel writers explicitly call Jesus "God" so seldom, if at all?* It's true that only John's Gospel explicitly calls Jesus "God," and it does so only a few times (John 1:1, 18; 20:28). In fact, Jesus is directly called "God" only a handful of times in the entire New Testament. But this hardly dulls the force of such affirmations. As R. T. France, former principal of Wycliffe Hall, Oxford University, notes, we shouldn't be surprised that

> explicit use of God-language about Jesus is infrequent in the New Testament, and is concentrated in the later writings. . . . It was such shocking language that, even when the beliefs underlying it were firmly established, it was easier, and perhaps more politic, to express these beliefs in less direct terms. The wonder is not that the New Testament so seldom describes Jesus as God, but that in [a radically monotheistic] milieu it does so at all.[14]

Indeed, as W. L. Schutter observes,

> The incarnation first scandalized the Jews, because it threat-
> ened their commitment to radical monotheism. Christian
> Jews, like Paul or John, had to wrestle with the possibility
> that they were compromising that faith. What is more, the
> doctrine surely represented an obstacle in the church's mis-
> sion to Judaism. Hence, the Jewish leadership of the infant
> church had to have had very deep convictions about the in-
> carnation or they would have abandoned it.[15]

In light of these observations by France and Schutter, we should
expect to see roundabout depictions of Jesus as God outnumber direct statements to the same effect. The indirect approach was stra-
tegic. And, as we will see, it was just as compelling.

MASTER IMAGES: TWO POWERFUL SCENES FROM THE "SECOND" GOSPEL

Jesus' miracles are not ends in themselves. They point beyond the
power to the *person*, revealing the extraordinary identity of one exercising the authority of God.[16] Thus, we might think of these miracles as "theological audiovisuals," illustrating spiritual truths about
the one performing them. Sometimes these truths were lost on eyewitnesses to the miracles; other times, they were not.

The theological audiovisual was loud and clear in Mark 2:1–12.
The scene is Capernaum, on the northern shore of the Sea of Galilee.
Jesus was inside a house teaching those who had gathered there. The
account tells of a lame man who was lowered through the roof of the
house by his friends because the crowd was so big it was blocking the
doorway. The friends, eager for the man to be healed, went out of
their way to get to Jesus. Moved by their show of faith, Jesus did—
and said—an astonishing thing. To the amazement of the crowd, he
restored the lame man's limbs. But even more remarkably, Jesus told
the man, "Son, your sins are forgiven" (v. 5).

Some religious leaders in the crowd immediately recognized a theological problem in Jesus' statement: "Why does this man speak this way?" they thought. "He is blaspheming! Who can forgive sins but God alone?" (Mark 2:7). They were half right: God alone can forgive sins. But Jesus was not blaspheming. He was implicitly and authoritatively claiming equality with God.[17]

Jesus himself made clear that the healing of the lame man pointed to a greater reality when he asked his enemies,

> Which is easier, to say to the paralytic, "Your sins are for-given," or to say, "Stand up, take your stretcher, and walk"? But so that you may know that the Son of Man has authority on earth to forgive sins . . . (Mark 2:9–10)

Jesus let his actions speak where his words trailed off. Indeed, everyone within eyeshot of the man's restored legs saw that Jesus' proclamation stood: the paralytic's sins had been forgiven. Significantly, it was this claim that caused Jesus' enemies to scoff. They made no attempt to explain away the miracle itself. We thus have strong historical witness to a miracle that, in turn, gives powerful theological testimony to Jesus' divine identity.

Another powerful affirmation of Jesus' own belief in his divinity took place at his trial before the Jewish council on the eve of his execution (Mark 14:53–64). Looking to pin a charge on Jesus that would stick until Jesus could be brought before Pilate, the high priest Caiaphas asked, "Are you the Christ [Messiah], the Son of the Blessed One?" (Mark 14:61b). Jesus' answer jarred the high priest and his associates:

> "I am," said Jesus, "and you will see *the Son of Man sitting at the right hand* of the Power and *coming with the clouds of heaven*." Then the high priest tore his clothes and said, "Why do we still need witnesses? You have heard the blasphemy! What is your verdict?" They all condemned him as deserving death. (Mark 14:62–64)

At first blush, the reaction of Caiaphas and the council seems extreme. After all, there was nothing inherently blasphemous about the claim to be Messiah.[18] But, as we will see, Jesus claimed far more than that.[19]

Jesus claimed to be more than the King of the Jews when he identified himself as the "Son of Man" (Mark 14:62). It's often wrongly assumed that the title "Son of Man" refers simply to Jesus' humanity. However, Jesus' interrogators, who were saturated in the Hebrew Scriptures, wouldn't have had Jesus' earthly qualities in mind. They would have been thinking of the heavenly vision in Daniel 7:13–14:

> I was watching in the night visions,
> And with the clouds of the sky
> > one like a son of man was approaching.
> He went up to the Ancient of Days
> > and was escorted before him.
> To him was given ruling authority, honor, and sovereignty.
> All peoples, nations, and language groups were serving him.
> His authority is eternal and will not pass away.
> His kingdom will not be destroyed.

Obviously, human frailty was far from the mind of Daniel, who portrayed the Son of Man as an exalted, humanlike figure possessing all judgment authority and ruling over an everlasting kingdom. Daniel's vision also revealed the Son of Man to be *more* than human. In other Old Testament writings, the image of riding on clouds was used exclusively for divine figures (Exod. 14:20; 34:5; Num. 10:34; Ps. 104:3; Isa. 19:1).[20] Daniel employed this image, and Jesus embraced it as his own.

Jesus made an even more staggering claim when he said that he—a divine-human figure with all judgment authority—would be seen "*sitting at the right hand* of the Power" (Mark 14:62). This imagery was not unfamiliar to the Jewish council, which was intimately familiar with the Psalms:

Here is the LORD's proclamation to my lord:
"Sit down at my right hand until I make your enemies your footstool!" (Ps. 110:1)

That Jesus would apply this text to himself was astonishing. Only a few significant figures in Judaism ever entered God's presence. Even fewer *sat* in it.[21] But up to this point, no one in Jewish literature was ever afforded the privilege of sitting *at God's right side.* Yet Jesus personally insisted on his right to do so.

Jesus in Mark 14:62	Old Testament Allusions
"I am, . . . and you will see <u>the Son of Man</u> <u>sitting at the right hand</u> of the Power and <u>coming with the</u> <u>clouds of heaven.</u>"	"The LORD says to my lord, <u>'Sit at my right hand.'"</u> (Ps. 110:1 NRSV) "And behold, <u>with the clouds of</u> <u>heaven</u> One like a <u>Son of Man was</u> <u>coming.</u>" (Dan. 7:13 NASB)

The priests of the Jewish council, before whom Jesus made this radical claim, could not, as a rule, even go into the inner sanctum of the temple. The Holy of Holies—God's earthly dwelling place—could only be entered on a specific day in a specific way by a specific person. On the annual Day of Atonement, the high priest was allowed to enter the Holy of Holies to offer the blood of a bull for personal purification and the blood of a goat for the people's atonement. This was preceded by a change of garments and ritual washings (Lev. 16). In other words, God's presence in the temple was entered *cautiously.* Failure to proceed with caution resulted in death.[22]

With such restrictions for entry into the *earthly* Holy of Holies, we can imagine what went through the priests' minds when Jesus claimed the right to enter God's *heavenly* presence.[23] And we can only begin to imagine what they thought when Jesus said he would enter into the heavenly Holy of Holies *and sit down.* He might as well have claimed that he owned the place![24]

Jesus' response was too much for the religious leaders to swallow. He had claimed to exercise the authority of God, implying that he sat in judgment over the Jewish council—not the other way around. He also had committed blasphemy by threatening the uniqueness of God's presence.[25] Jesus spoke brashly about going directly into the heavenly Holy of Holies and staying there, thus occupying a place far above even the angels, for "the place on the throne of God at the right hand of the Father is the highest place in heaven."[26] Jesus' words staggered the Jewish council; their reaction strongly suggests that they understood him to be claiming divinity. No doubt, this is how Mark understands Jesus. And this is how Jesus understood himself.[27] We are thus safe in concluding with Richard Bauckham that "the earliest Christology was already the highest Christology."[28]

Chapter 13

SUPREME DEVOTION

Jesus in the Larger New Testament

For Paul . . . the Christ represents the one awareness that is the true identity of all of us.

—TIMOTHY FREKE AND PETER GANDY,
The Laughing Jesus, 62

We have seen that the Gospels clearly portray Jesus as more than a man, as truly divine. That should settle the issue. Someone might argue, however, that the disciples were awestruck by Jesus' majesty and miracles and that they went over the top in their descriptions of him. Or that the Gospels are late productions and have no historical credibility. We have already answered these charges, but in this chapter we will take a different tack. We will look at what the rest of the New Testament writings have to say about Jesus. And we'll start with a former enemy of the gospel, a man who ended up writing almost half the books of the New Testament.

THE APOSTLE PAUL

Paul was not one of the original twelve disciples. He never sat at Jesus' feet, never witnessed any of his miracles, never even met him in the flesh. When the Christian movement began, Paul (or Saul) vehemently opposed it. He was, as he put it, "a Hebrew of Hebrews," a Pharisee who persecuted the church (Phil. 3:5–6).

What was the reason Paul was so hostile to this new sect known as Christians? The apostles were proclaiming that God had raised Jesus from the dead. But Paul—who had been rigorously trained by the great rabbi Gamaliel—knew the Scriptures. He knew the Deuteronomic curse: "anyone hung on a tree is under God's curse" (Deut. 21:23 NRSV). If Jesus was raised from the dead, the Scriptures were wrong. After all, how could God bless a man by raising him from the dead if he had cursed him by hanging him on a tree? This was the dilemma that the early Christians needed to answer and what drove Paul the Pharisee to persecute them.

On the way to Damascus to hunt down more members of this new sect, Paul had a remarkable experience. He met the risen and ascended Christ. When the heavenly voice asked, "Saul, Saul, why are you persecuting me?" (Acts 9:4), Paul was puzzled. He must have thought, *Who in heaven could possibly think that I was persecuting him? I'm doing God's will by rounding up these heretics and putting them in prison!* So he asked, "Who are you, Lord?" The heavenly voice shot back a response that changed the face of history: "I am Jesus whom you are persecuting!" (v. 5). Paul now knew two things. First, the persecution of the church was ultimately the persecution of one who occupied heaven, Jesus himself; second, Jesus was *alive!*

Now Paul was in conflict. As a pious Jew, he believed the Old Testament Scriptures. The Deuteronomic curse *must* be true. But his Damascus Road experience could not be denied.[1] After this encounter Paul's answer to this conundrum was the key to unraveling the identity of Jesus Christ. He soon recognized that Jesus could not have been cursed for his own sins; otherwise, he would still be in the grave. Yes, God cursed him—and he cursed him for sins. But those sins were not his own.

By the time of the apostle Paul's first letter, written to the Galatian churches in about 49, he had already come to this conviction. He notes in Galatians 3:13 that "Christ redeemed us from the curse of the law by becoming a curse for us (because it is written, 'Cursed is *everyone who hangs on a tree')*." This is the language of substitutionary atonement: a perfect, sinless person was sacrificed in our place. By definition, if Christ was without sin, then he was no ordinary man, no "mere mortal."

Paul never changed in that assessment of Christ. Over the next several years, he wrote frequently of Christ's death in our place. He was not just mimicking what the Gospels say, for some of his letters were written before any of the four Evangelists put pen to papyrus. Since Paul died sometime around the year 64, his letters were all written within little more than three decades from the time of Jesus. Although Paul did not know Jesus in the flesh, Paul's dramatic experience on the road to Damascus brought him face-to-face with the ascended Lord.

According to Paul, who exactly was Christ? The apostle tells us in several places, three of which we will treat here. The first passage is Romans 10:9–13, where Paul discusses saving faith:

> Because if you confess with your mouth that Jesus is Lord and believe in your heart that God raised him from the dead, you will be saved. For with the heart one believes and thus has righteousness and with the mouth one confesses and thus has salvation. For the scripture says, *"Everyone who believes in him will not be put to shame."* For there is no distinction between the Jew and the Greek, for the same Lord is Lord of all, who richly blesses all who call on him. For *everyone who calls on the name of the Lord will be saved.*

In Romans 10:9, we have an explicit ascription of the title "Lord" to Jesus. What does Paul mean by this? Note in this paragraph that his argument begins with a confession about Christ and continues: "Everyone who believes in him will not be put to shame." The object of belief ("him") is still Christ.[2] In verse 12, Paul again mentions "Lord": "There is no distinction between the Jew and the Greek, for the same Lord is Lord of all." The Lord of verse 9 ("Jesus is Lord") is the "him" of verse 11 ("Everyone who believes in him"), who is also the "Lord" of verse 12 ("the same Lord is Lord of all"). Finally, Paul wraps up his argument by quoting from Joel 2:32: "Everyone who calls on the name of the Lord will be delivered." In the Hebrew text of Joel, "Lord" is YHWH. Thus, there is continuity from verse 9 through verse 13; in view throughout is "the same Lord," Jesus Christ, YHWH himself. Here we see Paul making a startling statement: confessing Christ as Lord means confessing Christ as God. As such, this is explicit identification of Jesus with the God of Israel.[3]

The second passage is in Paul's letter to the Philippians. In 2:6–11, we read a text that may well have been part of an ancient hymn, incorporated into the letter by Paul.[4]

> Who though he existed in the form of God
> did not regard equality with God
> as something to be grasped,
> but emptied himself
> by taking on the form of a slave,
> by looking like other men,
> and by sharing in human nature.
> He humbled himself,
> by becoming obedient to the point of death—
> even death on a cross!
> As a result God exalted him
> and gave him the name
> that is above every name,
> so that at the name of Jesus
> every knee will bow—
> in heaven and on earth and under the earth—
> and every tongue confess
> that Jesus Christ is Lord
> to the glory of God the Father.

Several important issues surface in this passage, only three of which will be touched on here. First, Christ existed in "the *form* of

God." Today when we think of *form*, we often think of appearances that lack substance: "She's beautiful on the outside, but she has a cold heart"; "there's no depth to his character—he's all show." Form, to us, means something that does not correspond to reality. That is not the case in this text. Note the parallel between the expression "the form of God" and "taking on the *form* of a slave [or servant]." The same Greek word rendered "form" *(morphē)* is used both times.[5] Paul here draws a contrast between Jesus' heavenly mode of existence, in which he had "the form of God," and his earthly mode of existence, in which he had "the form of a slave." Jesus was not a mere man to whom his followers later accorded divine honors. Rather, Paul says, Jesus was a divine person, existing in the form of God, who "humbled himself" by becoming a man in order to effect our salvation. His point here is similar to Jesus' statement in Mark 10:45, "The Son of Man did not come to be served but to serve, and to give his life as a ransom for many." Now if Jesus was truly a servant on earth, then he was truly God in heaven. The inherent lexical meaning of *morphē* also suggests this. Although the precise nuance of what Paul meant by this word has been hotly debated, it's safe to say that it indicates a form that fully and accurately corresponds to the being that underlies it.[6] If we think of *form* as an exact replica, or rather, as identical to the original, we get a good sense of what this means here. Thus, in a most succinct manner, Paul here indicates both Christ's deity and his humanity ("form of God . . . form of a slave").

The second important issue is that *universal* worship must be given to Christ: "every knee will bow . . . and every tongue confess that Jesus Christ is Lord." In this assertion we find a conceptual link to Exodus 20:4–5, the second commandment, which expressly forbids worship to any except the Lord (YHWH), the God of Israel. In Philippians 2, Jesus receives not only worship, but the same kind of worship that the second commandment restricts to God himself. Notice the parallels between Exodus 20:4 and Philippians 2:10.

Exodus 20:4:	Philippians 2:10:
"You shall not make for yourself a carved image or any likeness of anything that is	"At the name of Jesus every knee will bow—
in heaven above	in heaven
or that is on the earth beneath,	and on earth
or that is in the water below."	and under the earth."

In one respect, the Philippian hymn employs even stronger, more explicit language than Exodus. The commandment is not to make a "carved image," with the *implication* that such an image would be worshiped. In Philippians, Jesus is *explicitly* the object of worship—and not just of some, but of all. It is unthinkable that the early church, comprised at first only of Jews, would forget about the second commandment. Instead, they incorporated it into a hymn for Christ. To put it mildly, this is not the kind of thing that could be said of a mere man.

Third, not only is Exodus 20 in the background of this hymn but so is Isaiah 45:23.[7] Here God declares, "I solemnly make this oath— what I say is true and reliable: 'Surely every knee will bow to me, every tongue will solemnly affirm.'" In this passage, "the uniqueness of the God of Israel is proclaimed and his universal triumph is hailed. The Lord, who has already declared that he will not share his name or his glory with another, swears solemnly by his own life that 'every knee will bow before me; by me every tongue will swear.'"[8] Earlier, in his letter to the Romans, Paul used this very passage to refer to God (Rom. 14:11). He knew the Old Testament context, that God and God alone was in view. Consequently, his application of Isaiah 45:23 to Christ is not sloppy and unwitting; it is intentional. And his intention is to show that Jesus Christ is God himself and is to be worshiped as such. Such usage by New Testament writers of the Old Testament texts that speak clearly of YHWH is neither cavalier nor accidental. Their use of such texts to point to Jesus Christ occurs so frequently and in such lofty contexts that the intention is unmistakable.

The third passage from Paul is Colossians 1:15–20, which is likely another ancient hymn to Christ.[9]

> He is the image of the invisible God, the firstborn over
>   all creation,
> for all things in heaven and on earth were created
>   by him—all things,
> whether visible or invisible,
> whether thrones or dominions,
> whether principalities or powers—
> all things were created through him and for him.
> He himself is before all things and all things are held
>   together in him.
> He is the head of the body, the church,
> as well as the beginning, the firstborn from among the dead,
> so that he himself may become first in all things.
> For God was pleased to have all his fullness dwell in the Son
> and through him to reconcile all things to himself
> by making peace through the blood of his cross—
> through him, whether things on earth or things in heaven.

Note that in verses 16–17, Paul emphasizes Christ's role as Creator: "for all things in heaven and on earth were created by him." As if to make sure that the reader does not miss the point, the apostle first defines what "all things" includes: "all things, whether visible or invisible, whether thrones or dominions, whether principalities or powers." Remarkably, the accent is not on the mundane or the lowly things in life but on the greatest potentates on earth and in heaven—the thrones, dominions, principalities, and powers. Christ is Lord over them all.

Paul then defines in what sense Christ is Creator and Ruler of the cosmos: "all things were created through him and for him. He himself is before all things and all things are held together in him." As Richard Bauckham has noted, in the Jewish literature of the day, what distinguished the God of the Bible is that he "is sole Creator of all things and sole Ruler of all things."[10] That early Christians could sing to Christ as, in some measure, both Creator and Ruler at the least puts him in the same ballpark with YHWH. Although it is disputed as to exactly what Christ's role was in Creation, the traditionally hard-drawn Jewish lines with regard to God get fuzzy when Christ enters the picture. It is of course impossible for the language of Colossians 1:15–20 to describe a mere man. Mere men do not create the universe or sustain it.

Several other passages in Paul's letters could be mentioned, but the three we have examined are sufficient to show that the apostle consciously and intentionally embraced the deity of Christ.[11]

THE WRITER OF HEBREWS

In Hebrews 1, the author[12] presents a case for the supremacy of Christ. First, Christ is superior to any prophets (vv. 1–2). This opening gambit proves beyond question how ludicrous it is to think of the early church as embracing Jesus only as a man, a prophet. Like Paul in Colossians, the author of Hebrews speaks of Christ as both Creator and Sustainer of all things: He is the one whom God "appointed heir of all things, and through whom he created the world. The Son is the radiance of his glory and the representation of his essence, and he sustains all things by his powerful word" (vv. 2b–3). Now if Christ is on this plane, one can correctly conclude that he is above even the angels. And in the best tradition of Jewish monotheism, the author refuses to allow angels to share credit with God for creating or ruling the universe. The former concept he implies in verses 2–3; the latter he makes explicit in verses 6–8:

> But when he again brings his firstborn into the world, he says,
> *"Let all the angels of God worship him!"*
> And he says of the angels,
> *"He makes his angels spirits and his ministers a flame of fire,"*
> but of the Son he says,
> *"Your throne, O God, is forever and ever,*
> *and a righteous scepter is the scepter of your kingdom."*

There is an obvious contrast here between the angels and Christ. The description of angels in Hebrews 1:6–7 speaks of their subordinate role (of worship for God—or in this context, Christ) and their inferior essence ("He *makes* his angels . . . a flame of fire"). But the description of Christ does the opposite: He is the one being worshiped, and his reign is forever. Indeed, the author goes so far as to explicitly identify Christ with God: "Your throne, O God, is forever and ever."[13]

The writer of Hebrews continues his affirmations of Jesus' exaltation with a quotation from the Old Testament about the Lord God as Creator, which he also applies to Jesus: "You founded the earth in the beginning, Lord, and the heavens are the works of your hands" (Heb. 1:10; quoting Ps. 102:25). With this quotation, the author is giving biblical context for his earlier statement that God made the world through his Son (Heb. 1:2).

In Hebrews 1 the author presents Jesus Christ as superior to the prophets and the angels. In so doing, the author makes some astounding claims: (1) Christ is the Creator; (2) angels are commanded to worship him; (3) he is God, sitting on the throne; and thus (4) he is both Ruler and Judge. There is hardly a more explicit way for the author of Hebrews to have indicated that Jesus is fully God.

AUTHOR OF THE APOCALYPSE

Finally, we take a quick look at the book of Revelation (the Apocalypse). Revelation was written no later than 96. As such, it is most likely the last book of the New Testament to be written. What is interesting is that both in Philippians 2 and Revelation 5, we see the *universal* worship of Christ. In Philippians 2:10, we are told that everyone "in heaven and on earth and under the earth" will worship Christ as Lord. Revelation 5 says the same thing, though the setting is heaven itself:

> Then I heard every creature—
>   in heaven, on earth, under the earth, in the sea,

and all that is in them—
  singing:
"To the one seated on the throne and to the Lamb
  be praise, honor, glory, and ruling power forever and ever!"
And the four living creatures were saying "Amen,"
  and the elders threw themselves to the ground and worshiped.
(Rev. 5:13–14)

If proper worship is practiced anywhere, it is in the very throne room of God. And it is here, in that throne room, that the Lamb, Christ, is worshiped together with God. This chapter is sometimes labeled "The Christology of Heaven." Heaven's assessment of Christ is of course the right assessment. Remarkably, Revelation 5:13, like Philippians 2:10, alludes to Exodus 20:4 ("You shall not make for yourself a carved image or any likeness of anything that is in heaven above, or that is on earth under it, or that is in the water below"). And if the worship of Christ is not a violation of this commandment, it can only be because he, too, is considered to be God.

Again, we are forced to conclude that the New Testament authors are neither sloppy in their wording nor unaware of what they are saying. When they describe their devotion to Christ, they use reverential, worshipful, unmistakable language, for they are describing their devotion to God.

POSTSCRIPT: WORSHIP IN THE NEW TESTAMENT

The New Testament references to worship of Jesus Christ invite the question, Could the New Testament Christians have accorded worship to anyone other than God? Were first-century Christians comfortable assigning divine titles and honors to exalted creatures? The consistent answer given throughout the New Testament is an emphatic no, beginning with Jesus himself. When the Devil tempted Jesus in the Judean wilderness by offering him the kingdoms of the world if he would only worship Satan, Jesus quoted Deuteronomy 6:13, *"You are to worship the Lord your God and serve* only *him"* (Matt. 4:10).

It is all the more surprising, then, to see Jesus' response to Thomas's confession in John 20:28—"My Lord and my God!" Thomas exclaims this to the risen Christ, as we saw earlier. But what is Jesus' response? Remarkably, Jesus does not rebuke Thomas but instead says, "Have you believed because you have seen me? Blessed are the people who have not seen and yet have believed" (v. 29). Jesus affirms the rightness of Thomas's response. Now perhaps Jesus was just being polite; perhaps he was so glad that Thomas came to believe in the Resurrection that he didn't want to squelch the moment or quench Thomas's zeal. No, this answer won't do, as we'll see in the following passages. When God's honor is on the line, politeness is not an option.

About a dozen years later, King Herod Agrippa I, the grandson of Herod the Great, had a dispute with the people of Tyre and Sidon. He came to Caesarea and met with a gathering of citizens in the theater. The citizens were eager to solve the dispute because Agrippa controlled their food supply (Acts 12:20). He made a grand entrance followed by a speech, inciting in the crowd an exuberant response: "On a day determined in advance, Herod put on his royal robes, sat down on the judgment seat, and made a speech to them. But the crowd began to shout, 'The voice of a god, and not of a man!'" (Acts 12:21–22).

The praise offered to Agrippa is not nearly as strong as that offered by Thomas to Jesus: "a god" versus "my God." Further, Jesus explicitly accepted this praise from Thomas, while Herod only implicitly did, as far as the record in Acts tells us. Yet, there was divine judgment on Agrippa, and it came swiftly: "Immediately an angel of the Lord struck Herod down because he did not give the glory to God, and he was eaten by worms and died" (Acts 12:23). How is it possible that Jesus could accept *higher* praise from Thomas and yet not be struck down by God? The contrast makes no sense unless Jesus is indeed God in the flesh.

Two chapters later in Acts we see another instance of people worshiping men as though they were gods. Paul and Barnabas had come to Lystra to preach the gospel. And there, Paul healed a lame man.

"So when the crowds saw what Paul had done, they shouted in the Lycaonian language, 'The gods have come down to us in human form!' They began to call Barnabas Zeus and Paul Hermes, because he was the chief speaker" (Acts 14:11–12). Apparently, the crowd came and reported to the local pagan priest that the gods had visited them, for he, in turn, began preparing animal sacrifices. "But when the apostles Barnabas and Paul heard about it, they tore their clothes and rushed out into the crowd, shouting, 'Men, why are you doing these things? We too are men, with human natures just like you!'" (Acts 14:14–15a).

We see here a similar situation to that of Acts 12: Men are worshiped as gods without recognition of *the* God. Agrippa accepts the worship and is struck down. Paul and Barnabas are repulsed by the honor extended to them. In fact, their initial reaction was to tear their clothes. Recall that this was the response of Caiaphas to Jesus' proclamation that the Son of Man would be sitting at the right hand of God, coming on the clouds. Judaism taught that tearing one's clothes was the appropriate reaction upon hearing blasphemy.[14]

Paul and Barnabas's reaction to their deification is exactly the opposite of Agrippa's reaction. It is also the opposite of Jesus' reaction when Thomas worships him. In light of Paul and Barnabas's abhorrence to being worshiped, why did Jesus react differently? If what Thomas said was blasphemy, shouldn't Jesus have torn his clothes too? The contrast between Paul's and Jesus' reactions to being worshiped is startling and inexplicable on any grounds other than that Jesus Christ was, in fact, true deity.

Now perhaps a distinction needs to be made here. Even though it is not permissible for mere men to receive worship, perhaps *angels* may be worshiped. After all, they are not mortals. They have superhuman powers. And they are unlike us, thus naturally eliciting a reverent response from human beings.

We again turn to the last book of the Bible, the book of Revelation, for some help on this question. In chapter 19, we read that John, the author, is overcome with emotion in the presence of an imposing angel. He says, "So I threw myself down at his feet to worship him."

The angel reacted quickly and decisively: "Do not do this! I am only a fellow servant with you and your brothers who hold to the testimony about Jesus. Worship God, for the testimony about Jesus is the spirit of prophecy" (Rev. 19:10). The angel's reaction shows unequivocally that neither men nor angels may receive worship. There is no exception. We already noted in Matthew 4:10 that Jesus told Satan, the chief of the fallen angels, to worship only God. And yet, in Hebrews 1:6, God tells the *angels* to worship Christ (*"Let all the angels of God worship him!"*). How is it possible that Christ—and only Christ—is excluded from the divine punishment for being worshiped? The only way to make sense of the New Testament's witness to Christ is that these writers embraced him as true deity. Nothing short of that does justice to their words.

As we have seen in just a handful of representative texts, the New Testament clearly and forcefully presents Jesus Christ as more than a mere man. In fact, it presents him as more than an angel: he is God himself. The notion that his divinity was invented nearly three hundred years after his time on earth is an absurd fable, created out of thin air. Although *The Da Vinci Code* is a fascinating tale, that is *all* it is: a tale, a fable, a good yarn spun by a master storyteller.

Chapter 14

FROM THE PENS OF FATHERS AND FOES

Jesus Outside the New Testament

If we were to take away all the miraculous events surrounding the story of Jesus to reveal a human, we would certainly find no one who could have garnered huge crowds around him because of his preaching. And the fact is that this crowd-drawing preacher finds his place in "history" only in the New Testament, completely overlooked by the dozens of historians of his day, an era considered one of the best documented in history.

—ACHARYA S, *The Christ Conspiracy*, 100

Jesus' place in history is secure. We've seen that the biblical Gospels are generally reliable witnesses to his life, that core New Testament teachings about his person and work have remained intact, and that the bulk of New Testament writings made the canonical cut without much ado. In short, the New Testament is historically credible.

That credibility is confirmed in part by noncanonical references to Christ, both Christian and non-Christian.[1] Several non-Christian writers supply surprising detail about the life of Jesus and his extraordinary impact upon the ancient Mediterranean world.[2] Comments like those of Acharya S that imply that Jesus never existed because he is not mentioned outside the New Testament are remarkable for their bluster. This would be an interesting topic to pursue fully,[3] but our goals are more focused.

In this chapter, we will explore what friends and foes of Christianity had to say about the deity of Christ. Surveying the period after the apostles (c. 100) and up to the Council of Nicea (325), we'll take a brief look at three non-Christian writers who show that anti-Christian rhetoric was well aware of belief in Jesus' divinity. Significantly, each of these writers predates the Nicene Council by *at least* 125 years.

We'll also sample writings from early Christian thinkers known as the *ante-Nicene Fathers*. Their works were penned after the close of the New Testament era and before the Council of Nicea. Though the Fathers (or patristic writers, as they're sometimes called) drew heavily from the New Testament and so can't be seen as purely non-canonical witnesses, many deserve attention as careful scholars in their own right.[4] Indeed, it is their reflection on the teachings of the New Testament about Christ that most interest us in this chapter. Highlighting second- and third-century Fathers, our sampling will reveal continuity between their convictions about Christ's deity and biblical affirmations of the same.

TESTIMONY FROM CHRISTIANITY'S OPPONENTS

It is a remarkable thing that we have *any* statements about Jesus by non-Christian writers. After all, he was a Jewish carpenter who spent most of his time on the shores of the Sea of Galilee, occasionally journeying to Jerusalem with his disciples. What's more, writers in the Roman Empire were typically upper-class men who looked down on Eastern religions and gazed back on Rome's celebrated past. So why would they ever pay attention to a Nazarene who founded a religion embraced by the lowest rungs of society? Simply put, he couldn't be ignored. The rise of the religion bearing Christ's name was rapid, widespread, and revolutionary. And it turned the Roman Empire upside down. Although we may not have extensive non-Christian sources about Jesus, some writers recognized that the early Christians treated Jesus as divine, threatening pagan culture as a result.

It's axiomatic that skeptics rise with scorn whenever Christians bow before Christ. And what's true in the second millennium was even truer in the second century. Take, for example, the Greek satirist Lucian of Samosata. Writing around 170, Lucian blasted Christians for their devotion to Jesus, "whom they still worship, the man who was crucified in Palestine because he introduced this new cult into the world."[5] Lucian used his pen to poke fun at followers of Christ, "poor wretches" who revealed their gullibility "by denying the Greek gods and by worshiping that crucified sophist [i.e., philosophical huckster] himself."[6] In addition to confirming basic facts about the life and impact of Jesus, Lucian's writings supply that which is of most interest to us here: non-Christian testimony that Jesus was treated as divine *long* before the Council of Nicea.

Despite severe ridicule, Christians stubbornly refused to stop worshiping Jesus. Around 177, the Roman philosopher Celsus wrote a treatise that revealed both his ignorance of early Christian doctrine and the intensity of early Christian devotion. Celsus scoffed at Christians who were worshiping a man as God:

> Now, if the Christians worshiped only one God they might have reason on their side. But as a matter of fact they worship a man who appeared only recently. They do not consider what they are doing a breach of monotheism; rather, they think it perfectly consistent to worship the great God and to worship his servant as God. And their worship of this Jesus is the more outrageous because they refuse to listen to any talk about God, the father of all, unless it includes some reference to Jesus: Tell them that Jesus, the author of the Christian insurrection, was not his son, and they will not listen to you. And when they call him Son of God, they are not really paying homage to God, rather, they are attempting to exalt Jesus to the heights.[7]

Celsus, himself a monotheist, didn't see how Christians could revere Jesus as God without retreating into polytheism. Further, he found it absurd to imagine that God himself came down to earth, since that would, in Celsus's mind, require alteration of God's nature.[8] Of course, the early Christians did not believe that God *changed* into a man; they believed that he *added* humanity to his divine nature. Nevertheless, Celsus's complaints spurred church leaders to devise clearer expressions of doctrine and supplied us with more non-Christian testimony of early belief in Jesus' divinity. And, as Celsus noted above, that belief was unswerving.

Early Christians refused to veer from their devotion to a divine Jesus, even when it put them on the road to martyrdom. And rulers like Pliny the Younger stood eager to point the way. Pliny, governor of Bithynia (a secluded Roman province in Asia Minor, or modern-day Turkey) from about 111–113, didn't care for the impact Christianity was having on business in pagan houses of worship. Demand for sacrificial animals was down, sacred holidays were set aside, and sanctuaries were boarded up. If Pliny's religious industry was going to survive, Christians would have to die. But on what grounds?

Pliny admitted that the Christians lived good, clean lives. He could not pin a standard felony on them. So he took a creative angle and ran it by the emperor. In a letter written around 112, Pliny informed Trajan of his dealings with the "wretched cult" of Christianity:

> For the moment this is the line I have taken with all persons brought before me on the charge of being Christians. I have asked them in person if they are Christians, and if they admit it, I repeat the question a second and third time, with a warning of the punishment awaiting them. If they persist, I order them to be led away for execution; for, whatever the nature of their admission, I am convinced that their stubbornness and unshakeable obstinacy ought not to go unpunished.[9]

Pliny, however, was lenient in the case of those who denounced their faith:

Among these I considered that I should dismiss any who denied that they were or ever had been Christians when they repeated after me a formula of invocation to the gods and had made offerings of wine and incense to your statue . . . and furthermore had reviled the name of Christ: none of which things, I understand, any genuine Christian can be induced to do.[10]

Eventually, Pliny revealed the specific crime to which the Christians had admitted: "They had met regularly before dawn on a fixed day to chant verses alternately among themselves in honour of Christ as if to a god."[11] In other words, the martyred Christians were guilty of *worshiping Jesus.*

The writings of Lucian, Celsus, and Pliny make clear that early Christian beliefs about Jesus can't be reduced to mere reminiscences of a great man. Rather, belief in the divinity of Jesus was the heart of early Christian confession. For believers like those in Bithynia, that confession was a matter of life and death.[12] To suggest that Jesus' divinity was the convenient creation of a fourth-century council does more than make a mess of history; it sullies the graves of martyrs—second century or otherwise—who staked their lives on the conviction that Jesus is God.

THE REAL QUESTION: WAS JESUS REALLY A MAN?

In the first century A.D., a form of thought known as Platonism was growing in popularity throughout the Greco-Roman world.[13] The defining feature of Platonism was its distinction between two levels of reality: the physical world, experienced through the ordinary senses; and the "spiritual" world, where *ideas* represented ultimate reality. In Platonic thought, the spiritual world was actually more real than its physical counterpart. At best, the physical world was inferior; at worst, it was devoid of anything good. This philosophy, coupled with others, influenced some in the early church to adopt a view of Christ that was far removed from that of the New Testament.[14]

The early second century witnessed the growth of a Christological heresy known as *Docetism*. Named after the Greek verb meaning "to seem or appear," Docetism taught that Jesus only *looked* human. Speaking of Jesus as if he were some sort of phantom, proponents of this heresy argued that it would have been impossible for Jesus to truly suffer in life and experience death on the cross.[15]

The church father Ignatius vehemently opposed Docetism and warned Christians not to accept anyone who "blasphemes my Lord by not confessing that he was clothed in flesh."[16] Even with such strong condemnation of the Docetic heresy, it became the prevailing position of Gnostic thinkers and writers.

What's the upshot of all this? Simply that second-century debates over the nature of Christ were far more concerned with his earthly qualities than his heavenly status. In the world in which the church Fathers lived and wrote, embracing the divinity of Jesus wasn't the problem.[17] Embracing his *humanity* was. It shouldn't surprise us, then, to find a lack of *articulation* of Jesus' divinity in the patristic writings. Nonetheless, in their defense of Jesus' humanness, the Fathers left us several *affirmations* of their belief that Jesus was far more than a man.

TESTIMONY FROM THE APOSTOLIC FATHERS

The first patristic writers, active from the 90s through the first half of the second century, are known as the Apostolic Fathers. They were given this name because some of them had known the apostles or those who had learned directly from the apostles. The Fathers' proximity to the apostles and apostolic doctrine made them influential in the ancient church and makes them important to modern church historians. We'll look briefly at some representative Fathers and their affirmations of Christ's deity.

Though the Apostolic Fathers didn't spend time speculating *how* Jesus was divine or systematizing arguments for his deity, they did make statements that reveal belief in Jesus as a sovereign figure who existed before time.

Clement of Rome, writing at the end of the first century, speaks of Jesus as the "majestic scepter of God,"[18] emphasizing his role as God's instrument of divine sovereignty.[19] Thus, according to Clement, the resurrected Jesus is afforded divine honor in the presence of the Father.[20] Such honor is apparently equal to that given the Father, since Clement speaks of Jesus (as well as the Spirit) as existing on the same plane with God: "For as God lives, and the Lord Jesus Christ lives, and the Holy Spirit . . ."[21] Similarly, 2 Clement (a second-century sermon by a different author) exhorts its readers "to think of Jesus Christ, as we do of God, as 'Judge of the living and the dead.'"[22] Both Clements clearly ascribe to Jesus activities and honors belonging to God.

Clement also affirmed his belief in the preexistence of Jesus Christ, who spoke through the Spirit in the Old Testament Psalms.[23] The author of the Epistle of Barnabas (written sometime between 70 and 135) goes even further, proclaiming that the preexistent Christ shared creative duties with the Father:

> For the Scripture speaks about us when he says to the Son: "Let us make man according to our image and likeness, and let them rule over the beasts of the earth and the birds of the air and the fish of the sea." And when he saw that our creation was good, the Lord said, "Increase and multiply and fill the earth." These things he said to the Son.[24]

Not surprisingly, the same author declares that Jesus is "Lord of the entire Cosmos."[25] Such a statement not only affirms that Jesus Christ existed before time; it also implies his identity as God.

Ignatius did not feel compelled to merely imply such a thing; he stated it explicitly. As the bishop of Antioch, Ignatius wrote seven epistles to various churches in Asia Minor while on his way to martyrdom in Rome (c. 107–110). In those epistles, he spoke of Christ as one who "before the ages was with the Father,"[26] who was "the mind of the Father,"[27] and who can properly be called "our God."[28] Of course, since Ignatius was an outspoken opponent of Docetism, he was sure to note that Jesus Christ was "God [who] was revealed in human form."[29] He further unpacks the idea of God's union with human flesh:

> There is only one physician, of flesh and of the Spirit, generate [born] and ingenerate [unborn], God in man, life in death, Son of Mary and Son of God, first passible [subject to suffering] then impassible [beyond suffering], Jesus Christ our Lord.[30]

The above quotation clearly shows that Ignatius saw Jesus as both God and man. But his statement is even more precise than it may first appear. When he calls Jesus *ingenerate*, Ignatius uses a technical term that distinguishes the eternal Creator from his creatures.[31] In other words, when Ignatius calls Jesus "God," he uses the title in its fullest sense.

Although the Apostolic Fathers do not have a highly articulated doctrine of the Incarnation, they clearly embrace Jesus' divinity. That they were generally well connected to the apostles suggests continuity between the New Testament view of Christ and their own. That continuity continued into the next era.

TESTIMONY FROM THE APOLOGISTS

During the early decades of the church's existence, there was little formal theological development. The Apostolic Fathers simply asserted truths like the deity and humanity of Christ and resisted speculation. But when attacks—arising both inside and outside the church[32]—were leveled against cherished beliefs, a different kind of resistance was needed. Enter the Apologists—church Fathers who lived and wielded their pens in defense of the faith between the middle of the second century and the end of the third.

The most prominent early apologist was Justin Martyr (c. 100–165). Justin argued vigorously for the divinity of Christ and his preexistence, featuring proofs from the Old Testament. For example, he claimed that Old Testament manifestations of God were actually appearances of the preincarnate Christ,[33] and he identified Jesus as "Wisdom" speaking in the book of Proverbs.[34] Additionally, he saw "Let us" statements in the creation text of Genesis 1 as dialog between the persons of the Trinity, one of whom was, of course, the preincarnate Christ.[35] Throughout his writings, Justin distinguished between the Father and the Son, while maintaining the true and eternal deity of both.[36]

The greatest theologian of the second century was Irenaeus (c. 130–200), Bishop of Lyons (in modern-day France). As a youth he sat under the tutelage of Polycarp (martyred c. 155), who was in turn a disciple of the apostle John. Only one generation removed from the apostles, Irenaeus was passionate about defending the apostolic faith. Significantly, he is best known for emphasizing the God-man as the crux of all theology.

Irenaeus unequivocally affirms the deity of Christ when he writes "the Father is God and the Son is God; for He who is born of God is God."[37] Ever concerned with the heretical Christologies of Docetism and Gnosticism, Irenaeus also asserts the true humanity of Christ with vigor:

> But in every respect, too, [Christ Jesus our Lord] is a man, the formation of God: and thus he took up man into himself, the invisible becoming visible, the incomprehensible being made comprehensible, the impassible becoming capable of suffering, and the Word being made man.[38]

As J. N. D. Kelly notes, Irenaeus's writings insist "almost monotonously on the unity of the God-man."[39] He clearly thought it was a point to be stressed. So did others.

During the third century, affirmations of Christ's deity increasingly stood alongside the defense of his humanity. This approach characterized apologists in both the Latin-speaking West and the Greek-speaking East. Western apologist Hippolytus (c. 170–236), a disciple of Irenaeus, took for granted that the Incarnation involved a joining together of true deity and true humanity.[40] Taking a page from the Gospel of John, Hippolytus declared that "the Word [pre-incarnate Christ] was made incarnate and became man"[41] and was "manifested as God in a body."[42] That body was one of flesh and blood according to Hippolytus, who was careful to note that "[the Word] became man really, not in appearance or in a manner of speaking."[43]

Another Western apologist, Tertullian (c. 160–225), describes the eternal union of the preincarnate Christ with God the Father:

> The Word, therefore, is both always in the Father, as He says, "I am in the Father"; and is always with God, according to what is written, "And the Word was with God"; and never separate from the Father, or other than the Father, since "I and the Father are one."[44]

In addition to his affirmation that Jesus shares the divine nature of the Father, Tertullian declares that Jesus shares the human nature of the Virgin Mary.[45] Mary was not, as some avowed, a mere conduit through which some sort of spiritual body passed—like "water through a pipe."[46] To the contrary, Jesus received his flesh directly from her.[47] Emphasizing both the divine and human natures of Jesus, Tertullian's Christology can be stated simply: "one person . . . God and man."[48]

When it came to the deity of Christ, writings of the Eastern apologists were essentially in harmony with those of their Western colleagues. Clement of Alexandria (c. 155–220) insisted that "the Word Himself has come to us from heaven,"[49] and that Jesus is "alone . . . both God and man."[50] Similarly, Origen (c. 185–254) insists that the Son is begotten, not created, by the Father and that the begetting was in eternity past so that the Son was eternally generated: "His generation is as eternal and everlasting as the brilliancy which is produced from the sun."[51] Their belief in "the eternal generation of the Son" has not been shared by all orthodox writers, but it did not diminish their conviction that Jesus Christ was both man and God. Indeed, theologians have sometimes criticized them for stressing Christ's deity in a way that overpowers his humanity. The details of such criticism are not important to our discussion here. Suffice it to say that the church Fathers were eager—perhaps overly eager in the case of Eastern apologists—to emphasize the divinity of Jesus.

Much more evidence could be cited to show that the church Fathers believed Jesus to be divine. Our brief survey has shown that as the third century drew to a close, there was agreement that Christ was sovereign, existed before time, and participated in Creation. Indeed, he was viewed as true God and true man united in one person. And the Council of Nicea was still on the horizon.

Chapter 15

SIMPLY DIVINE?

The Real Issue at Nicea

By officially endorsing Jesus as the Son of God, Constantine turned Jesus into a deity who existed beyond the scope of the human world, an entity whose power was unchallengeable.

—DAN BROWN, *The Da Vinci Code*, 233

No one with a seat at the Nicene Council thought that the fact of Jesus' divinity was on the table. It was simply assumed. By the time the bishops had convened at Nicea on May 20, 325, the divinity of Jesus had been affirmed by the majority of Christians for almost three centuries (see chaps. 12–14). Like their forefathers in the faith, each of the participating bishops—and the congregations they represented—actively worshiped Jesus, prayed to him, and confessed him as universal Lord. These actions, of course, presupposed faith in a man who was out of this world.

Current popularity of the claim that Jesus' divinity was invented at Nicea is a sign of our historically illiterate times. Ironically, such a claim would have been viewed by fourth-century Christians as seriously *behind* the times—nearly three hundred years out-of-date. This is not to say that the Council of Nicea was not a trendsetting event. Indeed, the council launched a new campaign—complete with catchwords, slogans, and a position paper—to articulate and promote its new *official* stance on Jesus. Its impact resonates to this day. But this begs the question: If Jesus' divinity had been a pillar of Christian belief for so long, then what made the council's proceedings and pronouncements so monumental? What more could be said about a Jesus already viewed as divine? In other words, what was the *real* issue at Nicea?

LIKE FATHER, LIKE SON?

The road to Nicea began in Alexandria. Situated on the Mediterranean Sea in northwest Egypt, Alexandria boasted the ancient world's largest library and a reputation as the intellectual center of its day. It was also home to some of the most prominent theologians of old.

One of those theologians was Alexander, the archbishop of Alexandria from 313 to 328. Alexander, who took his role as an overseer with utmost seriousness, regularly held seminars for the senior clergy under his watch. A member of that senior clergy, Arius, the presbyter of an important church district in Alexandria, was at odds with Alexander over the precise way to describe Jesus' divine status. In what would prove to be a pivotal lecture, Alexander unequivocally proclaimed that Christ shared all of the divine attributes of the Father—including eternality. Arius, who denied that the Son was timeless, was pushed to his limits.

Arius believed that Jesus was divine inasmuch as he was *like* the Father. Jesus was like the Father in that he existed before creation, played a role in the origin of creation, and was exalted over all creation. Yet the Son himself was a *creature*. According to Arius, the Father created the Son *ex nihilo* ("out of nothing") in eternity past and, in turn, commissioned the Son to create the universe. So while Jesus was *like* the Father in his divinity, their divine natures were not *identical*. Jesus was divine in a lesser sense.

Alexander vigorously maintained that divinity was like pregnancy; it was absolute. Just as a woman cannot be more or less with child, Jesus must be all that divinity is or he is not divine at all. Sensing that Jesus' deity was the head domino in a line of essential Christian truths (especially truths related to salvation), Alexander used his pulpit and his pen to challenge Arius's teachings. But Arius was persistent, so something had to be done. If the head domino fell, all the rest would fall with it. Even though Alexander was a gentle leader who loathed conflict, he knew he could not avoid it when it came to the nature of Christ. So in 318 Alexander gathered a hundred or so bishops in Alexandria to discuss the matter and formally defrock Arius.

Arius was outraged. He rejected the defrocking, retreated to Nicomedia (in modern-day Turkey), and rallied his supporters. His strongest backer, Eusebius of Nicomedia, was related by marriage to the emperor, Constantine, and was the theologian of the imperial court. Together Arius and Eusebius embarked on a letter-writing campaign to bishops who had not presided over Arius's defrocking. A savvy publicist, Arius also set his teachings to rhymes[1] and put them into "songs to be sung by sailors, and by millers, and by travelers."[2] It wasn't long before graffiti were covering walls, pamphlets were blanketing public squares, and violence was spreading in the streets. With the help of his well-connected friend, Arius had ignited a cause with an explosive effect.

The reverberation was felt throughout the imperial territory. Constantine, who had toppled his final challenger and emerged as the sole ruler of the Roman Empire in 324, was embarrassed by the bickering among his bishops. More than anything else, the new monarch wanted unity in his empire. And he would seek it on the twentieth anniversary of his ascent to a Roman throne.

In 325 Constantine summoned all of his bishops to what would be the first ecumenical council in the history of the church. Constantine, who normally resided in Byzantium (later renamed Constantinople; now modern-day Istanbul, Turkey), stayed at his lakeside palace in Nicea while renovating the city that would later bear his name. It would be the perfect setting for the bishops, who were treated like royalty. Constantine's honored guests arrived at Nicea on the imperial transport system, reserved for official imperial mail and the travel of imperial officials.[3] The all-expenses-paid trip included welcome gifts, fine meals, and luxurious, secured living quarters. Indeed, the accommodations were "splendid beyond description."[4] Constantine was going out of his way to bring unity to the church in his empire. But the final say did not belong to him.

NOT ONE IOTA

The bishops at Nicea were more accustomed to persecution than pampering. Many of them had lived through the injustices of Emperors Diocletian (ruling c. 284–305) and Maximian (ruling c. 286–305). Diocletian was eager to confiscate Christian writings, burn Christian buildings, and arrest Christian clergy. Maximian didn't hesitate to execute, disable, or exile those who refused to renounce Christ. At least one of the bishops at Nicea had personally experienced Maximian's cruelty. Paphnutius lost his right eye and gained a limp in his left leg—before being banished to the mines—as a result of confessing his faith.[5] There were more victims of persecution at the hands of others. Some lost use of their fingers because their nerves had been seared with hot pokers. Still others lost limbs altogether. The marks of persecution were so prevalent that one ancient writer said, "The council looked like an assembled army of martyrs"![6] Of course, men who had suffered such physical injuries for the sake of spiritual integrity were not about to be told what they should believe about Christ—imperial pressure or not.

Indeed, the bishops at Nicea were more preoccupied with preaching than politics. Their burdens were for their congregations and for faithfulness to "the Holy Fathers," to whom they often referred. They were keener on apostolic tradition than theological innovation, and they sought the Spirit's witness to truth in the context of *community.* In other words, the council was not a collection of individuals with isolated opinions. To the contrary, they brought under one roof the collected wisdom of the church Fathers who had gone before them in understanding the nature of Christ. The bishops momentarily left the practice of theology in their congregations to join the broader Christian community in discussing such practice. The upshot of this should not be overlooked: the council was informed—no, driven—by the devotional life of the church at large. Constantine knew that whatever solution came about would have to reckon with the deeply held convictions of the majority of bishops and the churches they represented.

The emperor wasn't much of a theologian, so he relied on his theological advisor, Hosius, to get him up to speed before the bishops arrived. Hosius would have known that the majority of three hundred or so[7] bishops expected at Nicea would not be quick to side with Arius. In fact, less than thirty would have come prepared to say that the Son was a created being. Many more, perhaps even most, entered the meeting hall straddling the fence. They did not yet have a clear understanding of the issues.

Concerned more with imperial unity than theological precision, Constantine was eager to adopt a solution that would appeal to the largest number of bishops—no matter what that solution might be.[8] The Arians unwittingly helped him on this front. Shortly after the council went into session, a call was made for a clarification of the Arian position. Arius's friend and stand-in (Arius could not sit on the council since he was not a bishop), Eusebius of Nicomedia, took the opportunity to present the Arian position in no uncertain terms. He strenuously asserted that the Son was in no way equal to the Father and was, in fact, a finite creature. The bishops were scandalized. Church historian Roger E. Olson describes the scene:

> Some of the bishops were holding their hands over their ears and shouting for someone to stop the blasphemies. One bishop near Eusebius stepped forward and grabbed the manuscript out of his hands, threw it on the floor and stomped on it. A riot broke out among the bishops and was stopped only by the emperor's command.[9]

The bishops straddling the fence were suddenly staring at Arius from the other side. Apparently, they didn't previously understand how black-and-white the issue really was. Jesus was either finite, or he was not. The majority of bishops couldn't stand the thought of the former. Constantine had the council sitting right where he wanted it—or so he thought.

As things in the meeting hall quieted down, talk of an official statement against Arianism picked up. The bishops didn't like what Arius and his followers said about the finite nature of the Son. They knew what they *did not* believe. But how precisely should they articulate what they *did* believe about the deity of Christ? Therein lay the real issue at Nicea: determining *how*—not *if*—Jesus was divine.

Eventually the bishops and the emperor agreed that a formal statement would be crafted and signed by all of the bishops. Those who refused to sign the document would be deposed from their positions of leadership within the church.[10] Constantine immediately appointed Hosius as secretary of the new document, but talks with the bishops stalled over the matter of language. The handful of Arians on the council insisted that only terminology found in the Bible be used; those opposed to Arius argued that extrabiblical language was needed to unpack the meaning of words used in Scripture. Constantine, most likely at the prompting of Hosius, proposed a solution.

The emperor suggested that the Son be described as possessing the "same substance" (Greek *homoousios*) as that of the Father. Constantine apparently believed this label would identify Jesus as full deity (thus pleasing those opposed to Arius) without implying too much beyond that (thus alleviating the concerns of the Arians). If this proved to be the case, the emperor would have a catchword that unified all of the bishops—regardless of their views of Christ's divinity. Indeed, the majority of bishops seemed eager to adopt the description. But hard-core Arians thought the word was too pregnant with meaning. In their view, it gave Jesus equality with the Father but didn't adequately explain how that equality fit into the framework of belief in one God.

Despite the loud objections of a few—including those of his nephew, the court theologian—Constantine forged ahead with the majority to create a new creed declaring Christ to be identical in substance to the Father. The resulting article of faith stated:

> We believe in one God, the Father almighty, maker of all things, visible and invisible;
>
> And in one Lord Jesus Christ, the Son of God, begotten from the Father, only-begotten, that is, from the substance of the Father, God from God, light from light, true God from true God, begotten not made, of one substance *[homoousios]* with the Father, through Whom all things came into being, things in heaven and things on earth, Who because of us men and because of our salvation came down and became incarnate, becoming man, suffered and rose again on the third day, ascended to the heavens, and will come to judge the living and the dead;
>
> And in the Holy Spirit.
>
> But as for those who say, There was when He was not, and, Before being born He was not, and that He came into existence out of nothing, or who assert that the Son of God is from a different hypostasis or substance, or is created, or is subject to alteration or change—these the Catholic Church anathematizes.[11]

All of the bishops signed the creed—with the exception of Theonas of Marmarica and Secundus of Ptolemais. Some who signed did so reluctantly, but the overall message was clear: Arianism was inconsistent with the historic faith and practice of the church. Those who embraced it would find themselves on the outside looking in.

Some who were unwilling to embrace Arianism were nevertheless uneasy with the term *homoousios.* They were worried that a word meant to suggest that the Father and Son shared the same *substance* could be twisted to say that the Father and Son were the same *person.*[12] These folks suggested that a slight modification to the term *homoousios* might solve the problem.

In the Greek language, the difference between the words for "same" *(homo)* and "like" *(homoi)* is the letter *iota.* By changing *homo-ousios* to *homoi-ousios,* some anti-Arians described the Son as sharing "like substance" with the Father. In so doing, they affirmed the Son's divinity and yet treated him as a person distinct from the Father. But other anti-Arians objected to the blander term, arguing that it didn't do full justice to Christ's essential equality with God. What's more, Arius and his followers were all too eager to use the term in describing a created Christ. For these reasons, many anti-Arians stood resolutely behind the decision to describe Jesus with the term *homoousios*. Athanasius was one such man who would not budge—not one *iota*.

THE EMPEROR STRIKES BACK

Athanasius was in his twenties when he accompanied Bishop Alexander to the Council of Nicea. Three years later, in 328, he would succeed his mentor as the bishop of Alexandria. Four decades later, he would prove to be the church's greatest champion of Nicene Christianity.

Indeed, a champion was needed if the decisions at Nicea were going to stand. Despite the clear pronouncement of the council that Jesus shared the Father's exact nature, in-house squabbles over the terms *homoousios* and *homoiousios* continued. Some members of the council proclaimed the wording as a triumph of Sabellianism—that view of the Godhead that did not distinguish its persons. The ousted Arians played this to their advantage, arguing that the creed had gone too far. Quickly, they gathered steam and were able especially to persuade secret sympathizers of Arianism to speak up. Even many of the anti-Arians began to waffle about the wording. Yes, Jesus Christ was truly God. But did the Nicene Creed open the door to saying more? By jumping out of the frying pan of Arianism with this creed, they may have inadvertently landed in the fire of Sabellianism. Precise clarification would be needed on the nature of Christ and his relationship to the Father, but the church would have to wait over fifty years to get it (at the Council of Constantinople in 381).

The prolonged debate over how to describe Christ's divinity both showed that Constantine lacked the power to force a decision upon the church and set the stage for him to act out his real agenda.

In 328, an assembly of bishops restored Arius and his followers to fellowship. These bishops also began to lobby the emperor for Arius's formal reinstatement as an Alexandrian presbyter. Constantine, who just a few years earlier had condemned Arius as a heretic, acquiesced. In 332, the emperor pronounced Arius a presbyter in good standing and ordered the new bishop of Alexandria—a young Athanasius—to accept Arius back into the fold. Athanasius rebuffed Constantine's command and rejected Arius's confirmation. For staying true to the Nicene Creed and standing against those the emperor had earlier condemned, Athanasius was rewarded with exile to the outer limits of the western empire. In this act Constantine revealed that doctrinal precision was far less important to him than imperial unity.

Athanasius would find himself banished four more times, spending a total of seventeen years in exile. Not once would he waver from the Nicene pronouncement that Jesus shared the exact same nature as the Father. Athanasius would stand against the world, if need be, in defense of this truth.

Constantine, on the other hand, would die embracing Arians before letting go of his vision for unity. His alternating favor toward Athanasius then Arius makes sense when we realize that Constantine's main agenda was not to support orthodoxy or suppress heresy. It was to promote harmony. To suggest that Constantine had the ability—or even the inclination—to manipulate the council into believing what it did not already embrace is, at best, a silly notion. At worst, the emperor was merely a speed bump in the church's march toward a deeper understanding of the nature of Christ. And although Constantine may have called himself "bishop of the bishops," the church was going to believe what it knew it must believe—with or without him. And it believed, as it had from the beginning, that Jesus is God.[13]

PART 5

STEALING THUNDER

Did Christianity Rip Off Mythical Gods?

Chapter 16

PARALLELOMANIA

Supposed Links Between Christianity and Pagan Religions

Why should we consider the stories of Osiris, Dionysus, Adonis, Attis, Mithras, and the other Pagan Mystery saviors as fables, yet come across essentially the same story told in a Jewish context and believe it to be the biography of a carpenter from Bethlehem?

—TIMOTHY FREKE AND PETER GANDY, *The Jesus Mysteries*, 9

Jesus was a Pagan god . . . and Christianity was a heretical product of Paganism!

—TIMOTHY FREKE AND PETER GANDY, *The Jesus Mysteries*, 9

Nothing in Christianity is original.

—DAN BROWN, *The Da Vinci Code*, 232

The traditional history of Christianity cannot convincingly explain why the Jesus story is so similar to ancient Pagan myths.

—TIMOTHY FREKE AND PETER GANDY,
The Laughing Jesus, 61

The title of this chapter, "Parallelomania," is drawn from Samuel Sandmel's influential article in the *Journal of Biblical Literature* 81 (1962): 1–13. This article dealt with scholars' desires to find parallels where none exist. We borrow it for this chapter since it speaks to the same ongoing situation in comparative studies.

What makes Christianity unique among world religions is that it is grounded in history. More specifically, the Christian faith rests on the person of Jesus Christ as a real, historical man. The notion that God became man in space-time history, that he lived among us, that he died on a Roman cross and rose from the dead is the core of the Christian proclamation. Indeed, one implication of the Incarnation—of God becoming man—is that the Incarnation invites us and even requires us to examine its historical credibility. The Gospels go to great lengths to speak to the where, who, and when of Jesus' ministry. They practically beg the reader to check out the data, to see if these things are so. To think that one can be a Christian without embracing the historicity of Jesus Christ is pure fantasy. Christianity *is* Christ. Without him, the Christian gospel has no meaning. Or as Paul put it in his first letter to the Corinthians, "If Christ has not been raised, then our preaching is futile and your faith is empty" (1 Cor. 15:14).

But there is a problem. The ideas of the Incarnation, the Virgin Birth, and the Resurrection might not be new with the Christian faith. Some claim to find these concepts in pagan religions *before* the advent of Christianity. As Freke and Gandy argue in their recent book, *The Laughing Jesus*, "The Jesus story has all the hallmarks of a myth. The reason for this is quite simple. It is a myth. Indeed, not only is it a myth, it is a Jewish version of a Pagan myth!"[1] These authors outline thirteen points of comparison between the deities of mystery religions and Jesus Christ:

- His father is God, and his mother is a virgin girl.
- He is hailed by his followers as the saviour, God made flesh and Son of God.
- He is born in a cave or humble cowshed on the twenty-fifth of December in front of shepherds.
- He surrounds himself with twelve disciples.
- He offers his followers the chance to be born again through the rites of baptism.
- He miraculously turns water into wine at a marriage ceremony.

- He rides triumphantly into town on a donkey while people wave palm leaves to honour him.
- He attacks the religious authorities who set out to destroy him.
- He dies at Easter time as a sacrifice for the sins of the world, sometimes through crucifixion.
- On the third day he rises from the dead and ascends to Heaven in glory.
- His followers await his return as the judge during the Last Days.
- His death and resurrection are celebrated by a ritual meal of bread and wine, which symbolize his body and blood.
- By symbolically sharing in the suffering and death of the Godman, initiates of the mysteries believed they would also share in his spiritual resurrection and know eternal life.[2]

These parallels, if genuine, suggest that Christianity is based on nothing but thin air. But are they true parallels? Is Christianity just a myth, having no historical foundation at all? Did Christianity rip off the tales of pagan gods? In this chapter we cannot deal with all the issues, but we will offer a framework for interpreting the data.

The idea that Christianity stole its basic content from pagan religions is not new. It finds its roots in the "history of religions school," which developed in the second half of the nineteenth century.[3] By the mid-twentieth century, this viewpoint had been largely debunked, even by scholars who saw Christianity as a purely natural religion. But in recent years, the notion that Christianity simply baptized pagan deities and applied their characteristics to Jesus of Nazareth has found a new following. What has caused this shift? How could the idea that there is nothing unique in Christianity gain a footing today?

A combination of factors contributed to this resurgence. The postmodern interest in spirituality, coupled with its increasing lack of historical grounding, has been the main ingredient. But the icing on the cake is ready access to unfiltered information via the Internet and the influential power of this medium. The result is junk food for the mind—a pseudointellectual meal that is as easy to swallow as it is devoid of substance.[4] One online article posted at an influential anti-Christian site states:

> After Osiris came many other virgin-born, resurrected savior gods: Dionysus (Grecian), Krishna (Hindu), Mithra (Persian), Tammuz (Sumerian-Babylonian). . . . Since Krishna allegedly lived centuries before Jesus, this is sufficient reason to suspect that Jesus was merely a counterfeit of Krishna and the other savior-gods who were worshiped throughout the pagan world long before Jesus.[5]

Irresponsible statements of this sort can trouble Christians deeply. Such statements do not go unchallenged, but because the Internet creates all opinions equal, it is difficult to know where to look to find adequate responses.

In this section we will note the faulty assumptions behind the alleged parallels and then outline the nature of the mystery religions. Finally, we will look at the two most commonly cited examples of Christianity's borrowing from pagan religions—the Virgin Birth and resurrection of Jesus Christ. Much more could be said in this section, but this overview should help the reader think through Christianity in relation to the ancient pagan religions.

The Faulty Assumptions Behind the Alleged Parallels

Five basic assumptions underlie parallel allegations:

1. Parallels between Jesus Christ and pagan deities can be found in any mystery religion.
2. Terms used of the Christian message just as naturally fit pagan religions.
3. Parallels indicate wholesale dependency.

4. Fully developed mystery religions existed before the rise of Christianity.
5. The purpose and nature of key events are the same in each of these religions.

These assumptions overlap, but this may be a helpful way to think about the methodological fallacies of those who claim that Jesus was just a mythical god put in Jewish garb.

The Composite Fallacy

One of the fallacies regarding parallels between pagan deities and Jesus Christ is that the pagan religions are often lumped together as though they were one religion—and one that is virtually identical to Christianity in many of its most important features. This is the *composite fallacy*. By combining features from various mystery religions, a unified picture emerges that shows strong parallels with the gospel. The only problem is, this unified religion is artificial, a fabrication of the modern writer's imagination.

Albert Schweitzer, writing early in the twentieth century, observed, "Almost all the popular writings fall into this kind of inaccuracy. They manufacture out of the various fragments of information a kind of universal Mystery-religion *which never actually existed*, least of all in Paul's day."[6] Unfortunately, the composite fallacy has been repeated in modern times too. Bruce Metzger reminds us that the form of a particular mystery cult would be different from place to place, and from century to century.[7] If this is the case *within* the same mystery religion, how much more would it be the case for *all* mystery religions?

To take one example among many, in his careful study of alleged parallels with Christian baptism, Günter Wagner concluded, "The mystery religion *par excellence* has never existed, and quite certainly did not in the first century A.D."[8] Or consider the Christian doctrine of rebirth. After an examination of the evidence, Ronald Nash declares:

We find that there was no pre-Christian doctrine of rebirth for the Christians to borrow.... The claim that pre-Christian mysteries regarded their initiation rites as a kind of rebirth is unsupported by any evidence contemporary with such alleged practices. Instead, a view found in much later texts is read back into earlier rites, which are then interpreted quite speculatively as dramatic portrayals of the initiate's "new birth." The belief that pre-Christian mysteries used *rebirth* as a technical term is unsupported by even one single text.[9]

Thus, when Freke and Gandy suggest that the gods of the mystery cults offered their followers "the chance to be born again through the rites of baptism,"[10] they have committed the composite fallacy of reading such ideas into the mystery religions as a whole. Examination of the thirteen alleged parallels makes one justifiably suspicious that these authors have been a bit too casual in fitting Christian elements into mystery religion data.

The Terminological Fallacy

Freke and Gandy assert: "Each mystery religion taught its own version of the myth of the dying and resurrecting Godman, who was known by different names in different places."[11] Examination of the thirteen-point list of parallels between Jesus Christ and pagan deities shows a conscious pattern around the life of Christ that is stated in explicitly Christian terms. This in itself should raise red caution flags that Christian vocabulary is being manipulated. This improper redefining of terms to prove a point is the *terminological fallacy*.

By way of analogy, suppose you go to a college football game. One team suffers badly in the first two quarters and is down by twenty-one points at halftime. In the third quarter, however, the players make adjustments and come back strong. Finally, late in the fourth quarter, they tie the game. With less than a minute to go, they score a field goal and hold on to win. The next day the local newspaper reports on the game. The writer adds a little flair to his description when he says that the home team was "dying" in the first half but was "resurrected" in the second half. The team went on to "glory," which led to "salvation" for their fans. To think in such specifically Christian terms might never have occurred to you before reading the article. And upon reading it, you might consider the wording of the article a bit cheesy. To use specifically Christian terminology to describe the mystery religions strikes us as the same kind of thing.

Nash makes the insightful observation that "one frequently encounters scholars who first use Christian terminology to describe pagan beliefs and practices and then marvel at the awesome parallels they think they have discovered."[12] Bruce Metzger, the preeminent New Testament scholar and emeritus professor at Princeton Seminary, summarized the parallels as follows: "It goes without saying that alleged parallels which are discovered by pursuing such methodology evaporate when they are confronted with the original texts. In a word, one must beware of what have been called, 'parallels made plausible by selective description.'"[13]

With reference to the use of language, Nash gives the example of the Isis-Osiris myth. His statement is worth quoting in full.

> The basic myth of the Isis cult concerned Osiris, her husband during the earlier Egyptian and nonmystery stage of the religion. According to the most common version of the myth, Osiris was murdered by his brother who then sank the coffin containing Osiris's body into the Nile river. Isis discovered the body and returned it to Egypt. But her brother-in-law once again gained access to the body, this time dismembering it into fourteen pieces which he scattered widely. Following a long search, Isis recovered each part of the body. It is at this point that the language used to describe what followed is crucial. Sometimes those telling the story are satisfied to say that Osiris came back to life, even though such language claims far more than the myth allows. Some writers go even further and refer to the alleged "resurrection" of Osiris. One

liberal scholar illustrates how biased some writers are when they describe the pagan myth in Christian language: "The dead body of Osiris floated in the Nile and he returned to life, this being accomplished by a baptism in the waters of the Nile."

This biased and sloppy use of language suggests three misleading analogies between Osiris and Christ: (1) a savior god dies and (2) then experiences a resurrection accompanied by (3) water baptism. But the alleged similarities, as well as the language used to describe them, turn out to be fabrications of the modern scholar and are not part of the original myth. Comparisons between the resurrection of Jesus and the resuscitation of Osiris are greatly exaggerated. Not every version of the myth has Osiris returning to life; in some he simply becomes king of the underworld. Equally far-fetched are attempts to find an analogue of Christian baptism in the Osiris myth. The fate of Osiris's coffin in the Nile is as relevant to baptism as the sinking of Atlantis.[14]

When it comes to parallels between Jesus Christ and pagan gods, too often the terms used by modern writers come from specifically Christian vocabulary, even though such terms have nothing to do with the pagan religions. Such language reveals the prejudices of the modern writer more than the substance of the ancient parallels.

The Dependency Fallacy

The *dependency fallacy* occurs when interpreters believe that Christianity borrowed not only the form but also the substance of the mystery religions and turned this into a new religion. But how one defines dependency is absolutely crucial. Not only this, but the presence of parallels does not necessarily indicate any kind of borrowing.

As noted above, the history of religions school launched the notion that Christianity borrowed heavily from pagan religions. The core proposition of this school is that Christianity is dependent for its content (stories and important doctrines) on the Hellenistic mystery religions. Yet even when the history of religions movement was most influential, not all liberal scholars embraced this viewpoint. For example, Adolf von Harnack, the premier liberal German historian of early Christianity during the first three decades of the twentieth century, wrote:

> We must reject the comparative mythology which finds a causal connection between everything and everything else.... By such methods one can turn Christ into a sun god in the twinkling of an eye, or one can bring up the legends attending the birth of every conceivable god, or one can catch all sorts of mythological doves to keep company with the baptismal dove ... the wand of "comparative religion" triumphantly eliminate(s) every spontaneous trait in any religion.[15]

The first thing to note is that *dependence* can be used in two ways.[16] Was the origin of Christianity dependent on existing Greek philosophical and religious ideas? That question hinges upon how one is using the word "dependent." Nash argues that dependency can be weak or strong and that the difference is a vital one. A strong dependency would mean that the idea of Jesus as a dying and rising savior-god would never have occurred to early believers if they had not become aware of it first in pagan thought. It would be admitting that Paul and the other new Christians came to believe that Christ was a resurrected God-man who made an atoning sacrifice for the sins of the world *because* such notions were already part of pagan ideas. Proving a strong dependency of Christianity on Greek thought would be very damaging to those who hold to the general historicity of the Gospels.

A weak dependency may mean that the followers of Jesus used common religious terminology to tell their story in a way understandable in the Hebrew and Greek cultures, or they simply may have used language that was coincidentally parallel to other religions, for reasons discussed below. As Nash states, "The mere presence of parallels in thought and language does not prove any dependence in the strong sense."[17] Oxford University historian Robin Lane Fox asserts that nearly all the supposed parallels between pagan practices and Christianity are spurious.[18] Fox challenges the thesis that Christianity was "not so very novel in the pagan world."[19] His research led him to conclude that there is, in Leon McKenzie's words, only "a marginal and weak connection between paganism and Christianity."[20]

Second, those who press for parallels and dependence often ignore the universal similarity of human experiences that underlie specific cultural forms. In his carefully researched article, "Methodology in the Study of the Mystery Religions and Early Christianity," Metzger observed, "The uniformity of human nature sometimes produces strikingly similar results in similar situations where there can be no suspicion of any historical bridge by which the tradition could have been mediated from one culture to the other."[21] For example, "The two facts that all human beings eat and that most of them seek companionship with one another and with their god account for a large percentage of similarities among the examples from around the world."[22] Metzger then quotes S. G. F. Brandon with regard to the parallels between the Egyptian Osiris cult and Jesus Christ: "Any theory of borrowing on the part of Christianity from the older faith is not to be entertained, for not only can it not be substantiated on the extant evidence, but it is also intrinsically most improbable."[23]

We might add that all religions, if they are to gain any converts, must appeal to universal human needs and desires. Should we be surprised, then, to discover parallels between Christianity and any other religion regarding the offer of life after death, identification with the deity, initiation rites, or a code of conduct? No, but in such cases, it can hardly be maintained that parallels indicate dependence. As Walter Künneth argued in *The Theology of the Resurrection*,

> The fact that the theme of the dying and returning deity is a general one in the history of religion, and that a transference

of this theme is possible, must not be made the occasion for speaking at once of dependence, of influence, or indeed of identity of content. Rather, the scientific task is not to overlook the essential differences in form, content and ultimate tendency, and even in cases of apparent formal analogy to work out the decisive difference of content.[24]

Third, one has to take into account the *accommodating language* of the early Christians. This seems to take at least two forms, language articulated by a "missionary motive"[25] and language motivated by a desire to be accepted by the culture at large. The apostle Paul fits the first model; the second-century writer Justin Martyr, the second.

Paul told the Corinthians, "I have become all things to all people, so that by all means I may save some" (1 Cor. 9:22). Paul knew how to speak the language that would best communicate to his particular audience. He did this when he addressed the philosophers in Athens (Acts 17) and the recently converted Christians in Thessalonica.[26] The real question is, "Does the fact that some New Testament writer knew of a pagan belief or term prove that what he knew had a formative or genetic influence on his own essential beliefs?"[27] The language Paul used is meant to be a point of departure—to show that Christianity is not in any of its essentials like the pagan religions.[28]

Justin Martyr (c. 100–165) was motivated by impulses that find their antecedents in Philo of Alexandria (c. 20 B.C.–A.D. 50), the Jewish writer who packaged Judaism in Greek philosophical terms. Does this mean that Judaism was indebted to Greek philosophy? Hardly. But it does show the lengths to which an ancient writer might go to make his religion winsome, understandable, and palatable to outsiders.

Similarly, Justin Martyr came from a pagan home and was weaned on Greek philosophy. "Justin was forced by his conversion to Christianity to seek connection between his pagan, philosophical past and his Christian, theological present. This biographical quest would come to expression as he sought to mediate between the worlds of Greek and Christian thought."[29] For example, Justin defends the Virgin Birth as follows: "And if we even affirm that He was born of a virgin, accept this in common with what you accept of Perseus."[30] Obviously, there is a sense in which Justin wants to find commonality with other religions—in part, to lessen the attacks on Christianity (since it was an illegal religion at this time) and, in part, to present the gospel in a winsome manner, to show that it is not really unreasonable to embrace it.

It is true that Justin claimed that Satan had inspired the pagan religions to imitate some aspects of Christianity, but even this is a far cry from claiming that he saw the essential Christian proclamation duplicated in any other religion. As J. Gresham Machen argued, "We should never forget that the appeal of Justin Martyr and Origen to the pagan stories of divine begetting is an *argumentum ad hominem*. '*You* hold,' Justin and Origen say in effect to their pagan opponents, 'that the virgin birth of Christ is unbelievable; well, is it any more unbelievable than the stories that you yourselves believe?'"[31]

Whether this kind of accommodation was the best approach in spreading the gospel is a matter of debate. Tertullian (c. 160–c. 225), the North African defender of orthodoxy, felt that it was inappropriate. "Justin's view that philosophy is continuous with Christianity was emphatically not shared by" Tertullian, who "regarded philosophy as folly and the source of heresy."[32]

In sampling factors and nuances in regard to the issue of dependency, we noted that the New Testament only borrows concepts and occasionally wording from pagan religions for a variety of reasons. There was not a strong dependency—that is, there is no evidence that the New Testament writers were indebted to mystery religions for their essential message. We also observed that parallels are not the same as dependency and that a variety of reasons could produce similar parallels (not the least of which is the human condition and the fact that all religions address many of the same needs and desires).

We discussed accommodation as a motive to make the gospel palatable and understandable. In the New Testament, the apostle Paul shows that he accommodated his message for Gentile readers. *Never* was the gospel altered by such accommodation, however. And in the second century, Justin Martyr went so far as to concede certain parallels between Christianity and pagan religions—most likely as a way to bridge the gap between his pagan readers and the Christian faith. He did this in part because of his background in Greek philosophy and in part to legitimize Christianity as a religion that was not so different from other religions that it could not be embraced. At the same time, a careful reading of Justin shows that at every turn he sees the gospel as ultimately unique and thus superior to pagan religions. While Justin sought to win converts by accommodation, Tertullian sought to do so by showing the true distinctiveness of the Christian faith. This very issue of assimilation versus distinctiveness is a tension that evangelists and missionaries face even today.

The Chronological Fallacy

What is often overlooked when one considers parallels and dependence is whether Palestinian Jews of the first century A.D. would have borrowed essential beliefs from pagan cults. Remember that the church was at first composed almost entirely of Jews. Two factors need to be considered. First, there is so far no archaeological evidence today of mystery religions in Palestine in the early part of the first century. Norman Anderson asserted, "If borrowing there was by one religion from another, it seems clear which way it went. There is no evidence whatever, that I know of, that the mystery religions had any influence in Palestine in the early decades of the first century."[33] Second, the first-century Jewish mind-set loathed syncretism. Unlike the Gentiles of this era, Jews refused to blend their religion with other religions. Gentile religions were not exclusive; one could be a follower of several different gods at one time. But Judaism was strictly monotheistic, as was Christianity. As the gospel spread beyond the borders of Israel, the apostles not only found themselves introducing people to the strange idea of a man risen from the dead; they also came face-to-face with a polytheistic culture. But they made no accommodation on this front. Instead, John instructed his readers,

"Little children, guard yourselves from idols" (1 John 5:21), and Paul commended the Thessalonian church because they had "turned to God from idols to serve the living and true God" (1 Thess. 1:9). This was the Jewish and Christian mind-set.

The exclusivism extended to Jesus Christ. The apostles boldly proclaimed salvation in Christ alone: "There is salvation in no one else, for there is no other name under heaven given among people by which we must be saved" (Acts 4:12). Even Paul, when addressing Greek philosophers in Athens, did not accommodate his message to polytheism. "His spirit was greatly upset because he saw the city was full of idols" (17:16). In his proclamation, he identified God as the only God, and urged the Greeks to repent of their polytheistic ways (vv. 23–31). Although acknowledging that they were very religious, not once did he accommodate himself to the notion that there were, in reality, many gods. As Nash suggests, "The uncompromising monotheism and the exclusiveness that the early church preached and practiced make the possibility of any pagan inroads . . . unlikely, if not impossible."[34] This is a significant methodological issue that cannot be overlooked: To argue that early Christianity borrowed extensively from pagan religions looks more and more like unsubstantiated wishful thinking.[35]

If there are genuine parallels between Jesus Christ and pagan gods, when and how did they come about? Several contemporary scholars do see evidence of a dependent relationship between the mysteries and Christianity, but it is for the most part a *reversed* dependency.

Essentially, there are three periods of comparison between Christianity and the mystery religions:[36] A.D. 1–200; 201–300; and 301–500.

In the first period, the mystery religions were localized, having little influence on mainstream religions. If there is any influence between Christianity and the mystery religions, it must surely be in one direction: Christianity influenced the cults. This is evident by the fact that Christianity is essentially an *anti*-mystery religion. As such, its message would become known, its documents made public, and its basis in history strongly asserted. Further, since there is no evidence of syncretism in apostolic Christianity, while the mystery religions from their very beginning display syncretistic tendencies, the verdict has to be that Christianity influenced the mystery religions, beginning in the first century, not vice versa. In the second century, after the Christian faith had spread to all regions of the Roman world, the mystery religions became more eclectic, softening harsh elements, and consciously offering an alternative to Christianity. For example, "In competing with Christianity, which promised eternal life to its adherents, the cult of Cybele officially or unofficially raised the efficacy of the blood bath from twenty years to eternity."[37]

The second phase began in the third century. At this time the data come into clearer focus. The mystery cults take on definite forms as they interact and compete with Christianity. But the evidence that these same cults had all these features *prior* to the rise of the Christian faith is nonexistent. Nash observes:

> Far too many writers on this subject use the available sources to form the plausible reconstructions of the third-century mystery experience and then uncritically reason back to what they think must have been the earlier nature of the cults. We have plenty of information about the mystery religions of the third century. But important differences exist between these religions and earlier expressions of the mystery experience (for which adequate information is extremely slim).[38]

The sources skeptics typically cite as evidence that pagan religions influenced early Christian beliefs postdate the writings of the New Testament. But the chronology is all wrong. Attis, Mithras, and the others show evidence of a dependence upon Christianity.[39]

However, beginning in the fourth century, the situation reverses itself: Christianity began to adopt the terminology and modes of the mystery cults. This is important to keep in mind, since the parallels that some skeptics use are from *later forms of Christianity*. Thus, Freke and Gandy speak of December 25 as a date that Christians took over from mystery religions in celebration of the birth of Jesus.

This, of course, is likely,[40] but it is also beside the point. Nowhere in the New Testament do we read that Jesus' birth was on December 25. The use of this date was apparently picked to assimilate the cults into the now-dominant religion of the Roman Empire, Christianity. But that didn't officially occur until the fourth century.[41] Thus, we can readily admit that Christianity borrowed from the mystery religions, but *when* Christianity did this was hundreds of years after it began. Such borrowing has nothing to do with the core of the Christian proclamation.

The third stage of potential intersection between Christianity and the mystery cults was in the fourth and fifth centuries. Although the mysteries were dying out, they were able at this time to influence some of the modes of worship and terminology of the Christian church. Catholics and Protestants disagree over the appropriateness of such syncretism. But "the crucial question is not what possible influence the dying mysteries may have had on Christianity after A.D. 400 but what effect the emerging mystery cults may have had on the New Testament in the first century."[42]

Only after the rise of Christianity did mystery religions begin to look suspiciously like the Christian faith. Once Christianity became known, many of the mystery cults consciously adopted Christian ideas so that their deities would be perceived to be on a par with Jesus. The shape of the mystery religions prior to the rise of Christianity is vague, ambiguous, and localized. Only by a huge stretch of the imagination, and by playing fast and loose with the historical data, can one see them as having genuine conceptual parallels to the Christian faith of the first century.

The Intentional Fallacy

Finally, when one examines the purpose and nature of the mystery religions versus the purpose and nature of Christianity, huge differences surface. We will discuss these issues in some detail when we examine the virgin birth and the death and resurrection of Christ. Suffice it to say here that Christianity has a linear view of history—history is going someplace. But almost all mystery religions have a cyclical view of history linked to the harvest–vegetation cycle. The Christian proclamation offered genuine purpose in life, while the mystery religions looked at life as "a circular movement leading nowhere."[43]

WHAT MYSTERY RELIGIONS HAVE IN COMMON

The religions in the ancient world had strange names. Some folks worshiped a god named Mithra(s), others the deities of Osiris and Isis, and still others worshiped Dionysus. What makes things more interesting is that these religions borrowed heavily from each other. The same deity might end up having multiple names. It is difficult to speak of common features of these diverse religions because there were so many differences. Yet many skeptics of Christianity claim to see common elements between the mysteries *and* Christianity. The clear evidence is that this is not the case. Rather, the mysteries share far greater commonality with each other than they do with Christianity. In the Hellenistic[44] age, the common thread among these religions was that they all had *secret ceremonies*, mysteries to all but the initiated. These mysteries brought "salvation" to the participants. The major mystery religions included the Greek worship of Dionysus and Demeter and the later Eleusinian and Orphic mystery cults. In Phrygia (modern central Turkey) arose the cult of Cybele and Attis. Egypt contributed the cult of Isis and Osiris. From Palestine and Syria came the mystery worship of Adonis and finally Mithraism,[45] whose origin is disputed.[46] Strange names, strange places, and stranger deities. Do they have anything to do with Christianity?

The mysteries (excluding Mithraism)[47] had five characteristics in common:

1. At the core of each mystery was the annual vegetation cycle in which "life is renewed each spring and dies each fall. Followers of the mystery cults found deep symbolic significance in the natural processes of growth, death, decay, and rebirth."[48]

2. Each cult made "important use of secret ceremonies or mysteries, often in connection with an initiation rite ... every mystery religion also 'imparted a "secret," a knowledge of the life of the deity and the means of union with him.'"[49] This "knowledge" was always an esoteric or secret teaching, unattainable by anyone outside the circle of the cult.

3. The focus of the myth of each mystery was on the deity's victory over something. This could be a return to life or conquest over his enemies. "Implicit in the myth was the theme of redemption from everything earthly and temporal. The secret meaning of the cult and its accompanying myth was expressed in a 'Sacramental drama'" that appealed largely to the feelings of the initiates. Most importantly, the vegetation cycle dictated this sense of "rebirth" and new life.[50]

4. Doctrine and correct belief had little importance. Cults were primarily concerned with the emotions.[51] "Processions, fasting, a play, acts of purification, blazing lights, and esoteric liturgies" stirred emotional frenzy that brought one into union with the god.[52]

5. "The immediate goal of the initiates was a mystical experience that led them to feel they had achieved union with their god. ... Beyond this quest for mystical union were two more ultimate goals: some kind of redemption or salvation, and immortality."[53]

There are similarities to Christianity in these elements, but the differences are greater. Both recognized the triumph of their deity as an important aspect of the religion, and both placed an emphasis on salvation. Such features are common to most religions. But what set Christianity apart was (1) its insistence on historical credibility, which the mysteries didn't even pretend to have, versus the "going nowhere" view of the vegetation cycle; (2) Christian proclamation of the gospel as accessible to all people; (3) its insistence on right belief instead of emotional frenzy; and (4) the centrality of the death and resurrection of Jesus Christ and the coming resurrection of believers. As Robin Lane Fox has noted, while the mysteries "offered a myth of their god, Jews and Christians offered history; the pagan mysteries conveyed a secret experience, whereas Jews and Christians offered a 'revelation' based on texts."[54] Other differences could be mentioned, such as the Christian faith's exclusiveness. Christians proclaimed that there is only one legitimate path to God and salvation, Jesus Christ. The mysteries were inclusive. Nothing prevented a believer in one cult from following other mysteries as well.

The mystery religions had far more in common with each other than any of them had with Christianity. Yet, the mystery cults took note of the Christian movement and started to emulate it. Only after A.D. 100 did the mysteries begin to look very much like Christianity, precisely because their existence was threatened by this new religion. They had to compete to survive.

CONCLUSION: CHRISTIANITY THE ANTIMYSTERY

The alleged parallels between pagan gods and Jesus Christ do not argue that the Christian proclamation was based on fiction. That some modern authors continue to suggest that the gospel is based on myth is irresponsible at best and intentionally deceptive at worst. When Nash wrote his book, *The Gospel and the Greeks* (first published in 1992; second edition, 2003), he had to justify flogging a horse that was already mortally wounded. He gave the reason that, "even though specialists in biblical and classical studies know how weak the old case for Christian dependence was, these old arguments continue to circulate in the publications of scholars in such other fields as history and philosophy."[55] Remarkably, the ancient statements about the mystery religions were systematically examined by Christian August Lobeck in 1829. Bruce Metzger does not mince words in assessing Lobeck's accomplishment of revealing the real nature of the mystery religions: "A great deal of rubbish and pseudo-learning was swept aside, and it became possible to discuss intelligently the rites and teachings of the Mysteries."[56] Perhaps it is time to get out the broom again.

Chapter 17

THE VIRGIN BIRTH
OF ALEXANDER THE GREAT?

The notion that Jesus had no human father because he was the son of God . . . was originally a pagan notion.

—ROBERT J. MILLER,
Born Divine, 246

Is the Virgin Birth unique to Christianity? Or were there other virgin births in pagan literature, in Greek mythology, or in legendary accounts of great leaders? The charge that Christianity borrowed the concept of a virgin birth dates back to the second century. Justin Martyr, the first great apologist for Christianity, answered a similar charge in his *Dialogue with Trypho, a Jew*:

> And Trypho answered, "The Scripture has not, 'Behold, the virgin shall conceive, and bear a son,' but, 'Behold, the young woman shall conceive, and bear a son,' and so on, as you quoted. But the whole prophecy refers to Hezekiah, and it is proved that it was fulfilled in him, according to the terms of this prophecy. Moreover, in the fables of those who are called Greeks, it is written that Perseus was begotten of Danae, who

was a virgin; he who was called among them Zeus having descended on her in the form of a golden shower. And you ought to feel ashamed when you make assertions similar to theirs, and rather [should] say that this Jesus was born man of men. And if you prove from the Scriptures that He is the Christ, and that on account of having led a life conformed to the law, and perfect, He deserved the honour of being elected to be Christ, [it is well]; but do not venture to tell monstrous phenomena, lest you be convicted of talking foolishly like the Greeks."[1]

In this chapter we look at representative birth accounts that are compared with the biblical accounts of Matthew and Luke. The standard defense of the historicity of the Virgin Birth was written over sixty-five years ago by J. Gresham Machen. It was scholarly, interacted with all the relevant material, and was insightful. This powerful, sustained argument—a tome of over four hundred dense pages—has never been adequately answered. We will summarize some of the main points in Machen's *The Virgin Birth of Christ*.

THE VIRGIN BIRTHS OF PAGAN GODS

Besides birth accounts of pagan deities, skeptics also point to the stories of miraculous births of Greco-Roman heroes like Perseus, Heracles, and Romulus, or of deified kings Alexander the Great and the pharaohs, as further evidence that pagan parallels are the source of the belief in the virgin birth of Christ.

Perseus

In the Greek myth of Perseus, King Acrisius locked his daughter, Danae, in an inaccessible tower in order to thwart the prophecy that her son would kill his grandfather Acrisius. Although she was separated from any potential suitor, Zeus, chief god of the Greek pantheon, was taken with the beauty of this mortal woman and one night came to her as a shower of gold and impregnated her. Her child was the Greek hero Perseus, the son of a divine father and a (formerly) virgin human mother.[2]

Heracles

Heracles also was the product of a divine-human coupling. His mother, Alcmene, was the daughter of the king of Tiryns. While she was betrothed to Amphitryon, her brothers were killed in battle. She refused to consummate the marriage until her brothers' deaths were avenged. Zeus took advantage of her husband's absence and came to her *in her husband's likeness*. As a result she conceived. When her husband returned, she became pregnant by him as well. She bore twins—Heracles, the son of Zeus, and Iphicles, the son of Amphitryon.[3]

Romulus

According to the Roman historian Livy, Rome's legendary founder Romulus and his brother Remus were reputed to be sons of the god Mars.

> But the Fates were resolved, as I suppose, upon the founding of this great city, and the beginning of the mightiest of empires, next after that of Heaven. *The Vestal was ravished*, and having given birth to twin sons, named Mars as the father of her doubtful offspring, whether actually so believing, or because it seemed less wrong if a god were the author of her fault. But neither gods nor men protected the mother herself or her babes from the king's cruelty; the priestess he ordered to be manacled and cast into prison, the children to be committed to the river. It happened by singular good fortune that the Tiber having spread beyond its banks into stagnant pools afforded nowhere any access to the regular channel of the river, and the men who brought the twins were led to

hope that being infants they might be drowned, no matter how sluggish the stream. So they made swift to discharge the king's command, by exposing the babes at the nearest point of the overflow.[4]

From this desperate position, the twins were rescued by a she-wolf who nursed them; a woodpecker watched over and fed them as well. The wolf and the woodpecker are sacred to Mars, the twins' reputed father.

Alexander the Great

When we look at Alexander the Great, we have passed from legend to a historical figure. Yet according to legend, Olympias, the mother of Alexander the Great, conceived her son when Zeus, in the form of a thunderbolt from the sky, struck and impregnated her just before she was married to Philip of Macedon.[5]

The same thread connects all of these stories, yet the alleged parallels are completely at odds with the biblical accounts of the virgin birth of Christ.

The love of the gods for mortal women is the very point of the pagan stories—the thing without which they could not possibly exist. To mention any such thing in connection with the narratives in Matthew and Luke is to do violence to the whole spirit of those narratives. The truth is that when we read these narratives we are in a totally different world from that which produced the pagan stories of the loves and hates of the gods.[6]

Dionysus

The virgin birth of the pagan god Dionysus is attested only in post-Christian sources. It is significant that it is indeed Christians who speak of his virgin birth, but only several centuries after Christ.

We noted earlier that Justin Martyr, the second-century Christian apologist, referred to Perseus as virgin born. Not all Christian writers were so casual in their language or in their accommodation to pagan thought. Machen makes some astute observations in this regard:

> We have already seen that the application of the term "virgin" to pagan mothers by Christian writers is in general to be viewed with suspicion, since there was a tendency on the part of these writers to seek parallels for Christian beliefs in pagan religion. . . .
>
> The use of the term "virgin" by Christian writers, and particularly by Christian writers of such a late date, still remains open to the gravest suspicion; it is all too likely to be due simply to the well-established desire of such writers to find perverse imitations of Christian beliefs in pagan religion. We really have no valid evidence whatever to show that the term was actually used in the pagan worship of Dusares [Dionysus] three centuries before the time when Epiphanius lived. Furthermore, even if the term was used in the pre-Christian worship of Dusares, that would not show at all that it was used in the sense in which we use it and in which it was used by Matthew and Luke. . . . In other words, the term "virgin," if it really was applied in pre-Christian times to the mother of Dusares, meant, no doubt, almost the exact opposite of what that term means in the New Testament account of the birth of our Lord.[7]

THE BIBLICAL ACCOUNTS

The doctrine of the Virgin Birth was regarded as one of the fundamentals of the faith during the Fundamentalist-Modernist controversy, a divisive era in the North American church that began in the late nineteenth century but generated its greatest explosions after World War I. This doctrine is in fact explicitly mentioned only twice in the New Testament, in Matthew and in Luke:

Now the birth of Jesus Christ happened this way. While his mother Mary was engaged to Joseph, but before they came together, she was found to be pregnant through the Holy Spirit. Because Joseph, her husband to be, was a righteous man, and because he did not want to disgrace her, he intended to divorce her privately. When he had contemplated this, an angel of the Lord appeared to him in a dream and said, "Joseph, son of David, do not be afraid to take Mary as your wife, because the child conceived in her is from the Holy Spirit." (Matt. 1:18–20)

* * *

In the sixth month of Elizabeth's pregnancy, the angel Gabriel was sent by God to a town of Galilee called Nazareth, to a virgin engaged to a man whose name was Joseph, a descendant of David, and the virgin's name was Mary. The angel came to her and said, "Greetings, favored one, the Lord is with you!" But she was greatly troubled by his words and began to wonder about the meaning of this greeting. So the angel said to her, "Do not be afraid, Mary, for you have found favor with God! Listen: You will become pregnant and give birth to a son, and you will name him Jesus. . . ." Mary said to the angel, "How will this be, since I have not had sexual relations with a man?" The angel replied, "The Holy Spirit will come upon you, and the power of the Most High will overshadow you. Therefore the child to be born will be holy; he will be called the Son of God." (Luke 1:26–31, 34–35)

Comparing the biblical accounts with those of the surrounding pagan religions, we find both points of contact and sharp contrasts. This is in fact what we would expect to find. Throughout Scripture God accommodated himself to human understanding, employing as points of contact familiar concepts and then developing these points by pouring new meaning into them. Throughout the ancient world, greatness was often associated with physical generation by a god. Likewise the Old Testament, especially the Greek translation known as the Septuagint (LXX), hinted at the possibility of the Virgin Birth.[8] What is significant here is that Isaiah 7:14 is quoted by Matthew in the sense that Mary *was still a virgin when she conceived.* The LXX, which was produced before the birth of Jesus,[9] clearly spoke of the *virgin.* The idea of a virgin birth did not in any way have to derive from pagan religions. New Testament writers already saw it in the Old Testament. And as we noted earlier, the Judaism of Palestine in the first century A.D. was virtually untouched by pagan influences. Thus there is absolutely no reason to suspect that Matthew got this idea from pagan sources.

Some have argued that the Virgin Birth is a later mythical addition since it is mentioned only in two Gospels and is not spoken of by any other New Testament authors. Over a century ago one biblical scholar answered this objection with a very practical observation: If the Virgin Birth was common knowledge among the apostolic community, the New Testament authors "would have abstained from mentioning it for prudential reasons, lest they should expose the mother of our Lord to scandal during her lifetime—such scandals did in fact arise as soon as the virgin birth was declared."[10] Hence the apostles may have kept silent concerning the doctrine until after the death of Mary.[11]

The question of the Virgin Birth in Matthew becomes even more acute when we remember that first-century Judaism was radically monotheistic and abhorred anything that smacked of paganism. It is inconceivable that a Jew would incorporate any pagan mythological concept into his account, especially a concept that would compromise YHWH's utter transcendence and holiness.

It is generally agreed by conservative and most liberal biblical scholars that the Gospels are mid- to late-first-century compositions and that they rest upon earlier sources.

> The early provenance of the account and its features made it impossible to regard it as a mere legend. It was simply not

possible for a legend of this type to arise and gain adherence when Jesus' family was still alive to squelch it if it were false. [Briggs] concluded that the ultimate source of the account had to be Mary herself. At this point her testimony had to be accepted or rejected. Since her character as presented in the gospels was above reproach, her testimony had to be taken at face value.[12]

In *The Virgin Birth of Christ*, Machen concurs with this assessment: "The tradition of the virgin birth can easily be shown to have been in existence only a few decades from the time when Jesus lived upon earth. In the case of Jesus, therefore, we find a story of supernatural birth appearing at a time when information concerning Jesus' life may be supposed still to have been abundant."[13]

CONCLUSION

The pagan mythology of virgin births, which we have surveyed very briefly, reveals sharp contrasts with the biblical accounts. Mythology offers accounts of male deities taking physical form (sometimes human) and impregnating a woman through physical contact. In these stories, the women involved have some sort of sexual relations, so they are not virgins in the strict meaning of the term. By contrast, Gospel accounts of the Virgin Birth are decidedly non-sexual. Jesus is conceived by the creative power of the Holy Spirit in Mary's womb. He is born of a woman without the seed of man—or god.

One of the premier New Testament scholars of the twentieth century, Raymond Brown, observed:

Non-Jewish parallels have been found in the figures of world religions (the births of the Buddha, Krishna, and the son of Zoroaster), in Greco-Roman mythology, in the births of the pharaohs (with the god Amun-Ra acting through the father) and in the marvelous births of emperors and philosophers

(Augustus, Plato, etc.). But these "parallels" consistently involve a type of *hieros gamos* where a divine male, in human or other form, impregnates a woman, either through normal sexual intercourse or through some substitute form of penetration. They are not really similar to the non-sexual virginal conception that is at the core of the infancy narratives, a conception where there is no male deity or element to impregnate Mary.[14]

Brown's assessment is that "no search for parallels has given us a truly satisfactory explanation of how early Christians happened upon the idea of a virginal conception unless, of course, that is what really took place."[15]

Chapter 18

OSIRIS, FRANKENSTEIN, AND JESUS CHRIST

Jesus is the Pagan dying and resurrecting Godman under a new name.

—TIMOTHY FREKE AND PETER GANDY,
The Laughing Jesus, 57

The apostle Paul reminded the Corinthians that the foundation of their faith was the death and resurrection of Jesus Christ (1 Cor. 15:3–8):

> Christ died for our sins according to the scriptures, and . . . he was buried, and . . . he was raised on the third day according to the scriptures, and . . . he appeared to Cephas, then to the twelve. Then he appeared to more than five hundred of the brothers and sisters at one time, most of whom are still alive, though some have fallen asleep. Then he appeared to James, then to all the apostles. Last of all, as though to one born at the wrong time, he appeared to me also.

Paul insists that this is no myth. Not only does he relate the death and resurrection of Christ to the Old Testament prophecies (twice Paul says "according to the Scriptures"), but he also grounds his belief in history. He lists the apostles, five hundred other believers, James (the brother of the Lord), and himself as witnesses of the resurrected Christ. And he mentions that "most of [them] are still alive." The resurrection of Christ was *verifiable by eyewitnesses.* Paul reminds his readers of the fundamental importance of belief in the reality of the Resurrection: "If Christ has not been raised, then our preaching is futile and your faith is empty" (1 Cor. 15:14).

PAGAN "DYING-RISING" GOD MOTIF

Did Paul and the other apostles weave the tale of a dying and rising God-man on the loom of mystery religions? Some have said so. The idea of the dying-rising god as a parallel to the Christian concept of the death and resurrection of Christ was popularized by James Frazer in *The Golden Bough,* first published in 1906. Edwin Yamauchi, a scholar known for his extreme care and sober judgments with historical texts, has observed that, although Frazer marshaled many parallels, the foundation was very fragile and has been discredited by a host of scholars since his ideas were at the height of their popularity in the 1960s.[1] We need to examine the data to see whether the claims of Frazer—and others—have any substance.

We will briefly survey the three most influential myths of the mysteries—Isis and Osiris, Cybele and Attis, and Tammuz (Adonis)—to see what they say about a dying and rising god-man.

Isis and Osiris

Osiris was an ancient Egyptian god whose early mythology and worship were not associated with the mysteries. The Hellenistic form of Osiris worship developed into a mystery religion through innovations introduced by Ptolemy I (c. 300 B.C.). These changes involved a synthesis of the older Egyptian religion with Greek thought.[2] By the late first century, Plutarch identifies Osiris as the Egyptian manifestation of the god the Greeks identified as Dionysus.

Gary Habermas and Michael Licona summarize the Osiris myth thus:

> Osiris was killed by his brother, chopped up into fourteen pieces and scattered throughout Egypt. The goddess Isis collected and reassembled his parts and brought him back to life. Unfortunately she was only able to find thirteen pieces. Moreover, it is questionable whether Osiris was brought back to life on earth or seen by others as Jesus was. He was given status as god of the gloomy under world. So the picture we get of Osiris is that of a guy who does not have all his parts and who maintains a shadowy existence as god of the mummies. . . . Osiris's return to life was not a resurrection, but a zombification.[3]

One of the fundamental differences between YHWH, the God of the Jews, and the Egyptian gods is that YHWH was *transcendent* over nature, rather than identified with it, while the Egyptian gods were identified with the natural processes:

> The Egyptian gods seem captive within their own manifestations. They personify power but remain incomplete as personages. And yet these vague and grandiose gods were not distant and intangible; the Egyptians lived forever within the sphere of their activities. . . . [T]he Egyptians explained the daily appearance of the sun as its birth; the moon waned because it was the ailing eye of Horus. When barley was made into beer and bread, it was Osiris—manifest in the grain—who died. We shall meet such images at every turn, and we must not interpret them as allegories for we cannot abstract a meaning from them without falsifying the beliefs which they express.[4]

Henri Frankfort (see note 4) confirmed the identification of the gods with nature and its manifestations, as set out by Plutarch, the late-first-century biographer.[5] Plutarch warned his readers concerning the fables of the gods, "Whenever you hear the traditional tales which the Egyptians tell about the gods, their wanderings, dismemberments, and many experiences of this sort, . . . you must not think that any of these tales actually happened in the manner in which they are related."[6]

Regarding the Osiris myth, Metzger notes, "Whether this can rightly be called a resurrection is questionable, especially since, according to Plutarch, it was the pious desire of devotees to be buried in the same ground where, according to local tradition, the body of Osiris was still lying."[7] Yamauchi agrees:

> It is a cardinal misconception to equate the Egyptian view of the afterlife with the "resurrection" of Hebrew-Christian traditions. In order to achieve immortality the Egyptian had to fulfill three conditions: (1) His body had to be preserved, hence mummification. (2) Nourishment had to be provided either by the actual offering of daily bread and beer, or by the magical depiction of food on the walls of the tomb. (3) Magical spells had to be interred with the dead—Pyramid Texts in the Old Kingdom, Coffin Texts in the Middle Kingdom, and the Book of the Dead in the New Kingdom. Moreover, the Egyptian did not rise from the dead; separate entities of his personality such as his Ba and his Ka continued to hover about his body.[8]

Thus, to speak of Osiris as rising from the dead is a gross exaggeration. The Osiris myth has more to do with Frankenstein and *The Night of the Living Dead* than with Jesus.[9]

Cybele and Attis

While the Cybele and Attis myth exists in several forms, the core of each is the same. The mother goddess Cybele loved Attis, a handsome shepherd of Asia Minor. But Attis was unfaithful to his goddess lover, and in a jealous rage she made him insane. In that insanity Attis castrated himself and fled into the forest, where he bled to death. Cybele's overwhelming grief brought death to the world, but she then returned Attis to life, which in turn brought life back to the earth. Claims of "resurrection" in this myth are vastly overstated.[10] As J. Gresham Machen explains, "The myth contains no account of a resurrection; all that Cybele is able to obtain is that the body of Attis should be preserved, that his hair should continue to grow, and that his little finger should move."[11]

In the mystery cult of Attis, the notion of Attis's "resurrection" is not emphasized; rather his suffering and death are the focus. Evgueni Tortchinov notes,

> But the rite greatly stresses nothing else but suffering, death and the rising of the god; here lies the central point of the rite. This point lies in the very foundation of the cult of Attis itself and this point is the main cause of its popularity. So here it is correct to agree with Frazer's pointing out that myths have a secondary nature in comparison with the rites: the myths were invented to explain the rites and habits of the believers (Frazer, 1984, p. 327) . . . but it seems to me better to add to this opinion that the value of the rite itself was determined by its psychopractical aspect or intention, the purpose of which was the cathartic feeling realized through experience of death-rebirth. The psychopractical effect of the mystery rite was the magic power which changed the lovely boy-shepherd, the lover of two sacred female persons, into the Omnipotent Lord, Shepherd of Stars and the King of the Space beyond the world.[12]

Early worshipers of Cybele acted out the Attis myth to guarantee a good crop. It is only in the later Roman celebration, long after the establishment and spread of Christianity, that the idea of resurrection even *possibly* appears.[13] At the earliest, Attis appears as a "resurrected" god after the mid-second century A.D.[14] The dependence of the Attis cult on Christianity is thus a strong possibility.

Tammuz (Adonis)

Yamauchi notes that the evidence for two other major "dying-rising gods" put forward by Frazer has been discredited. The resurrection interpretation for the Mesopotamian Tammuz (Sumerian Dumuzi), who was supposedly raised by the goddess Inanna-Ishtar, had been read into the text in much the same way as the assertion that Jesus kissed Mary Magdalene on the mouth has been read into the Gospel of Philip. The end of the myth, both in the Sumerian and Akkadian texts of "The Descent of Inanna (Ishtar)," was lost. In 1960, ancient Mesopotamian religions expert Samuel Noah Kramer published a newly translated poem, "The Death of Dumuzi," which revealed that Inanna-Ishtar did not rescue Dumuzi from the underworld.[15]

Later in the story's development, Tammuz was syncretistically identified with the Phoenician Adonis, the handsome youth beloved by Aphrodite. Jerome tells us that the second-century emperor Hadrian consecrated a shrine of Tammuz-Adonis in the Bethlehem cave thought to be the birthplace of Jesus. While the Adonis cult spread from its birthplace in Byblos[16] to the Greco-Roman world, the cult never attained influence and was restricted to women. As with the texts of the other mysteries, there is no hint of the resurrection in the early texts or images of Adonis. The four surviving texts that do mention his resurrection are to be dated from the second to fourth centuries.[17]

The tale of a dying and rising god-man in the mystery religions prior to Christianity is itself a myth. According to Oxford historian Robin Lane Fox, "Thinking pagans had worried more about the beginning of the world than about its possible end. There was no question of a body being 'resurrected': the facts were obvious to anyone who opened a grave and saw bare bones."[18] Nash sums up the evidence about all these gods of the mystery religions and their alleged resurrections:

> Which mystery gods actually experienced a resurrection from the dead? Certainly no early texts refer to any resurrection of Attis. Attempts to link the worship of Adonis to a resurrection are equally weak. Nor is the case for a resurrection of Osiris any stronger. After Isis gathered together the pieces of Osiris's dismembered body, he became "Lord of the Underworld." As Metzger comments, "Whether this can be rightly called a resurrection is questionable, especially since according to Plutarch, it was the pious desire of devotees to be buried in the same ground where, according to local tradition, the body of Osiris was still lying." One can speak, then, of a "resurrection" in the stories of Osiris, Attis, and Adonis only in the most extended of senses. And of course no claim can be made that Mithras was a dying and rising god. French scholar André Boulanger concludes: "The conception that the god dies and is resurrected in order to lead his faithful to eternal life is represented in no Hellenistic mystery religion."[19]

CHRIST'S RESURRECTION

The idea of resurrection was a hard sell in a Jewish culture, and an even harder sell to the first-century Greco-Roman pagan culture. Although the idea of physical, bodily resurrection was deeply rooted in Jewish thought, the concept was tied inexorably to the final judgment at the end of time (cf. Dan. 12:1–2). The idea of a bodily resurrection *within time* would have been unthinkable to the Jew because it would not be associated in his mind with the end-times event. Likewise, the pagan world did not expect a resurrection. The Greco-Roman hope was escape from the body into the spiritual world, immortality of the soul rather than bodily resurrection. The theories that the resurrection was an idea incorporated into Christianity from pagan sources simply have no factual substance.

The New Testament in at least two places suggests that paganism had no concept of a resurrection. In Acts 17 Paul comes to Athens, the intellectual center of Greek philosophy and religion. There, he preached to philosophers at the Areopagus, men who were well informed on new philosophies and religions and were ready to hear the latest juicy tidbit (v. 21). Paul proclaimed the resurrection of Christ. But the philosophers scoffed (v. 32), presumably because such an idea was unheard of.

> It is of course quite possible that, when people in the wider world heard what the early Christians were saying, they attempted to fit the strange message into the worldview of cults they already knew. But the evidence suggests that they were more likely to be puzzled, or to mock. When Paul preached in Athens, nobody said, "Ah, yes, a new version of Osiris and such like." The Homeric assumption remained in force. Whatever the gods—or the crops might do, humans did not rise again from the dead.[20]

In the fourth chapter of 1 Thessalonians, Paul answers questions about the resurrection of the Christian dead. But he begins with a mild rebuke: he reminds them not to "grieve like the rest who have no hope" (v. 13). Paul had preached the resurrection of the dead when he was in Thessalonica (see 1 Thess. 1:10), but the Thessalonian believers now were acting like they didn't fully believe it. "The rest who have no hope" were their pagan neighbors. But the believers once had been idol-worshipers themselves (1 Thess. 1:9). They *knew* the pagan religions offered no real promise. These religions could give no hope because they did not teach a resurrection from the dead. Immortality of the soul was one thing, but resurrection of the body was a concept foreign to paganism.

As N. T. Wright put it, "Nobody actually expected the mummies to get up, walk about and resume normal living; nobody in that world would have wanted such a thing, either. That which Homer and others meant by resurrection was not affirmed by the devotees of Osiris or their cousins elsewhere."[21] Part of the uniqueness of Christianity is its insistence on the bodily resurrection of Jesus Christ and on the future bodily resurrection of believers in Christ. The reuniting of the soul with the body—a new, permanent body—is unheard of in the ancient mystery religions.

Ronald Nash's study on the mystery religions shows the contrast between them and Christianity. He notes six points of contrast between the death and resurrection of the savior-gods of the mysteries and the death and resurrection of Christ.

1. "None of the so-called savior-gods died for someone else. The notion of the Son of God dying in place of His creatures is unique to Christianity."[22]

2. "Only Jesus died for sin. . . . As Wagner observes, to none of the pagan gods 'has the intention of helping men been attributed. The sort of death that they died is quite different (hunting accident, self-emasculation, etc.).'"[23]

3. "Jesus died once and for all (Heb. 7:27; 9:25–28; 10:10–14). In contrast, the mystery gods were vegetation deities whose repeated death and resuscitation depict the annual cycle of nature."[24]

4. "Jesus' death was an actual event in history. The death of the god described in the pagan cults is a mythical drama with no historical ties; its continued rehearsal celebrates the recurring death and rebirth of nature. The incontestable fact that the early church believed that its proclamation of Jesus' death and resurrection was grounded upon what actually happened in history makes absurd any attempt to derive this belief from the mythical, nonhistorical stories of the pagan cults."[25]

5. "Unlike the mystery gods, Jesus died voluntarily. Nothing like the voluntary death of Jesus can be found in the mystery cults."[26]

6. "And finally, Jesus' death was not a defeat but a triumph. Christianity stands entirely apart from the pagan mysteries in that its report of Jesus' death is a message of triumph. Even

as Jesus was experiencing the pain and humiliation of the cross, He was the victor. The New Testament's mood of exultation contrasts sharply with that of the mystery religions, whose followers wept and mourned for the terrible fate that overtook their gods."[27]

Walter Künneth offers a fitting summary: "It is superficial and unfounded to say that the study of the history of religion has shown the dependence of the resurrection of Jesus on mythology. On the contrary, it is precisely the comparison with the history of religion that gives rise to the strongest objections to any kind of mythifying of the resurrection of Jesus."[28]

THE REAL JESUS

In the 1970s, the Ford Motor Company grabbed the attention of commercial viewers with the catchphrase, "The closer you look, the better we look." We can't comment on the veracity of such a statement about automobiles, but we have been driving toward a similar sentiment in this book: The closer you look, the better *Jesus* looks.

As we have taken a closer look at the historical person of Jesus, we've seen that:

- The Gospels are historically credible witnesses to the person, words, and deeds of Jesus Christ. What the evangelists wrote was based on a strong oral tradition that had continuity with the earliest eyewitness testimony. In essence, the gospel did not change from its first oral proclamation to its last written production.
- The original documents of the New Testament have been lost, but their contents have been faithfully preserved in thousands of copies. Today we are certain of about 99 percent of the original wording. In no place is the deity of Christ or his bodily resurrection called into question by textual variants. Although much of the wording of the text has undergone change over the centuries, the core truth-claims of Christianity have remained intact.

- The ancient church exercised careful scrutiny and sober judgment in determining which books belonged in the New Testament. They showed deep concern for authenticity—authentic authorship, history, and theology. And although the church wrestled with some of the books for centuries, a substantial core of books was accepted in the beginning. There is no evidence that the early church had to sort through various gospels to find the ones that agreed with the Christian community at large. Rather, the earliest Gospels prevailed precisely because they were written early, they were written by reliable eyewitnesses and/or historians, and they were not given to flights of fancy.
- The view that the divinity of Christ was invented in the fourth century is historically naïve. From the time that the New Testament was penned through the centuries that followed, the evidence is overwhelming that Jesus was consistently viewed as more than a man by his followers. Even the enemies of Christianity recognized that the early Christians worshiped Jesus Christ as deity.
- The Christian message did not plagiarize the writings of pagan religions. There is no substantiated connection between belief in the virgin birth and resurrection of Christ with the cults of Osiris, Dionysus, or Mithra. Alleged parallels between earlier religions and Christianity are not sustainable when the evidence is fairly examined.

In short, all of the evidence points to the biblical Jesus as the *real* Jesus.

At the same time, none of this suggests that we have *proved* the historical veracity of the Christian faith. After all, the events of history cannot be tested repeatedly in a controlled environment with consistently identical results. But when evidence that is strong and pervasive can be adduced, past events can be reasonably deemed *probable*. An ounce of evidence is worth a pound of presumption. But in this case, we have much more than an ounce of evidence! Indeed, probability is very much on the side of the Christian message.

We avoid two dangerous extremes when we ground our understanding of Jesus in probability. On the one hand, we avoid the unrealistic demand for historical certainty. If the evidence for the historicity of Christianity could be interpreted with 100 percent certainty, there would be no need for faith. And make no mistake: belief in the biblical Christ requires a *step* of faith. But a step is nowhere near a *leap*.

On the other hand, we avoid the foolish notion that all interpretations of Jesus are created equal. We would do well to remember that virtually every wrongheaded view of Jesus is based on a *possible* understanding of the ancient data. But such views have never been shown to be *probable*. Although speculation based on thin air and charges of conspiracy make for a good suspense novel, it has nothing to do with real history. Responsible historians and fiction writers may breathe the same air, but they do not share the same respect for historical evidence.

In the twenty-first-century world, many postmodernists claim to be evenhanded and open-minded. They loathe dogmatic convictions. But the irony is that they often become arrogant about their skepticism, about seeing all possibilities as equal. *Postmodern skepticism is the new dogma,* and it is not one that has much regard for historical probabilities.

So why all the present fuss about the historical Jesus? More specifically, why are so many people infatuated with reinterpretations of his life? Little attention is given to the scriptural portrait of Christ. However, when a new perspective on him—one that is decidedly out of sync with the Bible—is unveiled, it draws a crowd.

But why isn't society interested in reinventions of other major religious figures? Why not Muhammed, Buddha, Moses, or Confucius? Why Jesus? In a word, *accountability.* People in the civilized, Western world usually know something about Jesus and the gospel message, and their interest in him rises whenever a new theory comes along that can ease their consciences. People gravitate toward a tame Jesus—a Jesus who can be controlled, a Jesus who is nonthreatening, a Jesus who values what they value and does not demand anything of them at all. In other words, a Jesus who is not Lord and Savior. Frankly, it's hard to escape the feeling that our culture has taken Jesus' question "Who do you say that I am?" and changed it to "Who do you want me to be?" But the real Jesus doesn't ask that question; the real Jesus is not so tame.

In C. S. Lewis's *The Chronicles of Narnia*, the main character through the seven volumes is one named Aslan—a lion. He appropriately symbolizes Jesus Christ. Human children from another world in another dimension somehow come into the land of Narnia and learn about Aslan from some talking animals. Their introduction to Aslan sums up the power and majesty of Jesus Christ. One of the children, upon learning that Aslan is a lion, wants to know more:

> "Is he—quite safe? I shall feel rather nervous about meeting a lion."
>
> "That you will, dearie, and no mistake," said Mrs. Beaver, "if there's anyone who can appear before Aslan without their knees knocking they're either braver than most or else just silly."
>
> "Then he isn't safe?" said Lucy.
>
> "Safe?" said Mr. Beaver. "Don't you hear what Mrs. Beaver tells you? Who said anything about safe? 'Course he isn't safe. But he's good."[1]

The real Jesus is far from safe. We seem to know that instinctively. It's why we keep our distance. But something strange happens when we approach him fearfully and humbly in the words of Scripture. We hear the ring of authenticity in his voice. We witness the genuine authority in his actions. So we take a closer look.[2] And we see that he is good.

We want to hear from you. Please send your comments about this book to us in care of ReinventingJesus@kregel.com. Thank you.

ENDNOTES

INTRODUCTION: REINVENTING JESUS?

1. A quick survey of life-of-Jesus studies over the past two centuries appears in N. T. Wright, *Who Was Jesus?* (Grand Rapids: Eerdmans, 1993), 1–18.

2. Luke Timothy Johnson, quoted in David van Biema, "The Gospel Truth," *Time*, April 8, 1996: 57.

3. A few related topics do not fit the narrow purpose of this volume and so have not received much attention. Topics that have been treated on an easily understood level include (1) historical evidence for the Resurrection, Gary R. Habermas and Michael R. Licona, *The Case for the Resurrection of Jesus* (Grand Rapids: Kregel, 2004); (2) the relationship of Mary Magdalene to Jesus, Darrell L. Bock, *Breaking the Da Vinci Code: Answers to the Questions Everyone's Asking,* rev. ed. (Nashville: Nelson, 2006); and Ben Witherington III, *The Gospel Code: Novel Claims About Jesus, Mary Magdalene, and Da Vinci* (Downers Grove, IL: InterVarsity Press, 2004); and (3) the so-called "missing" gospels, Darrell L. Bock, *The Missing Gospels: Unearthing the Truth About Alternative Christianities* (Nashville: Nelson, 2006). We commend these works to you.

CHAPTER 1: THE GOSPEL BEHIND THE GOSPELS

1. The complete bibliography for this answer is too large to include in
a single endnote. The following is a select list of works undermining
radical skepticism in historical Jesus studies: (1) exposés of faddish
quests for the historical Jesus: Philip Jenkins, *Hidden Gospels: How
the Search for Jesus Lost Its Way* (Oxford: Oxford University Press,
2001); Luke Timothy Johnson, *The Real Jesus: The Misguided Quest
for the Historical Jesus and the Truth of the Traditional Gospels* (San
Francisco: HarperSanFrancisco, 1996); (2) methods for studying the
historical Jesus: Darrell L. Bock, *Studying the Historical Jesus: A Guide
to Sources and Methods* (Grand Rapids: Baker, 2002); (3) general
works related to the historical Jesus: Paul Barnett, *Jesus and the
Logic of History*, New Studies in Biblical Theology, ed. D. A. Carson
(Grand Rapids: Eerdmans; Cambridge, Leicester: Apollos, 1997);
Gregory A. Boyd, *Cynic Sage or Son of God? Recovering the Real Jesus
in an Age of Revisionist Replies* (Wheaton: Victor, 1995); C. Stephen
Evans, *The Historical Christ and the Jesus of Faith: The Incarnational
Narrative as History* (Oxford: Clarendon, 1996); Gary R. Habermas,
The Historical Jesus: Ancient Evidence for the Life of Christ (Joplin,
MO: College, 1996); Michael J. Wilkins and J. P. Moreland, eds., *Jesus
Under Fire: Modern Scholarship Reinvents the Historical Jesus* (Grand
Rapids: Zondervan, 1995); Ben Witherington III, *The Jesus Quest:
The Third Search for the Jew of Nazareth*, 2d ed. (Downers Grove, IL:
InterVarsity Press, 1997); (4) Christology of the early church: Richard
Bauckham, *God Crucified: Monotheism and Christology in the New
Testament* (Grand Rapids: Eerdmans, 1998); Martin Hengel, *Studies
in Early Christology* (Edinburgh: T & T Clark, 1995); (5) Jesus'
self-understanding: Ben Witherington III, *The Christology of Jesus*
(Minneapolis: Fortress, 1990); (6) Jesus traditions before the Gospels:
Paul Barnett, *The Birth of Christianity: The First Twenty Years* (Grand
Rapids: Eerdmans, 2005); James D. G. Dunn, *A New Perspective on
Jesus: What the Quest for the Historical Jesus Missed* (Grand Rapids:
Baker, 2005); (7) reliability of the Gospels: Craig Blomberg, *The
Historical Reliability of the Gospels* (Downers Grove, IL: InterVarsity

Press, 1987); (8) miracles of Jesus: Graham H. Twelftree, *Jesus the Miracle Worker: A Historical and Theological Study* (Downers Grove, IL: InterVarsity Press, 1999); (9) trial of Jesus before Jewish leadership: Darrell L. Bock, *Blasphemy and Exaltation in Judaism and the Jewish Examination of Jesus* (Tübingen: Mohr, 1998); (10) resurrection of Jesus: William Lane Craig, *Assessing the New Testament Evidence for the Historicity of the Resurrection of Jesus* (Lewiston, NY: Mellen, 1989); Gary R. Habermas and Michael R. Licona, *The Case for the Resurrection of Jesus* (Grand Rapids: Kregel, 2004); Grant R. Osborne, *The Resurrection Narratives: A Redactional Study* (Grand Rapids: Baker, 1984); and N. T. Wright, *The Resurrection of the Son of God* (Minneapolis: Fortress, 2003).

2. Earl Doherty, *The Jesus Puzzle: Did Christianity Begin with a Mythical Christ?* (Ottawa: Age of Reason, 1999), 229.

3. Robert W. Funk, Roy W. Hoover, and the Jesus Seminar, *The Five Gospels: The Search for the Authentic Words of Jesus* (New York: Macmillan, 1993), 4.

4. It is sometimes alleged by fringe scholarship that Jesus did not really exist because if he had, Paul would have commented more on his life, quoted more of his sayings, and made other references relating to him. Such allegations miss two important pieces of data. First, Paul does allude to quite a few of Jesus' sayings, some of which are not even found in the Gospels (see esp. David Wenham, *Paul: Follower of Jesus or Founder of Christianity?* [Grand Rapids: Eerdmans, 1995]). Second, that he does not speak very often about the life of Jesus no doubt is due to the fact that he was not an eyewitness to Jesus' life. Birger Gerhardsson in *Memory and Manuscript: Oral Tradition and Written Transmission in Rabbinic Judaism and Early Christianity*, rev. ed. (Grand Rapids: Eerdmans, 1998) notes that since Paul was an eyewitness to the resurrected Christ, this is what he focuses on (see chap. 15: "The Evidence of Paul," 262–323). Since his apostolic commission came later than that of the original apostles, he had to rely on their testimony about the words and deeds of Jesus. But he could say authoritatively that Jesus had indeed risen from the dead, since he met the ascended Lord on the road to Damascus. Yet, even here,

Paul speaks more of the life of Jesus than is sometimes recognized. Wenham, *Paul,* discusses this matter throughout.

5. See John W. Mauck, *Paul on Trial: The Book of Acts as a Defense of Christianity* (Nashville: Nelson, 2001).

6. J. A. T. Robinson, *Redating the New Testament* (Philadelphia: Westminster, 1976), 16.

7. Ibid., 25 (emphasis added).

8. For more on the dating of the Synoptic Gospels, see D. A. Carson and Douglas J. Moo, *An Introduction to the New Testament,* 2d ed. (Grand Rapids: Zondervan, 2005).

9. Robert W. Funk and the Jesus Seminar, *The Acts of Jesus: The Search for the Authentic Deeds of Jesus* (San Francisco: HarperSanFrancisco, 1998), 6.

10. This is not the standard definition of form criticism. Taylor was writing in 1933 when the shape of form criticism was far more skeptical about the historical Jesus than it is today. Form criticism is the study of identifiable literary forms to which the stories about Jesus belong. That these stories circulated in such forms during the oral period is quite likely. See Bock, *Studying the Historical Jesus,* 181–87. Bock notes that as a literary tool, form criticism is helpful, but it has little to say in the verifying of the historicity of the material (ibid., 187).

11. Vincent Taylor, *The Formation of the Gospel Tradition* (London: Macmillan, 1933), 41–43.

CHAPTER 2: ORAL TRADITION AND A MEMORIZING CULTURE

1. John Dominic Crossan, *The Birth of Christianity: Discovering What Happened in the Years Immediately After the Execution of Jesus* (San Francisco: HarperSanFrancisco, 1998), 47–93.

2. This is the fundamental premise in Robert W. Funk, Roy W. Hoover, and the Jesus Seminar, *The Five Gospels: The Search for the Authentic Words of Jesus* (New York: Macmillan, 1993), and stated explicitly on page 4 of *The Five Gospels.*

3. Remarkably, even Crossan agrees with N. T. Wright that the sayings of Jesus were most likely repeated multiple times: "The overwhelm-

ing probability is that most of what Jesus said, he said not twice but two hundred times with (of course) a myriad of local variations" (Crossan, *Birth*, 49, quoting N. T. Wright, *The New Testament and the People of God* [Minneapolis: Fortress, 1992], 423). Yet, Crossan does not seem to think that this made much of an impact on the apostolic proclamation of the gospel.

4. Birger Gerhardsson, *Memory and Manuscript: Oral Tradition and Written Transmission in Rabbinic Judaism and Early Christianity,* with *Tradition and Transmission in Early Christianity* (both volumes now together under one cover) rev. ed. (Grand Rapids: Eerdmans, 1998).

5. Gerhardsson, *Memory and Manuscript*, 134–35.

6. The basis for this approach to quoting sources can be found in Thucydides *History of the Peloponnesian War* 1.22.1.

7. For a popular treatment of this subject, see Darrell L. Bock, "The Words of Jesus in the Gospels: Live, Jive, or Memorex?" in *Jesus Under Fire: Modern Scholarship Reinvents the Historical Jesus,* ed. Michael J. Wilkins and J. P. Moreland (Grand Rapids: Zondervan, 1995), 73–99.

8. Several of these rabbis lived before the time of Christ, showing continuity with rabbinic education before and after the time of Christ.

9. Crossan argues that the best test for determining what stands behind the Gospels is "the intersection of memory, orality, and literacy from oral fieldworkers operating inductively, or from social psychologists operating experimentally" (*Birth*, 58). That this approach is restricted entirely to the modern era does not seem to matter to Crossan. And yet, when Gerhardsson's *Memory and Manuscript* first appeared in 1961, Jacob Neusner criticized the book for lacking genuine first-century parallels to the Gospels. In the revised version of 1998, Neusner took the opportunity to recant of his "uncompromising and unappreciative, indeed dismissive" review (in his foreword to *Memory and Manuscript,* xxv). Neusner discusses "why Gerhardsson was denied a hearing" (ibid.). Since the rabbinic materials were later than the New Testament, scholars simply rejected Gerhardsson's argument as irrelevant. The Mishnah, the earliest of the rabbinic sources, was codified in about 200, although it went back to oral sources that

were, in many cases, from before the time of Christ. Of course, we have no earlier materials from the Jewish side of things, so at least Gerhardsson was using the best available parallels, chronologically speaking. Yet, Crossan uses *modern* parallels, assuming that this is the scientifically proper approach. More conservative scholars are held to a significantly higher standard.

10. Contrasting this, Gerhardsson, *Memory and Manuscript,* at least begins with very close parallels in the following respects: (1) Jewish, (2) rabbis' relation to disciples, (3) ancient, (4) a culture that focused on memorization. Remarkably, there are two major differences that *favor* the retention of material by Jesus' disciples over that of rabbis' disciples: community reinforcement of memory, and eyewitnesses to certain events.

11. Kenneth E. Bailey's essays and his earlier books were hardly noticed by scholars until N. T. Wright and J. D. G. Dunn discussed them. See Bailey's essays, "Informal Controlled Oral Tradition and the Synoptic Gospels," *Asia Journal of Theology* 5 (1991): 34–54; and "Middle Eastern Oral Tradition and the Synoptic Gospels," *Expository Times* 106 (1995): 363–67, and his books, notably *Poet and Peasant* and *Through Peasant Eyes: A Literary-Cultural Approach to the Parables of Luke,* combined ed. (Grand Rapids: Eerdmans, 1983). See N. T. Wright, *Jesus and the Victory of God* (Minneapolis: Fortress, 1996), 133–37; and James D. G. Dunn, *Jesus Remembered* (Grand Rapids: Eerdmans, 2003), 206–10.

12. Dunn, *Jesus Remembered,* 210.

13. Bock, "Words of Jesus in the Gospels," 73–99.

14. Ibid., 77.

15. Gerhardsson, *Memory and Manuscript,* 123.

16. James D. G. Dunn, *A New Perspective on Jesus: What the Quest for the Historical Jesus Missed* (Grand Rapids: Baker, 2005), 35–36.

17. Bock, "Words of Jesus in the Gospels," 79. See pages 79–81. He quotes with approbation Rainer Riesner's quip about ancient Jewish society as a "culture of memory" ("Gedächtniskulturen"). See page 80. The original wording can be found in Rainer Riesner, "Jüdische Elementarbildung und Evangelienüberlieferung," in *Gospel Perspectives:*

Studies of History and Tradition in the Four Gospels, ed. R. T. France and David Wenham (Sheffield, England: JSOT, 1980), 1:218. For the entire essay, see pages 209–23.

18. Paul Barnett, *The Birth of Christianity: The First Twenty Years* (Grand Rapids: Eerdmans, 2005), 113–14; see also Gerhardsson, *Memory and Manuscript,* 136–56.

19. This point is argued in Barnett, *Birth of Christianity,* 114; H. Schürmann, *Traditiongeschichtliche Untersuchungen* (Düsseldorf: Patmos, 1968), 39–45; and many others. It is even admitted by Gerhardsson, *Memory and Manuscript,* 195, as a possibility, even though Gerhardsson is the champion of a strong oral tradition.

20. Barnett, *Birth of Christianity,* 114.

CHAPTER 3: AN ECCENTRIC JESUS AND THE CRITERIA OF AUTHENTICITY

1. Robert W. Funk, Roy W. Hoover, and the Jesus Seminar, *The Five Gospels: The Search for the Authentic Words of Jesus* (New York: Macmillan, 1993), 29.

2. Ibid., 31.

3. Darrell L. Bock, "The Words of Jesus in the Gospels: Live, Jive, or Memorex?" in *Jesus Under Fire: Modern Scholarship Reinvents the Historical Jesus,* ed. Michael J. Wilkins and J. P. Moreland (Grand Rapids: Zondervan, 1995), 91.

4. So Heinrich Schlier, "ἀμήν," in *Theological Dictionary of the New Testament,* ed. Gerhard Kittel, trans. Geoffrey W. Bromiley (Grand Rapids: Eerdmans, 1964), 1:335, though Schlier breaks this down into three categories.

5. Ibid., 338.

6. Funk, Hoover, and the Jesus Seminar, *The Five Gospels,* 36. Actually, three *different* definitions are used in *The Five Gospels,* 36–37. To the degree that these actually mean different things, the Jesus Seminar's fellows were voting within unclear, amorphous categories. The three definitions of gray are as follows: (1) "I would not include this item in the database, but I might make use of some of the content in

determining who Jesus was"; (2) "Jesus did not say this, but the ideas contained in it are close to his own"; (3) "Well, maybe." These seem to be three different definitions for "gray."

7. Regarding the system of voting, the Jesus Seminar notes that "black votes in particular could readily pull an average down, as students know who have one 'F' along with several 'A's. Yet this shortcoming seemed consonant with the methodological skepticism that was a working principle of the Seminar: when in sufficient doubt, leave it out" (Funk, Hoover, and the Jesus Seminar, *The Five Gospels*, 37). In addition to the shortcoming admitted here, it may be noted that at least one member of the Jesus Seminar, Robert Price, did not believe that Jesus even existed! Although he is not listed in the *Five Gospels* roster of scholars who worked on the words of Jesus, he is listed in a later volume, *The Acts of Jesus: The Search for the Authentic Deeds of Jesus*, by Robert W. Funk and the Jesus Seminar (San Francisco: HarperSanFrancisco, 1998), 540. The criteria, coloring system, and rationale are quite similar to that of the first volume, except for one notable difference: instead of "this shortcoming," we now read "this *feature*" (Funk and Jesus Seminar, *Acts of Jesus*, 37 [emphasis added]). Does this mean that it is *not* a shortcoming to have a member whose pockets are filled only with black beads?

8. C. F. D. Moule, "The 'Son of Man': Some of the Facts," *New Testament Studies* 41 (1995): 278.

9. Bock, "Words of Jesus in the Gospels," 91.

10. Ibid.

11. Ibid., 92. Some would distinguish multiple sources from multiple forms, treating each as a separate criterion (so Robert H. Stein, "The 'Criteria' for Authenticity," in *Gospel Perspectives: Studies of History and Tradition in the Four Gospels*, ed. R. T. France and David Wenham [Sheffield, England: JSOT, 1980], 1:229–33).

12. Bock, "Words of Jesus in the Gospels," 92.

13. See discussion in Scot McKnight, "Who Is Jesus? An Introduction to Jesus Studies," in *Jesus Under Fire*, 66 (whole essay on 51–72).

14. Bock, "Words of Jesus in the Gospels," 92.

15. Ibid., 92–93.

16. Funk, Hoover, and the Jesus Seminar, *The Five Gospels*, 5.

17. As evidence of this, one could consult the many comments on this text in the patristic writers. They struggled with how the theanthropic person—the God–man—could have limited knowledge of the future.

18. Funk, Hoover, and the Jesus Seminar, *The Five Gospels*, 114.

19. C. E. B. Cranfield, *The Gospel According to Saint Mark* (Cambridge: Cambridge University Press, 1959), 17.

20. Josephus (*Antiquities* 4.8.15 §219) says that women were disqualified because of their inherent "vanity and rashness." It is said in *mKet* 1.6–9; *Sifre Deut.* 190; *ySot* 6.4, 21a that the testimony of a hundred women was worth no more than the testimony of one man. Tal Ilan, *Jewish Women in Greco-Roman Palestine: An Inquiry into Image and Status* (Tübingen: Mohr, 1995), 163–66, summarizes her research on the matter: "We may conclude that the specific law disqualifying women as witnesses was formulated as a general *halakhic* principle, just as in other matters such as punishments, but that many exceptions arose from actual custom and practice. During a normal trial in court, women's testimony was not sought out and was in fact avoided whenever possible because 'no man wants his wife to degrade herself in court' (*bKet.* 74b), but testimony which could not otherwise be obtained was by all means accepted" (ibid., 165).

21. The Jesus Seminar places the statements about Jesus' baptism in red letters in the *Acts of Jesus*.

22. Funk, Hoover, and the Jesus Seminar, *The Five Gospels*, 5.

23. Ibid.

24. But see Paul Barnett, *The Birth of Christianity: The First Twenty Years* (Grand Rapids: Eerdmans, 2005), 57. He notes Paul's intersections with the person of Jesus.

25. McKnight, "Who Is Jesus?" 61.

26. James D. G. Dunn, *Jesus Remembered* (Grand Rapids: Eerdmans, 2003), 254.

Chapter 4: Can We Trust the New Testament?

1. Recently, some scholars have argued that the primary goal of New Testament textual criticism must be something other than seeking to determine the wording of the original. This is a shift from the objective that has held sway for centuries. For a brief critique, see Moisés Silva, "Response," in *Rethinking New Testament Textual Criticism*, ed. David Alan Black (Grand Rapids: Baker, 2002), 149.

2. We are not arguing here for what is often called the "doctrine of preservation." Rather, our point is simply that the historical data show that the New Testament has been preserved over the centuries. Without turning such a fact into a doctrine, the evidence is still significant. For more information, see Daniel B. Wallace, "Inspiration, Preservation, and New Testament Textual Criticism," *Grace Theological Journal* 12 (1991): 21–51.

3. Bruce M. Metzger, *Manuscripts of the Greek Bible* (Oxford: Oxford University Press, 1981), 53; and J. Harold Greenlee, *Introduction to New Testament Textual Criticism*, rev. ed. (Peabody, MA: Hendrickson, 1995), 134 n. 2.

4. E. C. Colwell, "Method in Evaluating Scribal Habits: A Study of P45, P66, P75," in *Studies in Methodology in Textual Criticism of the New Testament*, New Testament Tools and Studies 9, ed. Bruce M. Metzger (Leiden: E. J. Brill, 1969), 115–16.

5. See Kim Haines-Eitzen, "Girls Trained in Beautiful Writing: Female Scribes in Roman Antiquity and Early Christianity," *Journal of Early Christian Studies* 6.4 (1998): 629–46; and idem, *Women and Early Christian Literature: Gender, Asceticism, and the Transmission of Texts* (Oxford: Oxford University Press, forthcoming).

6. The example from Codex W is based on personal examination.

7. See the discussions in Gordon D. Fee, "The Use of the Definite Article with Personal Names in the Gospel of John," *New Testament Studies* 17 (1970–71): 168–83; J. Heimerdinger and S. Levinsohn, "The Use of the Definite Article before Names of People in the Greek Text of Acts with Particular Reference to Codex Bezae," *Filologia Neotestamentaria* 5.9 (1992): 15–44; Steve Janssen, "The Greek Article with

Proper Names in Matthew: Traditional Grammar and Discourse Perspectives" (Th.M. thesis, Dallas Theological Seminary, 2003).

8. Transpositions help scholars determine how much text a scribe is holding in memory before he or she writes it down. As we noted, the scribe of P[75] seems to have copied one or two letters at a time. His transpositions would involve just a couple of letters, resulting in nonsense wording. Other scribes copied out as many as eight or nine words at a time (such as are found in Codex Bezae, a fifth-century manuscript housed at Cambridge University), resulting in more extensive transpositions and accidental omissions.

9. Or, more technically, the pronouns and third person singular endings in the verbs.

10. See Gordon D. Fee, "Modern Textual Criticism and the Synoptic Problem: On the Problem of Harmonization in the Gospels," in *Studies in the Theory and Method of New Testament Textual Criticism,* by Eldon J. Epp and Gordon D. Fee (Grand Rapids: Eerdmans, 1993), 174–82. Even some advocates of what is called the "majority text" acknowledge that there are harmonizations in their preferred text-form. See Willem Franciscus Wisselink, *Assimilation as a Criterion for the Establishment of the Text: A Comparative Study on the Basis of Passages from Matthew, Mark, and Luke* (Kampen: Uitgeversmaatschappij J. H. Kok, 1989), 87–90.

11. Robert W. Funk, Roy W. Hoover, and the Jesus Seminar, *The Five Gospels: The Search for the Authentic Words of Jesus* (New York: Macmillan, 1993), 5–6.

12. Some might even object that three of these examples are not viable. In *The Greek New Testament,* 4th rev. ed. (Stuttgart: Deutsche Bibelgesellschaft, 1994), the texts of Romans 5:1; 1 John 1:4; and Mark 16:8 (i.e., without the longer ending) are regarded as "certain." That is, the editors have no doubt as to what the original wording is. In each of these instances, we agree with their textual decision, but our degree of certainty may not be as high.

13. For a helpful discussion of the issues, see the "tc" note at Romans 5:1 in the NET Bible.

14. See, for example, Galatians 4:19: "My children—I am again undergoing birth pains until Christ is formed in you!"

15. For a recent discussion on this problem, see J. A. D. Weima, "'But We Became Infants Among You': The Case for NHΠIOI in 1 Thessalonians 2.7," *New Testament Studies* 46 (2000): 547–64; and T. B. Sailors, "Wedding Textual and Rhetorical Criticism to Understand the Text of 1 Thessalonians 2.7," *Journal for the Study of the New Testament* 80 (2000): 81–98.

16. For discussion, see Bruce M. Metzger, *A Textual Commentary on the Greek New Testament,* 2d ed. (Stuttgart: German Bible Society, 1994), 639.

17. There are only two places in the New Testament where the text is uncertain to such a degree—Mark 16:9–20 and John 7:53–8:11. The next largest viable textual variant involves two verses.

18. For a discussion, see Metzger, *Textual Commentary,* 102–7; NET Bible "tc" note on Mark 16:8; N. Clayton Croy, *The Mutilation of Mark's Gospel* (Nashville: Abingdon, 2003); and Kelly R. Iverson, "A Further Word on Final Γάρ (Mark 16:8)," *Catholic Biblical Quarterly* 68 (2006): 79–94.

CHAPTER 5: MYTHS ABOUT MANUSCRIPTS

1. The dates and other relevant data of all known manuscripts are catalogued in Kurt Aland, *Kurzgefasste Liste der Griechischen Handschriften des Neuen Testaments,* 2d rev. and exp. ed. (Berlin: Walter de Gruyter, 1994).

2. For example, the KJV finds its descendants in the Revised Version (1881–85), the American Standard Version (1901), the Revised Standard Version (1952), the New American Standard Version (1960), and the New Revised Standard Version (1989). These are all conscious and deliberate revisions of the KJV—a translation that, itself, stands in the tradition of Tyndale's translation. Translations that are not revisions of earlier versions include the New International Version, the New English Bible, and the New English Translation.

3. This is because in the ninth and eleventh centuries conscious and

intentional editing took place. See T. J. Ralston, "The Majority Text and Byzantine Texttype Development: The Significance of a Non-Parametric Method of Data Analysis for the Exploration of Manuscript Traditions" (Ph.D. dissertation, Dallas Theological Seminary, 1994), 282–90, 93–98, 233–41, 244–68.

4. Lee Strobel, *The Case for Christ: A Journalist's Personal Investigation of the Evidence for Jesus* (Grand Rapids: Zondervan, 1998).

5. Earl Doherty, *Challenging the Verdict* (Ottawa: Age of Reason, 2001), 37.

6. Ibid., 39.

7. Robert W. Funk, Roy W. Hoover, and the Jesus Seminar, *The Five Gospels: The Search for the Authentic Words of Jesus* (New York: Macmillan, 1993), 6.

8. This chart was inspired by the comparisons made in F. F. Bruce, *The New Testament Documents: Are They Reliable?* 6th ed. (Grand Rapids: Eerdmans; Downers Grove, IL: InterVarsity Press, 1981), 11. Thanks are due to Greg Sapaugh for his work on updating the data found in Bruce, *The New Testament Documents.* Sapaugh's work was a term paper for the doctoral course "Advanced New Testament Textual Criticism," at Dallas Seminary, fall 2005, taught by Daniel B. Wallace. Our statistics are largely based on Sapaugh's study. The number of manuscripts for these ancient authors—including the New Testament—is growing substantially since Bruce reported on the matter in 1981. His data were as follows:

Histories	Oldest MSS	Number Surviving
Livy 59 B.C.–A.D. 17	4th Century	20
Tacitus A.D. 56–120	9th & 10th Centuries	3
Thucydides 460–400 B.C.	10th Century	8 + a few papyrus fragments
Herodotus 484–425 B.C.	10th Century	very few
New Testament	c. 100–150	over 5,000 (counting only Greek manuscripts)

9. There are two fragments from the first century. The earliest substantial text of Thucydides is from the tenth century.

10. This number may be a bit generous, but not all of the libraries that house ancient manuscripts have been carefully sifted. A few unknown copies may lurk in the shadows.

11. Homer was the earliest and most popular author of the ancient Greek world. Even with a nine-hundred year head start, the *Iliad* and the *Odyssey* couldn't catch up with the New Testament. Yet manuscripts of Homer are more plentiful than the average classical Greek author's by a hundredfold.

12. Doherty, *Challenging the Verdict*, 38.

13. Jacob Burckhardt, *The Age of Constantine the Great* (Berkeley: University of California Press, 1949), 244.

14. See ibid., 244–68. Bruce M. Metzger, *The Canon of the New Testament: Its Origin, Development, and Significance* (Oxford: Clarendon, 1987), 106–8, gives illustrations of how the Christian Scriptures were systematically rounded up and destroyed.

15. Eusebius *Life of Constantine* 4.36. See discussion in Bruce M. Metzger and Bart D. Ehrman, *The Text of the New Testament: Its Transmission, Corruption, and Restoration*, 4th ed. (New York and Oxford: Oxford University Press, 2005), 15–16.

    One indication of the success of Diocletian's persecution is found in a late-fourth-century or early-fifth-century Gospels manuscript, Codex Washingtonianus. The text is a patchwork compilation from four different text-forms, each coming from a different region of the Mediterranean world. The original editor, Henry Sanders, offered the plausible suggestion that the manuscript was put together from fragments of other Gospel manuscripts that, in turn, had become mutilated because of the Diocletian persecution. See Sanders's fascinating and plausible historical reconstruction in *Facsimile of the Washington Manuscript of the Four Gospels in the Freer Collection, with an Introduction by Henry A. Sanders* (Ann Arbor, MI: University of Michigan, 1912).

16. At the same time, we must not forget that in the decades prior to the reign of Diocletian, Christians enjoyed some immunity from perse-

cution even though the religion was not legal. But all this changed in 303.

17. Many Greek Orthodox monasteries include manuscripts of classical texts, giving eloquent testimony to the fact that the scribes copied not only the Scriptures but other Greek literature as well. For example, the monasteries on Mount Athos have more than twenty thousand manuscripts: "Most monasteries... have rich and important collections of medieval and later manuscripts. The majority of these are liturgical, biblical or patristic texts..., but an important minority are of ancient pagan literature" (Graham Speake, *Mount Athos: Renewal in Paradise* [New Haven, CT: Yale University Press, 2002], 8). In reality, the number of classical texts is almost equal to New Testament manuscripts, about 5 percent of the total (ibid., 248; see also the data listed in Aland, *Kurzgefasste Liste*, 441–52). See also S. Rudberg, "Les Manuscrits à contenu profane du Mont-Athos," *Eranos* 54 (1956): 174–85. When the Turks invaded Constantinople in 1453, the scribes fled with their manuscripts into Western Europe, thus providing the textual catalyst for both the Reformation and Renaissance (G. R. Potter, ed., *The New Cambridge Modern History,* vol. 1: *The Renaissance 1493–1520* [Cambridge: Cambridge University Press, 1961], 71, 192). Five years later, the first Greek course in Western Europe was offered at the University of Paris.

18. As if to anticipate Doherty's objections, Bruce (*New Testament Documents,* 10) offers the following arguments:

> The evidence for our New Testament writings is ever so much greater than the evidence for many writings of classical authors, the authenticity of which no one dreams of questioning. And if the New Testament were a collection of secular writings, their authenticity would generally be regarded as beyond all doubt. It is a curious fact that historians have often been much readier to trust the New Testament records than have many theologians. Somehow or other, there are people who regard a "sacred book" as *ipso facto* under suspicion, and demand much more corroborative evidence for such a work than

they would for an ordinary secular or pagan writing. From the viewpoint of the historian, the same standards must be applied to both. But we do not quarrel with those who want more evidence for the New Testament than for other writings; firstly, because the universal claims which the New Testament makes upon mankind are so absolute; and secondly, because in point of fact there *is* much more evidence for the New Testament than for other ancient writings of comparable date.

CHAPTER 6: AN EMBARRASSMENT OF RICHES

1. Martin Hengel, *Studies in Early Christology* (Edinburgh: T & T Clark, 1995), 57–58, makes a similar statement about the parallel dangers from "an uncritical, sterile apologetic fundamentalism" and "from no less sterile 'critical ignorance'" of radical liberalism. At bottom, the approaches are the same; the only differences are the presuppositions.

   A good illustration of radical liberalism's critical ignorance about, and abuse of, textual criticism can be found in Timothy Freke and Peter Gandy's book, *The Jesus Mysteries: Was the "Original Jesus" a Pagan God?* (New York: Three Rivers, 2001), 145. The authors rely on chapter 4, "How Reliable Are the Manuscripts of the Gospels?" of Graham Stanton's *The Gospel Truth? New Light on Jesus and the Gospels* (Valley Forge, PA: Trinity, 1995), 33–48. First, they quote the pagan Celsus's complaint (as recorded in Stanton, *Gospel Truth?* 35) that Christians had deliberately tampered with the text of the New Testament. Their comment on Celsus's complaint is that "modern scholars have found that he was right. A careful study of over 3,000 early manuscripts has shown how scribes made many changes" (Freke and Gandy, *Jesus Mysteries,* 145). The lone documentation for this assertion is Stanton's *Gospel Truth,* 35. But Stanton mentions nothing about three thousand manuscripts on this page—and in fact there are nowhere close to three thousand *early* manuscripts for the New Testament, let alone any other ancient literature! Indeed, Stanton himself does not agree with this assessment. Stanton goes on to quote

Origen's response to Celsus that such alterations were made only by heretics. This quotation and Stanton's subsequent discussion are conveniently left out of Freke and Gandy's treatment. Freke and Gandy's selective quoting of the data seems to be driven by the results the authors wish to achieve, rather than by an honest pursuit of truth.

In the next paragraph, they note that "scholars also know that whole sections of the gospels were added later." They give the same example we mentioned in chapter 5—Mark 16:9–20. By "whole sections" apparently they mean one or two verses—and verses that have been excised from modern translations. There is only *one* other large block of material that has affected modern translations of the New Testament, the story of the woman caught in adultery (John 7:53–8:11). While this passage is a favorite of many Christians, whether it is authentic makes no *doctrinal* difference. Yet, Freke and Gandy clearly give the impression that we simply cannot trust anything about these manuscripts, that skepticism must rule.

The reality is that they have not represented Stanton's treatment, the works of other scholars, or the evidence with anything that remotely resembles an honest appraisal. The most charitable verdict is that such works as Freke and Gandy's are sloppy and irresponsible.

The same kind of irresponsible use of sources and results-driven approach can be found in a host of "KJV only" literature. One of the most blatant offenders is G. A. Riplinger, *New Age Bible Versions* (Shelbyville, TN: Bible & Literature Missionary Foundation, 1993). See James White, "Why Respond to Gail Riplinger?" at bible.org/page.asp?page_id=664.

2. The official clearinghouse of Greek New Testament manuscript identifications, the *Institut für neutestamentliche Textforschung* (Institute for New Testament Textual Research) in Münster, Germany, catalogs the manuscripts, assigning them each a new number. The updated catalog can be downloaded from the institute's Web site as a pdf file at uni-muenster.de/NTTextforschung/KgL_Aktualisierung.pdf.

3. A few more manuscripts will be added soon, all discovered by the Center for the Study of New Testament Manuscripts. See csntm.org.

4. Not all agree with this dating, however. Most recently, see Brent

Nongbri, "The Use and Abuse of P[52]: Papyrological Pitfalls in the Dating of the Fourth Gospel," *Harvard Theological Review* 98.1 (January 2005): 23–48; cf. also A. Schmidt, "Zwei Anmerkungen zu P. Ryl. III 457," *Archiv für Papyrusforschung* 35 (1989): 11–12. However, this position seems to be way too skeptical of the usual dating of this fragment. C. H. Roberts (the man who discovered the fragment in the 1930s) gave evidence that the closest datable manuscript to P[52] was P. Fayyum 110 (A.D. 94). Leading paleographers have placed P[52] in the first half of the second century, among them Frederic G. Kenyon, W. Schubart, Harold I. Bell, Adolf Deissman, Ulrich Wilcken, W. H. P. Hatch, Kurt Aland, and E. G. Turner.

5. These manuscripts include P[52] (100–150), P[90, 104] (second century), P[66] (c. 175–225), P[46,] P[64+67] (c. 200), P[77], 0189 (second or third century), P[98] (second century [?]).

These nine manuscripts are the extent of those that the *Institut für neutestamentliche Textforschung* has identified as possibly or definitely from the second century. In addition to these, there are a few other candidates. Philip W. Comfort and David P. Barrett, *The Text of the Earliest New Testament Greek Manuscripts* (Wheaton, IL: Tyndale, 2001) argue for at least half a dozen other manuscripts as possibly from the second century. Comfort and Barrett's method, however, is generally to take the earliest date possible. Nevertheless, the date they suggest for P[4] (second century) is probably correct in light of some recent work done by T. C. Skeat of the British Library; and the date they offer for P[32] (late second century) has a lot going for it.

6. The analogy breaks down, however, at a crucial point: in each new generation of a family, there is always a 50 percent mixture from a foreign element—the marriage partner. Although manuscripts showed mixture, they didn't have this kind of rapid and significant addition to the mixture in every succeeding generation.

7. Bruce M. Metzger and Bart D. Ehrman, *The Text of the New Testament: Its Transmission, Corruption, and Restoration*, 4th ed. (New York and Oxford: Oxford University Press, 2005), 91.

8. See Gordon D. Fee, "P[66], P[75] and Origen: The Myth of Early Textual Recension in Alexandria," in *New Dimensions in New Testament Study*,

ed. R. N. Longenecker and M. C. Tenney (Grand Rapids: Zondervan, 1974), 19–45; and C. L. Porter, "An Evaluation of the Textual Variation Between Pap75 and Codex Vaticanus in the Text of John," in *Studies in the History and Text of the New Testament in Honor of Kenneth Willis Clark*, Studies and Documents 29, ed. Boyd L. Daniels and M. Jack Suggs (Salt Lake City: University of Utah Press, 1967), 71–80.

9. For example, in 1 Timothy 3:16, the original Greek text almost surely read, "who was manifest in the flesh." All but one of the Latin manuscripts have "which" for "who"; none have "God." Later Greek manuscripts have "*God* was manifest in the flesh." The difference between "who" ($\overline{OC}$) and "God" ($\overline{\Theta C}$) is just two horizontal strokes in the letters in the Greek manuscripts. But the Latin words "which" *(quod)* and Latin "God" *(Deus)* are quite different. It is evident that the Latin manuscripts originated by copying a Greek text that had "who" instead of "God."

10. Bruce M. Metzger, *The Early Versions of the New Testament: Their Origin, Transmission, and Limitations* (Oxford: Clarendon, 1977), 293, 334.

11. Metzger and Ehrman, *Text of the New Testament*, 276–77.

12. Ibid., 96–98.

13. Ibid., 126.

14. No complete count has been made, but judging from data supplied for the Latin Fathers alone, it is safe to say that there are well over one million quotations of the New Testament by the Fathers. By 1920, about seven hundred thousand quotations of the Bible by the Latin Fathers had been compiled by Father Joseph Denk. The Vetus Latina Institute in Beuron, Germany, has continued the work, almost doubling the number of quotations and allusions. See J. Lionel North, "The Use of the Latin Fathers for New Testament Textual Criticism," in *The Text of the New Testament in Contemporary Research: Essays on the* Status Quaestionis *(A Volume in Honor of Bruce M. Metzger)*, ed. Bart D. Ehrman and Michael W. Holmes (Grand Rapids: Eerdmans, 1994), 210n. 6.

15. See the essays by Gordon D. Fee in *Studies in the Theory and Method of New Testament Textual Criticism*, ed. Eldon J. Epp and Gordon D.

Fee (Grand Rapids: Eerdmans, 1993), 299–359; and Gordon D. Fee, "The Use of the Greek Fathers for New Testament Textual Criticism," in *Contemporary Research,* 191–207.

16. See Bruce M. Metzger, "The Practice of Textual Criticism Among the Church Fathers," in *New Testament Studies: Philological, Versional, and Patristic,* New Testament Tools and Studies 10 (Leiden: E. J. Brill, 1980), 189–97; and idem, "St. Jerome's Explicit References to Variant Readings in Manuscripts of the New Testament," in *New Testament Studies,* 199–210.

17. Fee, "Use of the Greek Fathers," 191.

CHAPTER 7: THE METHODS OF TEXTUAL CRITICISM

1. For a discussion of the Byzantine text-type and its place in textual criticism, see Daniel B. Wallace, "The Majority Text Theory: History, Methods and Critique," in *The Text of the New Testament in Contemporary Research: Essays on the* Status Quaestionis *(A Volume in Honor of Bruce M. Metzger),* ed. Bart D. Ehrman and Michael W. Holmes (Grand Rapids: Eerdmans, 1994), 297–320.

2. Since a large number of Wallaces immigrated to the United States from Germany, after moving to Germany from Scotland or Ireland, this is entirely plausible.

3. David C. Parker, *The Living Text of the Gospels* (Cambridge: Cambridge University Press, 1997), 1. The errors in the text and the displaced lines were intentional on Parker's part.

4. These guidelines are not applied mechanically. That is, other considerations are brought to bear on the problem. In particular, if a reading could have been created *unintentionally,* the canons of shorter and harder generally do not apply. The reason this is the case is that the bulk of unintentional readings will be harder (to the point that many are nonsense readings!). Many shorter readings are caused by writing once what should have been written twice (known as haplography), or they can be caused by such factors as scribal fatigue. Thus, unintentional possibilities need to be dispensed with before any level of certainty can be offered on the basis of shorter or harder readings.

5. J. R. R. Tolkien, *The Lord of the Rings,* part 1, *The Fellowship of the Ring* (New York: Ballantine, 1954), 233.

6. The translation "who was revealed in the flesh" is a literal rendering. Most modern versions render the pronoun as "he."

7. For an exception to this rule, see Matthew 27:16–17 and the "tc" note in the NET Bible on "Jesus Barabbas."

8. See James M. Hamilton Jr., "He Is with You and He Will Be in You" (Ph.D. diss., Southern Baptist Theological Seminary, 2003), 213–20.

9. Robert M. Price, *The Incredible Shrinking Son of Man: How Reliable Is the Gospel Tradition?* (Amherst, NY: Prometheus, 2003), 70.

10. Ibid. (emphasis added).

11. Darrell L. Bock, *Luke 1:1–9:50,* Baker Exegetical Commentary on the New Testament (Grand Rapids: Baker, 1994), 1:118.

12. Price, *Incredible Shrinking Son of Man,* 70.

13. Ibid., 22.

14. See Kurt Aland and Barbara Aland, *The Text of the New Testament: An Introduction to the Critical Editions and to the Theory and Practice of Modern Textual Criticism*, 2d ed. (Grand Rapids: Eerdmans, 1989) 280–81. Here they discuss "Twelve Basic Rules for Textual Criticism." Rules 5 and 7 are particularly relevant to our discussion: non-Greek witnesses are of secondary importance in establishing the text (rule 5 [280]), and the notion that the original text can be found in even a single version (let alone a single manuscript within a version!) "is only a theoretical possibility" which will do nothing to establish the wording of the original (rule 7 [281]).

CHAPTER 8: IS WHAT WE HAVE NOW WHAT THEY WROTE THEN?

1. Dan Brown, *The Da Vinci Code: A Novel* (New York: Doubleday, 2003), 231. Equally irresponsible statements can be found. For example, Frank Zindler, writing in the *American Atheists* magazine in 1986 ("The *Real* Bible: Who's Got It?" at atheists.org/christianity/realbible [accessed October 2005]), said:

Concerning the preferred text of the Greek Bible, readers may

wonder just who decides—and how—what the preferred readings should be? Space does not permit a discussion of the scientific (and sometimes very un-scientific) principles involved.
We can only observe that it is both laughable and sad to see the
more intelligent fundamentalists diligently learning Greek in
order to "read God's word in the original tongue." Little do
they suspect, while staring at the nearly footnote-free pages
of their Westcott-Hort Greek testaments, the thousands of
scientific and not-so-scientific decisions underlying what they
see—or don't see—on each page.

There is much wrongheadedness in this statement. It is by no
means only fundamentalists who are studying the Greek New Testament. The *Institut für neutestamentliche Textforschung* in Münster,
Germany, is anything but a fundamentalist institute. Yet it is the epi-
center of New Testament textual criticism and is responsible for the
highly touted Nestle-Aland, *Novum Testamentum Graece* (a Greek
New Testament now in its twenty-seventh edition that has well over
a century of scholarship behind it). Of the four doctoral courses on
New Testament textual criticism taught in the United States, not one
of them is taught at a fundamentalist school.

It is true that textual criticism is both a science and an art. Sometimes scholars need to employ creative thinking to make decisions
about what the internal evidence suggests. This does not in any sense,
however, suggest that their decisions have no basis in good historical
research principles. But the appellation *science* is sometimes applied
to historical studies only with disdain (especially by those who think
of science as what takes place only in a pristine lab). Historians cannot verify their views in a test tube that produces the same results
time after time. With history, we are dealing with partial data and
human activity. The determinations of good historical research may
not be as certain as those of some of the hard sciences, but this does
not mean that everything is up for grabs.

Furthermore, to suggest that the "footnote-free" Westcott-Hort
text is still used is misleading. That text was printed in 1881 and has

been out of print for decades. It is occasionally reprinted but is hard to find. We know of no school that uses the Westcott-Hort "footnote-free" text today. Most seminaries use one of two Greek New Testaments, both of which contain notes in the apparatus on thousands of textual variants. Whatever Zindler is critiquing, it is not part of the real world of today.

Finally, as we noted earlier, when one looks at the actual details of the textual problems, the vast majority are so trivial as to not even be translatable, while the meaningful and viable variants constitute only about 1 percent of the text. And even for this category, most scholars would say that 1 percent uncertainty is an overstatement. (The majority of New Testament scholars would say that the meaningful and viable variants constitute a small fraction of 1 percent of the text.) As we have said many times throughout this section, the dogma of absolute skepticism is unjustified in the field of textual criticism (just as the dogma of absolute certainty is).

2. F. F. Bruce, *The New Testament Documents: Are They Reliable?* 6th ed. (Grand Rapids: Eerdmans; Downers Grove, IL: InterVarsity Press, 1981), 11.

3. Miroslav Marcovich, *Patristic Textual Criticism*, part 1 (Atlanta: Scholars Press, 1994), ix.

4. Ibid.

5. There are two places in the New Testament where conjecture has perhaps been needed. In Acts 16:12 the standard critical Greek text gives a reading that is not found in any Greek manuscripts. But even here, some members of the UBS committee rejected the conjecture, arguing that certain manuscripts had the original reading. The difference between the two readings is only one letter. (See discussion in Bruce M. Metzger, *A Textual Commentary on the Greek New Testament*, 2d ed. [Stuttgart: Deutsche Bibelgesellschaft, 1994], 393–95; NET Bible "tc" note on Acts 16:12.) Also, in Revelation 21:17 the standard Greek text follows a conjecture that Westcott and Hort originally put forth, though the textual problem is not listed in either the UBS text or the Nestle-Aland text. This conjecture is a mere spelling variant that changes no meaning in the text.

6. Kurt and Barbara Aland, *The Text of the New Testament: An Introduction to the Critical Editions and to the Theory and Practice of Modern Textual Criticism,* 2d ed. (Grand Rapids: Eerdmans, 1989), 296 (emphasis added).

7. Ibid., 281.

8. Ibid., 280.

9. See G. D. Kilpatrick, "Conjectural Emendation in the New Testament," in *New Testament Textual Criticism,* ed. E. J. Epp and G. D. Fee (Oxford: Clarendon, 1981), 349–60. For a specific treatment on conjecture, in which the author rejects it outright, see D. A. Black, "Conjectural Emendations in the Gospel of Matthew," *Novum Testamentum* 31 (1989):1–15. On the other hand, on rare occasions a New Testament scholar will put forth a conjecture. But such proposals are few and far between and are self-consciously uphill battles. See, for example, J. Strugnell, "A Plea for Conjectural Emendation in the New Testament," *Catholic Biblical Quarterly* 36 (1974): 543–58.

10. For example, there are five known early copies of the Gettysburg Address. The two most authoritative copies were made by Lincoln's private secretaries, John Hay and John Nicolay. They do not agree completely with each other. But there is no need for conjecture.

11. See Earl Doherty, *Challenging the Verdict* (Ottawa: Age of Reason, 2001), 39. He argues:

> During formative periods, changes in theology as well as traditions about events which lay at the inception of the movement may be very significant. We have nothing in the Gospels which casts a clear light on that early evolution or provides us with a guarantee that the surviving texts are a reliable picture of the beginnings of the faith.
>
> In fact, the one indicator we do have points precisely in the opposite direction. The later gospels dependent on the earlier Mark show many instances of change, alteration and evolution of ideas.

To say that we cannot know anything that the original authors of the Gospels wrote, one must argue either that scribes introduced changes in Matthew and Luke that radically departed from Mark or that the manuscripts were terribly corrupted almost immediately by a radical harmonization. In answer to the former, we should note that neither Matthew nor Luke intended to duplicate Mark, so we should expect some differences. They felt free to shape the material as they saw fit. This is not the same as saying that they invented stories about Jesus; rather, they edited their sources for their own audiences. Still, if anything, Matthew and Luke more likely would be charged with plagiarism (a practice that was not an ethical issue in ancient literature) than with significantly changing the text.

What about the idea that harmonization of the manuscripts took place almost at the outset, rendering the original wording unknowable? If such were the case, we would hardly be able to distinguish among the Synoptic Gospels. The fact is that harmonization was a scribal tendency that increased over time, as we can see from later manuscripts. That the earliest manuscripts of the Gospels show the same differences among the Gospels suggests that the scribes in the earliest period copied them with relative accuracy.

12. Bart D. Ehrman's recent book, *Misquoting Jesus: The Story Behind Who Changed the Bible and Why* (San Francisco: HarperSanFrancisco, 2005), 109–12, discusses the role that Bengel played in the history of textual criticism. He gives Bengel high praise as a scholar: he was an "extremely careful interpreter of the biblical text" (ibid., 109); "Bengel studied *everything* intensely" (ibid., 111). Ehrman speaks about Bengel's breakthroughs in textual criticism (ibid., 111–12) but does not mention that Bengel was the first important scholar to articulate the doctrine of the orthodoxy of the variants. This is a curious omission because Ehrman is well aware of this fact, for in Bruce M. Metzger and Bart D. Ehrman, *The Text of the New Testament: Its Transmission, Corruption, and Restoration*, 4th ed. (New York and Oxford: Oxford University Press, 2005), which appeared just months before *Misquoting Jesus*, the authors note that Bengel collected the available manuscripts, and early translations. "After extended study, he came to the conclusions that the variant readings were fewer in number than

might have been expected and that they did not shake any article of evangelic doctrine" (158). On the other hand, Ehrman mentions J. J. Wettstein, a contemporary of Bengel, who, at age twenty, assumed that these variants "can have no weakening effect on the trustworthiness or integrity of the Scriptures" (Ehrman, *Misquoting Jesus,* 112). Years later, after careful study of the text, Wettstein changed his views after he "began thinking seriously about his own theological convictions" (ibid., 114). One is tempted to think that Ehrman may see a parallel between himself and Wettstein. Like Wettstein, Ehrman started out as an evangelical when in college but changed his views on the text and theology in his more mature years (see *Misquoting Jesus,* 1–15, where Ehrman chronicles his own spiritual journey). But the model that Bengel supplies—a sober scholar who arrives at quite different conclusions—is quietly passed over.

13. See D. A. Carson, *The King James Version Debate: A Plea for Realism* (Grand Rapids: Baker, 1979), 56, 65.

14. Kenneth W. Clark, "Textual Criticism and Doctrine," *Studia Paulina: In Honorem Johannis de Zwaan* (Haarlem: De Erven F. Bohn, 1953), 52–65; and idem, "The Theological Relevance of Textual Variation in Current Criticism of the Greek New Testament," *Journal of Biblical Literature* 85 (1966): 1–16.

15. In Bart D. Ehrman's provocative book, *The Orthodox Corruption of Scripture: The Effect of Early Christological Controversies on the Text of the New Testament* (Oxford: Oxford University Press, 1993), the author attempts to show that early "orthodox" Christians sometimes corrupted the original text of the New Testament by making it conform more *explicitly* to orthodoxy. But he is not arguing that the original New Testament taught anything *substantially* different from these scribally adjusted texts.

Nevertheless, his case is frequently overstated in especially one of two ways: either his interpretation of the original text or his textual basis is a bit strained. For critiques of Ehrman's work, see especially Gordon D. Fee's review in *Critical Review of Books in Religion* 8 (1995): 203–6; Bruce M. Metzger's review in *Princeton Seminary Bulletin* 15.2 (1994): 210–12; J. Neville Birdsall's review in *Theology*

97.780 (November–December 1994): 460–62. Ehrman's more recent, popular work, *Misquoting Jesus,* which to some degree is based on *Orthodox Corruption of Scripture,* is far more provocative and somewhat misleading. See the discussion below.

16. The very title of this book, *Misquoting Jesus,* is a misnomer. Almost none of the variants that Ehrman discusses involve *sayings* by Jesus.

17. Ehrman, *Misquoting Jesus,* 15. Apparently he does not count the several books written by "KJV only" advocates or the books that interact with them. It seems that Ehrman means that his is the first book on the general discipline of New Testament textual criticism written by a bona fide textual critic for a lay readership. This is most likely true.

18. Ibid., 208.

19. Ibid. These passages are especially discussed in chapters 5 and 6 of his book. Matthew 24:36 is mentioned five times in the book.

20. In the Greek text, if "nor the Son" is not authentic, then the preceding phrase can easily be translated "not even the angels in heaven" as in the NET Bible.

21. S. C. E. Legg, *Novum Testamentum Graece secundum Textum Westcotto-Hortianum: Euangelium secundum Marcum* (Oxford: Clarendon, 1935) lists only Codex X (a tenth-century Gospels manuscript) and one Vulgate manuscript for the omission. Nestle-Aland[27] adds to this *pc* (or *pauci,* "a few others"), but does not specify what they are.

22. See the discussion in the NET Bible's note on this verse.

23. When discussing Wettstein's views of the New Testament text, Ehrman argues that "as Wettstein continued his investigations, he found other passages typically used to affirm the doctrine of the divinity of Christ that in fact represented textual problems; when these problems are resolved on text-critical grounds, in *most instances references to Jesus' divinity are taken away*" (*Misquoting Jesus,* 113, emphasis added). He adds that "Wettstein began thinking seriously about his own theological convictions, and became attuned to the problem that the New Testament rarely, *if ever,* actually calls Jesus God" (ibid., 114, emphasis added). But these statements are misleading. Nowhere does Ehrman represent this conclusion as *only* Wettstein's; he seems to embrace such opinions himself (and confirmed this on NPR's *Diane*

Rehm Show on December 8, 2005). See discussion of early manuscript testimony to the deity of Christ in chapter 8.

24. For example, in *Orthodox Corruption of Scripture,* Ehrman devotes five pages to the textual problem in John 1:18. He forcefully argues that "only Son" must surely be the original reading (81):

> The more common expedient for those who opt for [ὁ] μονογενὴς θεός, but who recognize that its rendering as "the unique God" is virtually impossible in a Johannine context, is to understand the adjective substantivally, and to construe the entire second half of John 1:18 as a series of appositions, so that rather than reading "the unique God who is in the bosom of the Father," the text should be rendered "the unique one, who is also God, who is in the bosom of the Father." There is something attractive about the proposal. It explains what the text might have meant to a Johannine reader and thereby allows for the text of the generally superior textual witnesses. Nonetheless, the solution is entirely implausible.
>
> ... It is true that μονογενής can elsewhere be used as a substantive (= the unique one, as in v. 14); all adjectives can. But the proponents of this view have failed to consider that it is never used in this way when it is immediately followed by a noun that agrees with it in gender, number, and case. Indeed one must here press the syntactical point: when is an adjective *ever* used substantivally when it immediately precedes a noun of the same inflection? No Greek reader would construe such a construction as a string of substantives, and no Greek writer would create such an inconcinnity. To the best of my knowledge, no one has cited anything analogous outside of this passage.
>
> The result is that taking the term μονογενὴς θεός as two substantives standing in apposition makes for a nearly impossible syntax, whereas construing their relationship as adjective-noun creates an impossible sense.

Ehrman's grammatical argument is difficult to explain briefly. In

Greek, words are inflected for various grammatical features. For example, an adjective may be singular or plural; masculine, feminine, or neuter; and in the nominative, genitive, dative, or accusative case. The combination of these features means that a given adjective can have as many as twenty-four different forms. When it has *concord* with a noun that follows, this means that it agrees with that noun in number, gender, and case. At the same time, Greek adjectives (like English adjectives) can function substantivally—that is, like a noun. Thus, when we read "blessed are the poor," the adjective *poor* functions like a noun in that it does not modify any noun but takes the place of a noun. It is like saying "blessed are the poor people," even though "people" is not in the text.

Ehrman's grammatical point is that never in the New Testament does an adjective that has concord with a noun that follows it ever function substantivally. The problem is, this absolutizing of the grammatical situation is incorrect. There are, indeed, examples in which an adjective juxtaposed to a noun of the same grammatical concord is not functioning adjectivally but substantivally. Scores of texts can be mentioned (e.g., John 6:70; Rom. 1:30; Gal 3:9; Eph. 2:20; 1 Tim. 1:9; 1 Peter 1:1; 2 Peter 2:5). The 2 Peter text is instructive. Literally, it reads: "and if he did not spare the ancient world, but did protect an *eighth, Noah,* a herald of righteousness, when he brought a flood on an ungodly world." The adjective translated "eighth" has to be substantival rather than modify "Noah"; it meets all the qualifications that Ehrman says can only indicate one thing, and yet if we followed Ehrman's grammatical rule, the meaning here would be "an eighth Noah," as though there were seven other Noahs on the ark! If the construction that Ehrman says is "never used this way" is found in several examples in the New Testament, then what are we to make of John 1:18? A critique of Ehrman's treatment of verse 18 by Daniel B. Wallace was posted on the www.bible.org Web site several years ago and has influenced the wording of the NET Bible in verse 18. But either because it has not been noticed or has simply been ignored, Ehrman continues to make his claims that μονογενὴς θεός must mean "the unique God."

Now, if the adjective "unique" in John 1:18 does not have to modify "God," is there any other evidence that it acts substantivally here? In particular, are there sufficient *contextual* clues that μονογενής is in fact functioning as a noun? Ehrman has already provided both of them: (1) in John, it is unthinkable that the Word could become the *unique* God in 1:18 (in which he alone, and not the Father, is claimed to have divine status) only to have that status removed repeatedly throughout the rest of the Gospel. Thus, *assuming* that μονογενὴς θεός is authentic, we are in fact driven to the sense that Ehrman regards as grammatically implausible but contextually necessary: "the unique one, himself God . . ."; (2) that μονογενής is already used in verse 14 as a substantive becomes the strongest contextual argument for seeing its substantival function repeated four verses later. Immediately after Ehrman admits that this adjective can be used substantivally and is so used in verse 14, he makes his grammatical argument, which is intended to lay the gauntlet down or to shut the coffin lid (choose your cliché on the force of the connection with v. 14). But if the grammatical argument won't cut it, then the substantival use of μονογενής in verse 14 should stand as an important contextual clue. Indeed, in light of the well-worn usage in *biblical* Greek, we would almost expect μονογενής to be used substantivally *and* with the implication of sonship in 1:18. Thus, not only is the textual evidence strong for the wording μονογενὴς θεός here, but the linguistic evidence is strong that the meaning of this phrase is "the unique one, himself God."

These arguments were posted on bible.org some years ago, available to all. In addition, a student at Dallas Seminary wrote his master's thesis as a critique of Ehrman's *Orthodox Corruption of Scripture,* and included many more examples (Stratton Ladewig, "An Examination of the Orthodoxy of the Variants in Light of Bart Ehrman's *The Orthodox Corruption of Scripture*" [Th.M. thesis, Dallas Seminary, 2000). He corresponded with Ehrman about his work, so there is no reason why Ehrman would be unaware of it. Yet, Ehrman still maintains that if μονογενὴς θεός is read, it must mean "the unique God" (*Misquoting Jesus,* 161–62), even though substantial arguments were brought forth that the phrase should more properly be rendered "the unique one, himself God," as is found in the NET Bible. In the least, the strongest proof texts that Ehrman puts forth seem to lack either sufficient textual base or involve unwarranted interpretations. Although most of *Misquoting Jesus* is a decent lay introduction to the field of New Testament textual criticism, chapters 5 and 6 take the book one step further, especially giving the lay reader the clear impression that our Bibles today are quite untrustworthy as spiritual guides.

25. Peter Ruckman is perhaps the most extreme "KJV only" advocate, going so far as to argue that even the Greek and Hebrew text need to be corrected by the KJV! See Peter Ruckman, *The Christian's Handbook of Manuscript Evidence* (Pensacola, FL: Pensacola Bible Institute, 1970), 115–38; and idem, *Problem Texts* (Pensacola, FL: Pensacola Bible Institute, 1980), 46–48.

26. Not only has he influenced many laymen, but David Otis Fuller, ed., dedicated the book, *Counterfeit or Genuine[:] Mark 16? John 8?* 2d ed. (Grand Rapids: Grand Rapids International, 1978), to "Jasper James Ray, Missionary Scholar of Junction City, Oregon, whose book, *God Wrote Only One Bible* [(Junction City, OR: Eye Opener, 1955), v], moved me to begin this fascinating faith-inspiring study."

27. Ray, *God Wrote Only One Bible*.

28. Ibid., ii, 1, 32, 101, 122. For example, early in the book he likens modern translations to poison: "Put poison anywhere in the blood stream and the whole becomes poisoned. Just so with the Word of God. When words are added or subtracted, Bible inspiration is destroyed, and the spiritual blood stream is poisoned" (ibid., 9).

29. Fuller, *Counterfeit or Genuine*, 10.

30. Ibid., 9.

31. From a personal conversation with Herrick.

32. Zindler, "The *Real* Bible: Who's Got It?"

33. See, for example, 1 Timothy 3:16 and the "tc" note in the NET Bible. This verse was touched on in an earlier chapter.

34. See Mark 9:29 (and especially the "tc" note) in the NET Bible for one of these, as well as 1 Corinthians 14:34–35.

35. See, e.g., Carson, *King James Version Debate,* 65–66.

36. Michael Baigent, Richard Leigh, and Henry Lincoln, *Holy Blood, Holy Grail,* American Version (New York: Dell, 1983), 368–69.

37. The dates and other relevant data of all known manuscripts are catalogued in Kurt Aland, *Kurzgefasste Liste der Griechischen Handschriften des Neuen Testaments,* 2d rev. and exp. ed. (Berlin: Walter de Gruyter, 1994). There are thirty-five papyri from before the fourth century and another nine that are either from the third or fourth century. In addition, there are three uncial manuscripts from prior to the fourth century and two others that are either from the third or fourth century. Since the publication of this volume, a few more manuscripts have been discovered that are early, at least ten papyri and one uncial manuscript, bringing the total number of definitely pre-fourth-century Greek New Testament manuscripts to at least forty-eight and as many as fifty-nine. Keep in mind that the *Kurzgefasste Liste* only catalogs *Greek* New Testament manuscripts. It does not include the early versions or the pre-fourth-century patristic writers.

38. The other important uncial manuscript from the fourth century is Codex Sinaiticus. This is the oldest complete New Testament by five centuries. Both Sinaiticus and Vaticanus belong to the Alexandrian text-type. Yet they have a sufficient number of differences that it is impossible for them to have been copied from the same immediate ancestor. Some scholars believe that their common ancestor must be about ten generations removed, putting it very early in the second century. In the least, if these two documents were among the fifty Bibles that Constantine commissioned (as some believe), that commission did not extend to manipulation of the text. Vaticanus and Sinaiticus are too different to allow for the notion that Constantine's commission "enabled the custodians of orthodoxy to revise, edit, and rewrite their material as they saw fit, in accordance with their tenets" as Baigent, Leigh, and Lincoln allege (*Holy Blood, Holy Grail,* 368). These authors have capitalized on one fact in history (the commissioning of the production of fifty Bibles by Constantine) and have then read into it things that are not there. Ironically, their belief that

"The New Testament as it exists today is essentially a product of fourth-century editors and writers" (ibid., 369) describes the King James Bible and the Greek text it used more than the text that stands behind modern translations. Those used by modern translations go back substantially to the original text. Yet, even here, we have noted that there are no fundamental differences in doctrine between the KJV and most modern translations and that over time the New Testament text grew by only about 2 percent.

39. A good guide on the more meaningful and viable variants in the New Testament is the textual apparatus of the Nestle-Aland, *Novum Testamentum Graece,* 27th ed. (Stuttgart: Deutsche Bibelgesellschaft, 1993). This is the standard Greek New Testament used today. It lists no variants of any kind for John 1:1, two variants in John 20:28 ("and" at the beginning of the verse versus no conjunction, and "Thomas answered" versus "Thomas said"), no manuscript deviations in Romans 9:5, and four minor variants in Hebrews 1:8, all of which come *after* the affirmation of Jesus as God.

CHAPTER 9: THE RANGE OF THE CANON

1. This argument to include the Gospel of Thomas is implicit in Robert W. Funk, Roy W. Hoover, and the Jesus Seminar, *The Five Gospels: The Search for the Authentic Words of Jesus* (New York: Macmillan, 1993). The fifth gospel in this volume is the Gospel of Thomas. We have said that the Jesus Seminar assigned red letters to the words that they believed Jesus actually spoke, pink letters when an idea was thought to go back to Jesus, gray if the words (and thought) probably did not go back to Jesus, and black if the words (and thought) definitely did not go back to Jesus. Remarkably, there are more red and pink sayings in Thomas than there are in John (no red sayings and only one pink saying in John versus one red saying and thirty-five pink sayings in Thomas). The impression that the Jesus Seminar conveys is that Thomas is a more authentic witness to the life of Jesus than is John.

2. Bruce M. Metzger, *The Canon of the New Testament: Its Origin, Development, and Significance* (Oxford: Clarendon, 1987), 282.

3. William Barclay, *The Making of the Bible* (London: Lutterworth, 1961), 78.

4. Metzger, *Canon of the New Testament*, 287.

5. Dan Burstein, *Secrets of the Code: The Unauthorized Guide to the Mysteries Behind* The Da Vinci Code (New York: CDS Books, 2004), 116.

6. Even the Syrian church accepted all but 2 Peter, 2 and 3 John, Jude, and Revelation no later than the early part of the fifth century (Metzger, *Canon of the New Testament*, 219).

7. Most likely, this was due to the influence of the Trullan Synod (691–92), which "sanctioned implicitly, so far as the list of Biblical books is concerned, quite incongruous and contradictory opinions" (ibid., 216). Such confusion over the minor books of the New Testament continued for a long time.

8. The closest we come to one is the Council of Trent's declaration in 1546 as to what constituted the canon, but this applied only to the Roman Catholic Church, not the Protestant or Eastern Orthodox.

9. See Metzger, *Canon of the New Testament*, 271, for discussion. This proposal was added to Martin Luther King Jr.'s book, *Why We Can't Wait* (New York: Harper & Row, 1964), 77–100.

10. Paul Maier, "Chronology," in *Dictionary of the Later New Testament and Its Developments*, ed. Ralph P. Martin and Peter H. Davids (Downers Grove, IL: InterVarsity Press, 1997), 193.

11. D. F. Wright, "Docetism," in *Dictionary of the Later New Testament*, 307.

12. D. A. Carson and Douglas J. Moo, *An Introduction to the New Testament*, 2d ed. (Grand Rapids: Zondervan, 2005), 732.

13. Barbara Aland helped develop the argument that Marcion's theology was close to Gnosticism in her article, "Versuch einer neuen Interpretation," *Zeitschrift für Theologie unde Kirche* 70 (1973): 420–47.

14. According to Irenaeus, Marcion was influenced by the Gnostic teacher Cerdo (Irenaeus *Adversus Haereses* ["*Against Heresies*"] 1.27.1–3). Further, Marcion was excommunicated from his church in Rome in 144. Valentinus, one of the early Gnostics, was in Rome at this time promoting his views.

15. At the same time, it should be acknowledged that Marcion used only

Luke's Gospel, when Gnostics preferred John's Gospel for their own purposes. Marcion's preference for Luke, calling it "the Gospel," was most likely due to Luke's association with Paul. But this raises two other questions: First, why didn't Marcion list works like the Acts of John, a document that is most likely not Gnostic but simply docetic (J. K. Elliott, ed., *The Apocryphal New Testament*, rev. ed. [reprint, Oxford: Clarendon, 1999], 306), or the Gospel of the Adversaries of the Law and the Prophets (ibid., 24)? Second, why didn't Marcion list other works about or allegedly by Paul—such as the Acts of Paul, 3 Corinthians, the letter to the Laodiceans, the six letters to Seneca, or the Apocalypse of Paul? Again, the natural inference is that these books were either not yet in existence or, if they existed, were not considered credible because of their recent production.

16. See discussion in Metzger, *Canon of the New Testament*, 193–94.

17. In addition to the principal manuscript, named after the man who discovered it (Ludovico Antonio Muratori) and published it in 1740, four other manuscripts of this canon list have been located (ibid., 192–93).

18. See ibid., 194–99.

19. Text in ibid., 307.

20. See ibid., 199–201.

21. Ibid., 254.

22. Eusebius, *The Ecclesiastical History* 3.25, trans. Kirsopp Lake, Loeb Classical Library (Cambridge, MA: Harvard University Press, 1925), 1.257.

23. Carson and Moo, *Introduction to the New Testament*, 734.

24. Metzger, *Canon of the New Testament*, 287.

25. There was, however, strong external pressure, especially during the Diocletian persecutions, on the church's view of the canon.

26. Metzger, *Canon of the New Testament*, 287–88.

CHAPTER 10: WHAT DID THE ANCIENT CHURCH THINK OF FORGERIES?

1. Ignatius *Magnesians* 13:1, in *The Apostolic Fathers: Greek Texts and*

English Translations, ed. and rev. Michael W. Holmes (Grand Rapids: Baker, 1999). All quotations from the Apostolic Fathers are from this edition unless noted otherwise.

2. Ignatius *Trallians* 3.3. Ignatius *Romans* 4.3, is similar: "I do not give you orders like Peter and Paul: they were apostles, I am a convict." For other references to the apostles' authority, see *1 Clement* 42.1; Polycarp *Epistle to the Philippians* 3.2; Ignatius *Epistle to the Ephesians* 11.2; Ignatius *Trallians* 2.2; 7.1; 12.2; Ignatius *Letter to the Smyrnaeans* 8.1; the anonymous *Epistle to Diognetus* 11.6.

3. D. A. Carson and Douglas J. Moo, *An Introduction to the New Testament,* 2d ed. (Grand Rapids: Zondervan, 2005), 338–40, list other motives as well. But at bottom, almost all of these seem to include a desire for authority for one's views by claiming that the book was written by an apostle or some other leader of the early church.

4. Werner Georg Kümmel, *Introduction to the New Testament,* rev. English ed., trans. Howard Clark Kee (Nashville: Abingdon, 1975), 363, assumes that this was the impulse that drove much of the New Testament writings: "The only thing that is clear in relation to the pseudepigraphic material we encounter is that 'the decisive presupposition for pseudepigraphic writing in the New Testament [is represented by] the establishment of the apostolic as the norm' (cf. Eph. 2:20), so that literary fiction 'brings into play the authority' of an apostle." Whether or not this literary fiction is actually found in the New Testament is a different question, but Kümmel has identified what would have prompted it.

5. Martin Hengel, *The Four Gospels and the One Gospel of Jesus Christ* (Harrisburg, PA: Trinity Press International, 2000), 48–53, argues that the Gospels were not anonymous but, from the beginning, had the titles "the Gospel according Matthew," etc. Most New Testament scholars, however, have not accepted his view. For a balanced discussion, see Carson and Moo, *Introduction to the New Testament,* 140–42.

6. Papias, *The Fragments of Papias* 3.15.

7. See Donald Guthrie, *New Testament Introduction,* 4th ed. (Downers Grove, IL: InterVarsity Press, 1990), 85.

8. A similar motive to that of Irenaeus seems to have driven Augustine. In his *De doctrina Christiana* ("On Christian Learning") 2.13, he lists the twenty-seven books of the New Testament, but the order is unusual: He puts James at the end of the general letters, so as to give Peter first place!

9. Stevan L. Davies, *The New Testament: A Contemporary Introduction* (San Francisco: Harper & Row, 1988), 191.

10. It is an overstatement to say that this was not written to Hebrews. The "letter" has all the earmarks of being written to Jewish Christians who were sitting on the fence between Christianity and Judaism. Just because they were Jewish *Christians* does not mean they were not "Hebrews."

11. See, for example, Ben Witherington III, "The Influence of Galatians on Hebrews," *New Testament Studies* 37 (1991): 146–52.

12. There are two scholarly exceptions to this today: Eta Linnemann, "Wideraufnahme-Prozess in Sachen des Hebräerbriefes," *Fundamentum* 21 (2000): 101–12; 22 (2001): 52–65, 88–110; and David Alan Black, "On the Pauline Authorship of Hebrews," *Faith and Mission* 16.2 (1999): 32–51; 16.3 (1999): 78–86. One of the arguments is that the vocabulary of Hebrews is more similar to Paul's letters than to anything else in the New Testament. We could just as well say that 1 Peter was also written by Paul since its vocabulary is every bit as "Pauline" as that of Hebrews!

13. William Barclay, *The Making of the Bible* (London: Lutterworth, 1961), 78.

14. Carson and Moo, *Introduction to the New Testament*, 701.

15. Ibid., 706–7.

16. We have discussed these criteria in the first chapter in this section.

17. But see Robert Picirilli, "Allusions to 2 Peter in the Apostolic Fathers," *Journal for the Study of the New Testament* 33 (1988): 57–83.

18. Jerome *Epistle to Hedibia* 120.

19. Eusebius *Ecclesiastical History* 3.1.

20. As quoted by Eusebius *Ecclesiastical History* 6.12, trans. Kirsopp Lake, Loeb Classical Library (Cambridge, MA: Harvard University Press, 1925), 2.41.

21. As quoted in Bruce M. Metzger, *The Canon of the New Testament: Its Origin, Development, and Significance* (Oxford: Clarendon, 1987), 307.
22. Ibid.
23. Eusebius *Ecclesiastical History* 3.25, Loeb Classical Library, 1.257–59.
24. Carson and Moo, *Introduction to the New Testament,* 343.
25. E. Earle Ellis, *The Making of the New Testament Documents* (Leiden: Brill, 1999), 324. For an excellent discussion of the problem of pseudepigraphy and the canon that expands on this point, see Carson and Moo, *Introduction to the New Testament,* 337–50.
26. Timothy Freke and Peter Gandy, *The Jesus Mysteries: Was the "Original Jesus" a Pagan God?* (New York: Three Rivers, 2001), 224; cite Metzger, *Canon of the New Testament,* 13, in an endnote (311 n. 105) to back up their contention that "in the first four centuries every single document was at some time or other branded as either heretical or forged!" But that is not what Metzger says. He is citing a late seventeenth-century Irish author, one John Toland, who created a scandal when he made such a proclamation. The clear impression one gets when reading Metzger on this point is one of incredulity at, not agreement with, Toland's viewpoint. If Freke and Gandy are so careless in handling a modern author whose writings are well known and accessible, should we really trust them to handle ancient authors?
27. On local and temporary canons, see Metzger, *Canon of the New Testament,* 165–89.

CHAPTER 11: WHAT DID THE ANCIENT FORGERS THINK OF CHRIST?

1. Bruce M. Metzger, *The Canon of the New Testament: Its Origin, Development, and Significance* (Oxford: Clarendon, 1987), 165.
2. Ibid. Metzger cites both Jerome and Augustine on this point.
3. Ibid., 166.
4. Ibid., 166–67.
5. Dan Brown, *The Da Vinci Code: A Novel* (New York: Doubleday, 2003), 244.

6. Even in the Gospel of the Ebionites, composed by someone in a Jewish-Christian sect that emphasized the humanity of Christ and downplayed his divinity, we are told that Jesus "is not begotten by God the Father but created like one of the archangels, being greater than they." (The Gospel of the Ebionites is known only from quotations in patristic authors. This quotation is from Epiphanius, as translated in J. K. Elliott, ed., *The Apocryphal New Testament: A Collection of Apocryphal Literature in an English Translation*, based on M. R. James, rev. ed. [reprint ed., Oxford: Clarendon, 1999], 6). Remarkably, even though the Ebionites thought of Jesus as a human prophet, they nevertheless could speak of him as greater than any angel.

7. The difficulty in determining an exact number is that some of the gospels are known only by name or from allusions. Church Fathers may refer to the same books by different names. Some fragments may be portions of the very gospels that these patristic writers speak of. Also, a fragment might simply be one person's allusions to the gospel narratives, rather than a full-blown apocryphal gospel. To get a sense of how many apocryphal gospels there may have been, see Elliott, *The Apocryphal New Testament*. He lists ten lost gospels that are mentioned by name in the patristic writers, six fairly early infancy gospels, and five "gospels of the ministry and passion."

In addition, he mentions five other infancy gospels that "are in general far removed from the earlier apocryphal material" (ibid., 118), as well as a few fragments of Coptic narratives, some of which may belong to other lost gospels. This brings the total to about thirty or so apocryphal gospels. In addition, there are "the Pilate Cycles," books that can only loosely be called gospels. This includes twelve different books. More than forty gospels are thus mentioned in *The Apocryphal New Testament*. There may indeed be others, but most of them appeared so late that they had little impact. There may be fewer apocryphal gospels than forty if the same books were given different names by patristic writers or if some fragments are from the same book. It is quite impossible to speak definitively, as Dan Brown has done, of "more than eighty gospels," let alone to suggest that all such gospels were on the docket for canonical consideration.

8. Ibid., 47.
9. Edgar Hennecke and Wilhelm Schneemelcher, eds., *New Testament Apocrypha*, vol. 1, *Gospels and Related Writings* (Philadelphia: Westminster, 1963), 401, note:

> Perhaps infancy gospels were written by Gnostics at an early date. Certainly such material did not originate with them. But in order to be able to derive their speculations from Jesus Himself, they needed as a framework a setting in His life which could be lifted into the older gospel tradition, but without being controlled by its content. Besides the resurrection appearances during the forty days, there was available the whole childhood of Jesus left untouched by the older Gospels. We have seen how fruitful in this respect were the themes of Jesus at the age of twelve in the temple and of his education. What they now required, however, was a child Jesus who was only a child in appearance, but had in fact no need of development, since He possessed the full revelation in its entirety, and already had unlimited power to perform miracles.

10. Elliott, *Apocryphal New Testament*, 47.
11. Protevangelium 8.1; quotations from Hennecke and Schneemelcher, *New Testament Apocrypha,* 1:378.
12. Quotations from Hennecke and Schneemelcher, *New Testament Apocrypha,* 1:393.
13. Ibid.
14. Ibid., 1:394.
15. Ibid., 1:395.
16. Ibid., 1:400–401 (from Arabic Infancy Gospel and the Paris manuscript of the Gospel of Thomas).
17. Ibid., 1:409 (from Arabic Infancy Gospel 40).
18. Ibid., 1:412 (Pseudo-Matthew 22.1).
19. There was "the tendency to Docetism behind all the legends of the infancy" (ibid., 1:401).
20. So, for example, Pseudo-Matthew 18.2: "Have no fear, and do not

think that I am a child; for I have always been and even now am perfect . . ." (ibid., 1:410).

21. Brown, *Da Vinci Code*, 234.

22. One of the problems with identification is the problem of definition. In 1966 a highly publicized conference of scholars met in Messina to define Gnosticism. Unfortunately, at the end of the conference, there was still no consensus. The problem is generally that the looser the definition, the earlier we can date Gnosticism; the tighter the definition, the later we must date the origins of Gnosticism. If one wants to think of pre-Christian Gnostics, he has to define Gnosticism in such a loose way that it simply doesn't look like the Gnosticism that arose in the second century. But if a tighter definition is assumed, then there is no evidence that Gnosticism came into existence until *after* the rise of Christianity. For an excellent discussion about the problems of definition and date, see Edwin M. Yamauchi, *Pre-Christian Gnosticism: A Survey of the Proposed Evidences*, 2d ed. (Grand Rapids: Baker, 1983), 13–28. We will assume a tighter definition for Gnosticism in this book, with later origins.

23. D. M. Scholer, "Gnosticism," in *Dictionary of the Later New Testament and Its Developments*, ed. Ralph P. Martin and Peter H. Davids (Downers Grove, IL: InterVarsity Press, 1997), 401.

24. Ibid.

25. Robert E. Van Voorst, *Jesus Outside the New Testament: An Introduction to the Ancient Evidence* (Grand Rapids: Eerdmans, 2000), 186.

26. The infancy gospels were influenced by Gnosticism. Although they are fundamentally narrative gospels, their superman-like embellishments reveal a strong antipathy for the Incarnation. For the most part the Gnostic gospels portray conversations between Jesus and his disciples after his resurrection from the dead. This may be due to the emphasis in these gospels on secrecy, for Jesus' public ministry occurred only prior to his crucifixion.

27. Elliott, *Apocryphal New Testament*, 124.

28. Ibid.

29. Salome is even featured as much as Mary Magdalene in the Gospel of Thomas.

30. Timothy Freke and Peter Gandy, *Jesus and the Lost Goddess: The Secret Teachings of the Original Christians* (New York: Three Rivers, 2001), 95, quote from the Gnostic Gospel of Philip, 2.3.63–64, that "[Jesus] loved [Mary] more than the other disciples, and often used to kiss her on the lips." Freke and Gandy use this text as evidence that Jesus and Mary were married.

But there are a few problems with their conclusion. First, this gospel is late. It is probably a second-century gospel, even though the earliest copy comes from much later (Hennecke and Schneemelcher, *New Testament Apocrypha*, 1.276, 278). Second, it is a Gnostic gospel, which means that it discouraged marriage. As James Robinson, one of the world's leading Nag Hammadi experts, noted, "If one reads the entire Gospel of Philip it becomes clear that the writer disdains physical sex as beastly, literally comparing it to animals" (an interview with James Robinson, quoted in Dan Burstein, *Secrets of the Code: The Unauthorized Guide to the Mysteries Behind* The Da Vinci Code [New York: CDS Books, 2004], 99). To see Jesus and Mary as an item in this gospel is reading things between the lines that simply are not there.

Third, the line about Jesus kissing Mary *on the lips* is not in any known manuscripts! The Coptic text reads that Jesus "kissed her often on her _____." There is a lacuna, a gap, at exactly the point in dispute. Where, exactly, did Jesus kiss Mary? On the mouth, on the head, on the cheek, on the hands, on the feet? We are not told, but Freke and Gandy have filled in the blanks without so much as a footnote explaining that this is only their guess. This is misleading at best and certainly not in line with the Gnostic ascetic worldview. Their best guess and inferences do not take into consideration the nature of this "gospel." Again, Robinson notes that "too much has been made out of this kiss. It was also called the Kiss of Peace, somewhat analogous to a modern church service where they ask you to shake hands with everybody and say, 'May the peace of Christ be with you.'" He concludes with a sober observation: "I think the only relevant text for historical information about Mary Magdalene is the New Testament, and it does not go beyond saying that she was one of the circle of women who accompanied the wandering Jesus and his male followers. . . . No doubt the New Testament gives an accurate protrayal [*sic*] of all of these Marys" (ibid.).

To argue that Mary was married to Jesus makes about as much sense as arguing that Salome was married to Jesus. In the Gospel of Thomas 61, Salome says to the Lord, "You have mounted my bed and eaten from my table" (Elliott, *Apocryphal New Testament,* 143). But this can hardly be a reference to sexual intimacy. For one thing, the Coptic word for "bed" has been translated as "couch" or "bench" as well (as in other translations of this saying elsewhere). For another, in the immediate context, Jesus had just spoken of two resting on a couch. "Two on a couch probably refers to a dinner party or symposium . . . Jesus is here [in Salome's words] represented as an intruder at a dinner party" (Robert W. Funk, Roy W. Hoover, and the Jesus Seminar, *The Five Gospels: The Search for the Authentic Words of Jesus* [New York: Macmillan, 1993], 507). Finally, the whole of this gospel discourages marriage and sexual intimacy.

But if we wanted to take this one statement and strip it from its immediate and broader context, it would be possible to suggest that Jesus and Salome were married. This is precisely how many take the kiss in the Gospel of Philip.

31. For example, the Gospel of the Egyptians "was accepted as canonical in Egypt" (see Metzger, *Canon of the New Testament,* 171). Metzger discusses all such books in his brief chapter, "Books of Temporary and Local Canonicity: Apocryphal Literature" (165–89).

32. Jacob Burckhardt, *The Age of Constantine the Great* (Berkeley: University of California Press, 1949), 244.

33. The pogrom is described vividly in Eusebius, *Ecclesiastical History* 8.2.4. See also Burckhardt, *Age of Constantine,* 244–68. Metzger, *Canon of the New Testament,* 106–8, gives illustrations of how the Christian Scriptures were systematically rounded up and destroyed.

34. Metzger, *Canon of the New Testament,* 106–7.

35. Ibid., 107 n. 74.

36. Ibid., 167.

37. Ben Witherington III, *The Gospel Code: Novel Claims About Jesus,*

Mary Magdalene and Da Vinci (Downers Grove, IL: InterVarsity Press, 2004), 33.

38. All quotations from the Gospel of Thomas are from the translation in Elliott, *Apocryphal New Testament,* 135–47, unless otherwise noted.

39. Gospel of Thomas 13.

40. Elliott, *Apocryphal New Testament,* 150, notes that "most scholars date its composition to the second half of the second century," while Metzger, *Canon of the New Testament,* 172n. 18, notes that a couple of scholars date it to the first half of the second century.

41. Gospel of Peter 10.38–39 (translation in Elliott, *Apocryphal New Testament,* 156).

42. Gospel of Mary 8.18–19. All quotations of this gospel are from Esther A. de Boer, *The Gospel of Mary: Beyond a Gnostic and a Biblical Mary Magdalene* (London: T & T Clark, 2004), 19.

43. de Boer, *Gospel of Mary,* 21.

44. Metzger, *Canon of the New Testament,* 177 (citing Acts of John §93).

45. Ibid.

46. Ibid., 173.

Chapter 12: Divine Portraits

1. For a concise defense of the philosophical coherence of the Incarnation—God entering the time-space world as a man—see J. P. Moreland and William Lane Craig, *Philosophical Foundations for a Christian Worldview* (Downers Grove, IL: InterVarsity Press, 2003), 597–614. For a book-length treatment, see Thomas V. Morris, *The Logic of God Incarnate* (Ithaca, NY: Cornell University Press, 1986).

2. Dan Brown, *The Da Vinci Code: A Novel* (New York: Doubleday, 2003), 233.

3. Historic Christianity affirms that since the time of the Incarnation, Jesus Christ is fully God and fully man forever united in one person. A concise, accessible survey of the church's historic understanding of Christ as the God-man is found in John D. Hannah, *Our Legacy: The History of Christian Doctrine* (Colorado Springs: NavPress, 2001), 109–46.

4. Richard Bauckham, *God Crucified: Monotheism and Christology in the New Testament* (Grand Rapids: Eerdmans, 1998), 10.

5. Ibid., 10–11.

6. Two helpful, accessible resources on this front are Craig L. Blomberg, *Jesus and the Gospels: An Introduction and Survey* (Nashville: Broadman & Holman, 1997); and Darrell L. Bock, *Jesus According to Scripture: Restoring the Portrait from the Gospels* (Grand Rapids: Baker, 2002).

7. For a helpful listing of commentaries on New Testament books, including the four Gospels, see John Glynn, *Commentary and Reference Survey: A Comprehensive Guide to Biblical and Theological Sources* (Grand Rapids: Kregel, 2003). For books discussing Gospels and other New Testament texts that support the deity of Christ, see Robert M. Bowman Jr. and J. Ed Komoszewski, *Putting Jesus in His Place: The Case for the Deity of Christ* (Grand Rapids: Kregel, 2007); Murray J. Harris, *Three Crucial Questions About Jesus* (Grand Rapids: Baker, 1994); and Robert L. Reymond, *Jesus, Divine Messiah: The New and Old Testament Witness* (Fearn, Scotland: Christian Focus, 2003).

8. A few manuscripts, including one very important manuscript, Codex Sinaiticus, lack "Son of God" here. But other equally important witnesses have it, along with the rest of the witnesses in all three major textual traditions. The external evidence thus argues for the authenticity of the words. Internally, although the shorter reading is normally to be preferred, this rule cannot be applied mechanically. In cases where accidental omission is likely, the shorter reading canon is invalid. In this instance, there is a good likelihood that the words were omitted by accident in some witnesses: the last four words of verse 1, in uncial script, would have been written as two-letter contractions (known as *nomina sacra*), each ending in *upsilon*. With all the successive *upsilons*, an accidental deletion is likely. Even though Sinaiticus is in general one of the best New Testament manuscripts, its testimony is not quite as preeminent in this situation. There are several other instances in which it breaks up chains of genitives ending in *upsilon* (e.g., Acts 28:31; Col. 2:2; Heb. 12:2; Rev. 12:14; 15:7; 22:1), showing that there is a significantly higher possibility

of accidental scribal omission in a case like this. The first corrector of Sinaiticus added "Son of God," suggesting that the omission was simply an oversight. In light of the external and internal evidence, the original text of Mark 1:1 most likely included "Son of God."

9. The centurion is the first human in Mark's narrative to testify that Jesus was the Son of God. This is not to say, however, that the centurion was the first convert to Christianity. In all likelihood, the centurion didn't grasp the theological significance of what he was saying but was overwhelmed by the unique circumstance at Calvary (e.g., the unnatural darkness and Jesus' triumphant cry as he breathed his last) and recognized that Jesus was an extraordinary man with an extraordinary relationship to God. Nonetheless, it's clear that *Mark* intends his readers to understand this climactic confession as a reference to Jesus as the unique Son of God (cf. Mark 1:1, 11; 3:11; 5:7; 9:7; 12:6; 13:32; 14:61–62).

10. Luke stresses another unique aspect of Jesus' identity through the use of an additional *inclusio*. In both Luke 4:21 and 24:44, Jesus himself declares that he fulfills messianic prophecy. In the latter text, Jesus stresses that he fulfills the *totality* of the Old Testament writings ("the law of Moses and the prophets and the psalms"). In other words, Jesus claims to be the main character in the story line of the Hebrew Scriptures. Luke's *inclusio* invites the reader to view Jesus' life in light of that claim.

11. To the contrary, Luke makes clear that the category of "prophet" alone was too confining for Jesus. Whereas John the Baptist—prophet *par excellence* (Luke 7:26–27) and the greatest man ever born (v. 28)—was called "prophet of the Most High" (1:76), Jesus surpassed him as "Son of the Most High" (v. 32). In both the proclamation of heaven and the admission of John, Jesus was superior.

12. Although most scholars date John's Gospel in the 90s, a small but growing number see it as written in the 60s. Four reasons are given for the earlier date: (1) The literary dualisms (e.g., light vs. darkness) in John, which had seemed to suggest a late Hellenistic influence, were discovered in the Dead Sea Scrolls at Qumran (variously dated from 225 B.C. to A.D. 68). This shows that John's Gospel could be

both early and written by a Jew. (2) The date of P⁵², a fragmentary copy of John's Gospel and the earliest of all New Testament manuscripts, suggests an earlier date for the Gospel. Although some scholars have recently argued that the fragment should be dated later, the majority see it as copied between 100 and 150. Some even date it as early as the 90s. If P⁵² was produced in Egypt, then it suggests an earlier date for John since sufficient time was needed for the Gospel (originally penned in modern-day Turkey) to circulate to the Nile region. (3) The fact that the fall of Jerusalem is not mentioned in John has been taken to mean that it had not yet fallen. So momentous was the destruction of the temple and the fall of Jerusalem to any Jew that it surely would have been mentioned in the Gospels if it had already occurred. (4) Corroborating evidence for the third point is that in John 5:2 the author says that the pool of Bethesda *is* in Jerusalem. But since that pool was destroyed in A.D. 70, this note would seem to have been written prior to the Jewish war with Rome. See Daniel B. Wallace, "John 5, 2 and the Date of the Fourth Gospel," *Biblica* 71 (1990): 177–205.

13. Any translation of John 1 testifies to the belief in the first century that Jesus was much more than a mere man. On the grammar and translation of John 1:1, see Murray J. Harris, *Jesus as God: The New Testament Use of* Theos *in Reference to Jesus* (Grand Rapids: Baker, 1992), 51–71; and Daniel B. Wallace, *Greek Grammar Beyond the Basics: An Exegetical Syntax of the New Testament* (Grand Rapids: Zondervan, 1996), 256–70.

14. R. T. France, "The Worship of Jesus: A Neglected Factor in Christological Debate?" *Vox Evangelica* 12 (1981): 25.

15. W. L. Schutter, "A Continuing Crisis for Incarnational Doctrine," *Reformed Review* 32.2 (1979): 85.

16. For a fascinating look at the historicity and theology of Jesus' miracles, see Graham H. Twelftree, *Jesus the Miracle Worker: A Historical and Theological Study* (Downers Grove, IL: InterVarsity Press, 1999).

17. Mark 2:7 is not like 2 Samuel 12:13, where Nathan announces God's forgiveness of David. Jesus doesn't merely *announce* forgiveness of the paralytic; he *applies* it. Of course, the latter is a divine prerogative. See

C. E. B. Cranfield, *The Gospel According to Saint Mark* (Cambridge: Cambridge University Press, 1959), 99.

18. A point often made, sometimes as a historical criticism of Mark's account, e.g., S. G. F. Brandon, *The Trial of Jesus of Nazareth* (New York: Stein and Day, 1968), 89–90.

19. So Darrell L. Bock, *Blasphemy and Exaltation in Judaism: The Charge Against Jesus in Mark 14:53–65* (Grand Rapids: Baker, 2000), 230–31. We are indebted to Bock's research throughout this discussion.

20. Bock, *Jesus According to Scripture*, 345–46.

21. See a summary of such figures in Bock, *Blasphemy and Exaltation*, 234–35.

22. So precarious was his duty that one later Jewish source (possibly reflecting second temple tradition) says the high priest celebrated with friends if he survived the trip into the Holy of Holies: "And he made a feast for his friends because he had come forth safely from the Sanctuary" (Yoma 7.4 [Mishnah]). Translation taken from Philip Blackman, *Mishnayoth: Pointed Hebrew Text, English Translation, Introductions, Notes Supplement, Appendix, Addenda, Corrigenda*, 2d ed., rev., corrected, enlarged, 7 vols. (Gateshead: Judaica, 1977).

23. This claim would be especially shocking in light of the fact that, in Jewish thinking, the heavenly temple was the pattern for the earthly one. See Josephus *Antiquities of the Jews* 3.181–87.

24. As Bock has put it, Jesus' claim "would be worse, in the leadership's view, than claiming the right to be able to walk into the Holy of Holies in the temple and live there!" *Jesus According to Scripture*, 375.

25. Bock, *Blasphemy and Exaltation*, 204–5.

26. Martin Hengel, *Studies in Early Christology* (Edinburgh: T & T Clark), 155.

27. We can be confident that Mark 14:53–65 captures the historical gist of Jesus' sayings, as well as the setting in which they were uttered. See Bock, *Blasphemy and Exaltation*, 209–33.

28. Bauckham, *God Crucified*, viii.

CHAPTER 13: SUPREME DEVOTION

1. Not only were there companions with Paul who witnessed what happened to him, but he also had the physical proof: he was blinded temporarily. That this blinding was not psychosomatic was obvious three days later, when "something like scales fell from [Paul's] eyes" (Acts 9:18) after a follower of Jesus placed his hands on him.

2. Romans 10:11 is quoting Isaiah 28:16, a passage that Paul had quoted in 9:33 to refer to Christ. In verse 32, the apostle says that Israel has "stumbled over the stumbling stone," an obvious reference to Christ. This is followed by the quotation of Isaiah 28:16 mixed with 8:14, to the effect that belief in Christ is belief in "the stone."

3. For more discussion on the meaning of *Lord* as YHWH in Romans 10:9, see Daniel B. Wallace, *Greek Grammar Beyond the Basics: An Exegetical Syntax of the New Testament* (Grand Rapids: Zondervan, 1996), 187–88.

4. Not all scholars agree with this assessment, though it is the predominant and most likely interpretation. For a detailed discussion, see Ralph P. Martin, *A Hymn of Christ: Philippians 2:5–11 in Recent Interpretation and in the Setting of Early Christian Worship*, rev. ed. (Downers Grove, IL: InterVarsity Press, 1997), 24–41.

5. On this word, see J. H. Moulton and George Milligan, *Vocabulary of the Greek Testament* (Grand Rapids: Eerdmans, 1930), 417; Peter T. O'Brien, *Commentary on Philippians*, New International Greek Commentary (Grand Rapids: Eerdmans, 1991), 206–7; and David H. Wallace, "A Note on Morphē," *Theologische Zeitschrift* 22 (1966): 19–25.

6. Moulton and Milligan, *Vocabulary of the Greek Testament*, 417; O'Brien, *Commentary on Philippians*, 206–7; and Wallace, "A Note on Morphē," 19–25.

7. Cf. Richard Bauckham, *God Crucified: Monotheism and Christology in the New Testament* (Grand Rapids: Eerdmans, 1998), 51–53.

8. O'Brien, *Commentary on Philippians*, 241.

9. For a discussion on the hymnic nature of Colossians 1:15–20, see Peter T. O'Brien, *Colossians, Philemon*, Word Biblical Commentary 44 (Waco, TX: Word, 1982), 32–37.

10. Bauckham, *God Crucified,* 10–11.

11. Titus 2:13 is one of the clearest texts in the New Testament to affirm the deity of Christ, for it speaks of him as "our great God and Savior." We have not listed it in the section on Paul because some scholars dispute whether Paul wrote this letter. (For a defense of Paul's authorship of Titus, see D. A. Carson and Douglas J. Moo, *An Introduction to the New Testament,* 2d ed. [Grand Rapids: Zondervan, 2005]; and William D. Mounce, *Pastoral Epistles,* Word Biblical Commentary 46 [Nashville: Nelson, 2000]). Nevertheless, even if Paul did not write Titus, it still would have been written in the first century. And the Greek is unequivocal that the verse explicitly speaks of Christ as God. Cf. Murray J. Harris, *Jesus as God: The New Testament Use of Theos in Reference to Jesus* (Grand Rapids: Baker, 1992), 173–85; Wallace, *Exegetical Syntax,* 270–90; and Daniel B. Wallace, *Granville Sharp's Canon and Its Kin* (Bern: Peter Lang, forthcoming).

12. See discussion of Hebrews's authorship in chapter 10. The book of Hebrews is anonymous, and no one knows who wrote it. However, the author was a contemporary of the apostle Paul's protégé Timothy (Heb. 13:23), placing Hebrews in the first century.

13. On the suggested alternate translation "Your throne is God," see Harris, *Jesus as God,* 205–27; and Wallace, *Exegetical Syntax,* 59. This translation has very little to commend it. But even if we accepted it, it would in context elevate Jesus above all angels (note the contrast between the angels as God's servants who minister to us, vv. 7, 14, and the Son, who rules over angels and human beings, vv. 8–10).

14. Cf. the statement in the Mishnah (the Jewish document that codified conduct, written c. A.D. 200 but based on much earlier oral testimony) to this effect, *m. Sanhedrin* 7.5.

CHAPTER 14: FROM THE PENS OF FATHERS AND FOES

1. For helpful surveys and evaluations of noncanonical references to Christ, see Gary R. Habermas, *The Historical Jesus: Ancient Evidence for the Life of Christ* (Joplin, MO: College, 1996); Murray J. Harris, *Three Crucial Questions About Jesus* (Grand Rapids: Baker, 1994); and

Robert E. Van Voorst, *Jesus Outside the New Testament: An Introduction to the Ancient Evidence* (Grand Rapids: Eerdmans, 2000).

2. Concluding his discussion of ancient non-Christian sources for Jesus, Habermas, *Historical Jesus,* 224, notes that "it is quite extraordinary that we could provide a broad outline of most of the major facts of Jesus' life from 'secular' history alone."

3. Van Voorst, *Jesus Outside the New Testament,* 14, notes that although the question of Jesus' historicity is important to Christian faith, "the theory of Jesus' nonexistence is now effectively dead as a scholarly question." The nonexistence hypothesis is almost universally rejected by scholars as anemic and odd.

4. A point made by Habermas, *Historical Jesus,* 241–42.

5. Lucian, *The Passing of Peregrinus,* trans. A. M. Harmon, Loeb Classical Library (Cambridge, MA: Harvard University Press, 1936), 11 (5.13).

6. Ibid., 13 (5.15).

7. Celsus, *On the True Doctrine: A Discourse Against the Christians,* trans. R. Joseph Hoffmann (Oxford: Oxford University Press, 1987), 116.

8. Ibid., 77–78.

9. Pliny *Letters and Panegyricus,* trans. Betty Radice, Loeb Classical Library (Cambridge, MA: Harvard University Press, 1969), 10.96 (2.287).

10. Ibid., 2.288–89.

11. Ibid., 2.289.

12. For an enlightening and sobering look at the cost of devotion to Jesus in first-century culture, see Larry W. Hurtado, *How on Earth Did Jesus Become a God? Historical Questions About Earliest Devotion to Jesus* (Grand Rapids: Eerdmans, 2005), 56–82.

13. Especially in its newer form, Middle Platonism. The early first-century Alexandrian Jewish philosopher Philo illustrates Middle Platonism's attraction to educated Jews throughout the Greco-Roman world.

14. C. E. Arnold, "Syncretism," in *Dictionary of the Later New Testament and Its Developments,* ed. Ralph P. Martin and Peter H. Davids (Downers Grove, IL: InterVarsity Press, 1997), 1149–50.

15. The Alexandrian historian Basilides, writing 130–150, asserts that it was actually Simon of Cyrene who was crucified instead of Christ (cited in Irenaeus *Against Heresies* 1.24.4).

16. Ignatius *Letter to the Smyrnaeans* 5.2.

17. While the normative understanding of Jesus in the early church involved recognition of his deity, there were small enclaves that insisted that he was only human. Beginning in the late first century and continuing through the early third, the Ebionites, a Jewish Christian sect, viewed Jesus as merely a human prophet born of Mary and Joseph.

    In the late second century, a teaching arose among Gentile Christians known as Dynamic Monarchianism. This view insisted that Jesus was just a man but one upon whom the power *(dunamis)* of God had come in a special way. These adoptionists were a small and unrepresentative group within Gentile Christianity. They were most likely from a philosophical background that saw matter as inherently evil, and thus they found the idea repugnant that God himself would take up a fleshly body (J. N. D. Kelly, *Early Christian Doctrines,* rev. ed. [New York: Harper & Row, 1978], 116). Later, in mid-third-century Rome, adoptionism was revived briefly before it was condemned at the Synod of Antioch in 268.

    Thus, the idea that Jesus was just a man was a minor view that cropped up from time to time within the ancient church as an alternative to the prevailing Christian belief. It had minimal impact and was roundly rejected by the larger Christian community.

18. *1 Clement* 16.2.

19. Kelly, *Early Christian Doctrines,* 91.

20. *1 Clement* 32.4; 38.4; 43.6; 58.2; 63.3; 65.2.

21. *1 Clement* 58.2.

22. *2 Clement* 1.1.

23. *1 Clement* 22.1.

24. Epistle of Barnabas 6.12.

25. Ibid., 5.5; 12.7.

26. Ignatius *Magnesians* 6.1.

27. Ignatius *Epistle to the Ephesians* 3.2.

28. Ibid., 18.2.

29. Ibid., 19.3. Some translations have "appeared in human form." However, the verb φανερόω [phaneroō] in this text is better rendered "make known," "reveal." See W. Bauer, *A Greek-English Lexicon of the New Testament and Other Early Christian Literature*, 3d ed., rev. and ed. F. W. Danker, trans. W. F. Arndt, F. W. Gingrich, and F. W. Danker (Chicago and London: University of Chicago Press, 2000), 1048. Though the verb can be translated "appear," its meaning should not be confused with an appearance that does not correspond to reality or that merely *seems* to reflect reality.

30. Ignatius *Epistle to the Ephesians* 7.2.

31. Kelly, *Early Christian Doctrines*, 92.

32. Those who attacked the faith from outside were primarily Jews, pagan philosophers, and Roman authorities. The internal attacks that were ultimately judged to be heretical included the teachings of Marcion, a radically anti-Jewish teacher who saw the God of the Old Testament as evil and different from the God of the New Testament; Montanism, a visionary Christian sect that saw a continuing of prophecy and revelation that conceptually challenged the finality of apostolic revelation; and Dynamic Monarchianism (adoptionism) and Modalistic Monarchianism, which denied the Trinity by seeing the persons as modes of divine self-revelation rather than expressions of true eternal distinctions within the Godhead.

33. Justin Martyr *First Apology* 1.63, in *The Ante-Nicene Fathers* (hereafter cited as *ANF*), ed. Alexander Roberts and James Donaldson, 10 vols. (1885–1887; reprint, Grand Rapids: Eerdmans, 1978), 1.228: "For the sake of proving that Jesus the Christ is the Son of God . . . , being of old [i.e., during the Old Testament era] the Word, [who] . . . sometimes [appeared] in the form of fire, and sometimes in the likeness of angels."

34. Justin Martyr *Dialogue with Trypho* 61, *ANF*, 1.227.

35. Ibid., 62, 1.228.

36. Ibid., 63, 1.229.

37. Irenaeus *Proof of the Apostolic Preaching*, chap. 47.

38. Irenaeus *Against Heresies* 3, *ANF*, 1.443.

39. Kelly, *Early Christian Doctrines*, 147.

40. Hippolytus *Against the Heresy of One Noetus* 15, *ANF,* 5.229.
41. Ibid., 4, *ANF,* 5.225.
42. Ibid., 17, *ANF,* 5.230.
43. Ibid. Translation by Kelly, *Early Christian Doctrines,* 149.
44. Tertullian *Against Praxeas* 8, *ANF,* 3.603.
45. Ibid., 26, *ANF,* 3.622.
46. Tertullian *Against All Heresies* 4, *ANF,* 3.652.
47. Ibid.
48. Tertullian *Against Praxeas* 27, *ANF,* 3.624.
49. Clement of Alexandria *Exhortation to the Heathen* 11, *ANF,* 2.203.
50. Ibid., 1, *ANF,* 2.173.
51. Origen *De Principis* 1.2.4, *ANF,* 4.247.

CHAPTER 15: SIMPLY DIVINE?

1. The Arian slogan rhymed in Greek: *ēn pote hote ouk ēn* ("there was [a time] when he was not").
2. Philostorgius, *The Ecclesiastical History of Sozomen: Comprising a History of the Church from A.D. 324 to A.D. 440,* and *The Ecclesiastical History of Philostorgius,* trans. Edward Walford (London: Bohn, 1855), 2.2.
3. Philip Schaff, *History of the Christian Church* (New York: Scribners, 1882), 3.371.
4. Eusebius, *Life of Constantine,* chap. 15, in *The Nicene and Post Nicene Fathers* (hereafter cited as *NPNF*), 2d series, ed. Philip Schaff and Henry Wace (New York: Christian Literature, 1890), 1.792.
5. Rufinus of Aquileia, *Historia Ecclesiastica* (Excerpt on the First Council of Nicaea) 10.4, at http://www.tertullian.org/rpearse/rufinus_he.html (accessed March 2006).
6. Theodoret *The Ecclesiastical History of Theodoret* 1.6, *NPNF,* 3.67.
7. The number of bishops at the Council of Nicea is unclear in the ancient records. Schaff states, "This [318] is the usual estimate, resting on the authority of Athanasius, Basil (Ep. 114; Opera, t. iii. p. 207, ed. Bened.), Socrates, Sozomen, and Theodoret; whence the council is sometimes called the Assembly of the Three Hundred and

Eighteen. Other data reduce the number to three hundred, or to two hundred and seventy, or two hundred and fifty, or two hundred and eighteen; while later tradition swells it to two thousand or more" (*History of the Christian Church*, 3.205). According to ancient writers, "the number of bishops exceeded two hundred and fifty" (Eusebius *Life of Constantine* 3.12, in *NPNF*, 1.789), and went up to three hundred eighteen (Theodoret *The Ecclesiastical History of Theodoret* 1.6, *NPNF*, 3.67; Socrates Scholasticus *The Ecclesiastical History* 1.8, *NPNF*, 2.30). Socrates sometimes rounds the number up to three hundred and twenty, but is careful when quoting sources to reproduce the number of the bishops at Nicea as three hundred eighteen.

Some historians have doubted the accuracy of the number three hundred eighteen since it corresponds to the number of Abraham's troops reported in Genesis 14:14 when he defeated Kedorlaomer and the other kings who were his allies, yet there are a significant number who see no reason to doubt the traditional figure of three hundred eighteen, despite the coincidence with Genesis.

8. Justo González, *A History of Christian Thought*, vol. 1, *From the Beginnings to the Council of Chalcedon*, rev. ed. (Nashville: Abingdon, 1992), 266–67.

9. Roger E. Olson, *The Story of Christian Theology* (Downers Grove, IL: InterVarsity Press, 1999), 153–54.

10. See Eusebius *Life of Constantine* 3.12, in *NPNF*, 1.791.

11. Translation by J. N. D. Kelly, *Early Christian Doctrines*, rev. ed. (New York: Harper & Row, 1978), 232. The version of the Nicene Creed used today is an expansion of the creed by the Council of Constantinople in 381. Material added has to do with the full equality of the Holy Spirit with the Father and Son.

12. Two generations earlier, the heretic Paul of Samosata had used the term to suggest that the Father and Son were the same *person*—not just identical in *substance*. The Nicene Creed did not at all mean this, but the guilt by allusion to Paul of Samosata was enough to make some of the bishops nervous about the wording.

13. For an engaging narrative on the Council of Nicea and the historical

context in which it occurred, see Olson, *Story of Christian Theology,*
141–60; and Mark A. Noll, *Turning Points: Decisive Moments in the
History of Christianity,* 2d ed. (Grand Rapids: Baker, 2000), 47–64.

CHAPTER 16: PARALLELOMANIA

1. Timothy Freke and Peter Gandy, *The Laughing Jesus: Religious Lies
   and Gnostic Wisdom* (New York: Harmony, 2005), 55.
2. Ibid., 56–57.
3. As far back as the 1840s, Bruno Bauer began to publish views that
   the story of Jesus was rooted in myth. Bauer's greatest influence
   was on one of his students, Karl Marx, who promoted the view that
   Jesus never existed. This view eventually became part of communist
   dogma. See Robert E. Van Voorst, *Jesus Outside the New Testament*
   (Grand Rapids: Eerdmans, 2000), 8–10.
4. Probably the best accessible introduction to the subject is Ronald H.
   Nash, *The Gospel and the Greeks,* 2d ed. (Phillipsburg, NJ: Presbyterian and Reformed, 2003). Nash addresses the relationship of Christianity to Hellenistic philosophy, mystery religions, and Gnosticism.
5. "Is Jesus a Counterfeit?" at infidels.org/library/magazines/tsr/
   1994/3/3front94 (accessed August 2005).
6. Albert Schweitzer, *Paul and His Interpreters,* trans. W. Montgomery
   (London: Adam and Charles Black, 1912), 192 (emphasis added).
7. Bruce M. Metzger, ed., *Historical and Literary Studies: Pagan, Jewish,
   and Christian,* New Testament Tools and Studies 8 (Grand Rapids:
   Eerdmans, 1968), 6–7.
8. Günter Wagner, *Pauline Baptism and the Pagan Mysteries* (Edinburgh:
   Oliver and Boyd, 1967), 268.
9. Nash, *Gospel and the Greeks,* 167.
10. Freke and Gandy, *Laughing Jesus,* 56.
11. Ibid., 55.
12. Nash, *Gospel and the Greeks,* 116.
13. Metzger, *Historical and Literary Studies,* 9.
14. Ronald Nash, "Was the New Testament Influenced by Pagan Reli-
    gions?" at equip.org/free/DB109 (accessed August 2005). Essentially

the same statement is made in Nash, *Gospel and the Greeks,* 127–28.

15. Adolf von Harnack, *Wissenschaft und Leben,* 2 vols. (Giessen, Germany: Töpelmann, 1911), 2:191, translated and quoted by Nash, *Gospel and the Greeks,* 108–9.

16. The substance of this point is from Nash, *Gospel and the Greeks,* 8–9, where it is discussed in greater detail.

17. Ibid., 10.

18. Robin Lane Fox, *Pagans and Christians* (New York: Knopf, 1987), 22:

> Many of . . . [the] details [i.e., of pagan religions and culture] were set in Christian contexts which changed their meaning entirely. Other details merely belonged in contexts which nobody wished to make Christian. They were part of the "neutral technology of life" and it would be as unreal to expect them to change "as to expect modern man to Christianize the design of an automobile or to produce a Marxist wristwatch."

19. Ibid., 21.

20. Leon McKenzie, *Pagan Resurrection Myths and the Resurrection of Jesus* (Charlottesville, VA: Bookwrights, 1997), 46.

21. Metzger, *Historical and Literary Studies,* 10–11.

22. Ibid., 11 n. 1.

23. Ibid. Brandon also made this statement in his article "The Ritual Perpetuation of the Past," *Numen* 6 (1959): 128.

24. Walter Künneth, *The Theology of the Resurrection* (London: SCM, 1965), 59.

25. See Nash, *Gospel and the Greeks,* 251–52.

26. See especially Karl Paul Donfried, "The Cults of Thessalonica and the Thessalonian Correspondence," in Donfried's book, *Paul, Thessalonica, and Early Christianity* (Grand Rapids: Eerdmans, 2002), 21–48.

27. The wording of this question is from Nash, *Gospel and the Greeks,* 251.

28. Donfried ("Cults of Thessalonica and the Thessalonian Correspondence," 31) notes, for example, that

one should not overlook the obvious parallels between the following texts and the mystery cults: 1 Thess. 5.5–7 with its reference to darkness and drunkenness; 1 Thess. 5.19–22 where Paul explicitly urges his hearers not "to quench" the Spirit but "to test" it. Quite clearly the apostle does not wish the gift of the Spirit to be confused with the excesses of the Dionysiac mysteries; for Paul the Spirit does not lead to "Bacchic frenzies" but to joy precisely in the context of suffering.

29. Richard Plantinga, "God So Loved the World: Theological Reflections on Religious Plurality in the History of Christianity," in *Biblical Faith and Other Religions: An Evangelical Assessment,* ed. David W. Baker (Grand Rapids: Kregel, 2004), 108.

30. Justin Martyr, *First Apology,* in *The Ante-Nicene Fathers,* ed. Alexander Roberts and James Donaldson, 10 vols. (1885–1887; reprint, Grand Rapids: Eerdmans, 1978), 1:22.

31. J. Gresham Machen, *The Virgin Birth of Christ* (reprint; Grand Rapids: Baker, 1975), 330.

32. Plantinga, "God So Loved the World," 109. See Plantinga's sober conclusions about accommodation with pluralism on pages 133–37.

33. Norman Anderson, *Christianity and World Religions* (Downers Grove, IL: InterVarsity Press, 1984), 53–54. Cf. also Metzger, *Historical and Literary Studies,* 8: "Unlike other countries bordering the Mediterranean Sea, Palestine has been extremely barren in yielding archaeological remains of the paraphernalia and places of worship connected with the Mysteries." He details the earliest artifacts that had been found, all from the early second century A.D.

34. Nash, *Gospel and the Greeks,* 157.

35. Metzger (*Historical and Literary Studies,* 7) also makes this point:

Another methodological consideration, often overlooked by scholars who are better acquainted with Hellenistic culture than with Jewish, is involved in the circumstance that the early Palestinian Church was composed of Christians from a Jewish background, whose generally strict monotheism and traditional intolerance of syncretism must have militated against wholesale borrowing from pagan cults.

Regarding the contribution of Paul to theological formulation, Metzger writes,

> Psychologically it is quite inconceivable that the Judaizers, who attacked Paul with unmeasured ferocity for what they considered his liberalism concerning the relation of Gentile converts to the Mosaic Law, should nevertheless have acquiesced in what some have described as Paul's thoroughgoing contamination of the central doctrines and sacraments of the Christian religion. Furthermore, with regard to Paul himself, scholars are coming once again to acknowledge that the Apostle's prevailing set of mind was rabbinically oriented, and that his newly-found Christian faith ran in molds previously formed at the feet of Gamaliel.

36. So Nash, *Gospel and the Greeks,* 117–20. This section is based on his summary.
37. Metzger, *Historical and Literary Studies,* 11.
38. Nash, *Gospel and the Greeks,* 118.
39. Ibid., 133, 137; and Edwin M. Yamauchi, "Easter: Myth, Hallucination, or History?" *Christianity Today* 18.12 (March 15, 1974): 5.
40. Freke and Gandy commit both the composite fallacy and a form of the chronological fallacy in this assertion, for it was by no means all mystery religions that celebrated December 25. Rather, the Mithraic celebration of the sun-god occurred on this date. And to uncritically imply that December 25 was part of the *original* Christian proclamation is simply irresponsible and misleading (Metzger, *Historical and Literary Studies,* 23).
41. The date of December 25 was apparently first suggested as the day of Christ's birth by Hippolytus (165–235), about two hundred years after the birth of Christ. It did not achieve official status until 386 when Chrysostom declared that it was correct. It should be noted

that a midwinter date for the birth of Jesus is likely, and the Eastern church has traditionally celebrated January 6 as Christ's birthdate. Cf. Harold W. Hoehner, *Chronological Aspects of the Life of Christ* (Grand Rapids: Zondervan, 1977), 25–26.

42. Nash, *Gospel and the Greeks,* 120.

43. Metzger, *Historical and Literary Studies,* 23.

44. The terms *Hellenistic* and *Hellenism* in a restricted sense refer to the period beginning with the death of Alexander the Great in 323 B.C. to the conquest of Cleopatra's Egypt in 30 B.C., but they are used more generally to refer to the period that extends through the demise of the Roman Empire. This period was characterized by a unified government (Rome), a common language (Koine Greek), and a cosmopolitan culture in the Mediterranean basin with a Roman identity. The Hellenistic age was one of syncretism *par excellence.* Cultural and religious thought from Greece, Asia Minor, the Fertile Crescent, Persia, India, Palestine, and Egypt intermingled and morphed into innumerable individual expressions.

45. Nash, *Gospel and the Greeks,* 105–6.

46. David Ulansey, *Origins of the Mithraic Mysteries* (New York: Oxford University Press, 1989). Popular expositions of Mithraism, such as are found online, often posit the "copycat thesis," pointing to Mithraism as a pre-Christian religion that incorporates a virgin birth, a death and resurrection, and even a celebration of the god's birth on December 25. These proponents enlist the ancient nature of the religion— e.g., Mithra worship in Persia antedates Christianity by centuries.

While authorities of the nineteenth and early twentieth centuries have posited a continuum between the Persian deity Mithra and Mithraism as a Roman mystery religion, contemporary scholars assert that no such continuity exists. Rather, the recent assessment recognizes that Roman Mithraism arose as a mystery religion during the first century B.C. in Asia Minor. From there it spread throughout the empire to become one of the most successful mystery religions of late antiquity. Eliade notes, "When the Mysteries of Mithra are discussed, it appears inevitable to quote Ernest Renan's famous sentence: 'If Christianity had been halted in its growth by some mortal illness, the world would have been Mithraist'" (Mircea Eliade, *A History of Religious Ideas,* trans. Willard R. Trask [Chicago: University of Chicago Press, 1982], 2:326).

Eliade and others suggest that this is a vast overstatement. Although Mithraism was widespread and espoused a developed ethical standard, it was almost exclusively a religion of the soldiers and did not admit women to its membership. It would thus not appeal to the masses, women, or slaves.

Despite the claims of obvious and profound parallels between Christianity and Mithraism, when one looks at the evidence an entirely different picture emerges. First, Mithra was not thought of as virgin born in the most ancient myths; rather, he arose spontaneously from a rock in a cave (Edwin Yamauchi, *Persia and the Bible* [Grand Rapids: Baker, 1990], 498).

Second, "Mithra is the only god who does not suffer the same tragic destiny as the gods of the other mysteries, so we may conclude that the scenario of Mithraic initiation did not include ordeals suggesting death and resurrection" (Eliade, *History of Religious Ideas,* 2:324).

Third, the Mithraic concept of history is linear as opposed to the circular concept of the other mysteries. While the other mysteries were centered on the vegetation cycle (Nash, *Gospel and the Greeks,* 136), Mithraism was an astral religion filled with cosmic symbolism (Ulansey, *Mithraic Mysteries,* 46–66; Payam Nabarz, *The Mysteries of Mithras* [Rochester, VT: Inner Traditions, 2005], 24, 145; and Yamauchi, *Persia and the Bible,* 498).

Fourth, Roman Mithraism as a mystery religion apparently arose in the region of Tarsus in Asia Minor during the first century B.C. There is no evidence that the characteristic features of Mithras are in evidence before A.D. 100—several decades after the founding of Christianity (Walter Burkert, *Ancient Mystery Religions* [Cambridge, MA: Harvard University Press, 1987], 7).

47. See previous note for discussion.
48. Nash, *Gospel and the Greeks,* 113.
49. Ibid.
50. Ibid., 113–14.

51. Ibid., 114.
52. Ibid.
53. Ibid.
54. Fox, *Pagans and Christians*, 94.
55. Nash, *Gospel and the Greeks*, 2.
56. Metzger, *Historical and Literary Studies*, 1.

CHAPTER 17: THE VIRGIN BIRTH OF ALEXANDER THE GREAT?

1. Justin Martyr *Dialogue with Trypho* 67, in *The Ante-Nicene Fathers*, ed. Alexander Roberts and James Donaldson, 10 vols. (1885–1887; reprint, Grand Rapids: Eerdmans, 1978), 1:231. For easy access, see ccel.org/fathers2/ANF-01/anf01–48.htm#P4043_787325.

2. Michael Grant and John Hazel, *Who's Who in Classical Mythology* (London: Weidenfeld and Nicolson, 1973; reprint, New York: Routledge, 1994), 101. Cf. "Danae in Greek Mythology," *Mythography,* at loggia.com/myth/danae.html (accessed August 2005).

3. *Encyclopedia Britannica* 2002 on CD-ROM, s.v. "Amphitryon."

4. Livy *History of Rome* 1.4, trans. O. Foster, Loeb Classical Library (Cambridge, MA: Harvard University Press, 1952), 17, 19 (emphasis added).

5. Plutarch, *Life of Alexander.* Cf. *Plutarch's Lives,* trans. Bernadotte Perrin, Loeb Classical Library (New York: Putnam, 1919), 7:225, 227.

6. J. Gresham Machen, *The Virgin Birth of Christ* (reprint, Grand Rapids: Baker, 1975), 338–39.

7. Ibid., 347–48.

8. It is beyond our purpose here to debate whether ʿalmāh in Isaiah 7:14 means "virgin" or "young woman." The LXX translated the Hebrew ʿalmāh as *parthenos,* which means "virgin." See note in the NET Bible at Isaiah 7:14.

9. The LXX was not produced all at one time, but even the last portions were translated well over a century before the birth of Jesus.

10. C. A. Briggs, "The Virgin Birth of Our Lord," *American Journal of Theology* 12 (1908): 190. "The Jews asserted that Jesus' father was Ben Pandera. This is evidently a fiction based on Ben Parthena, son of

the virgin, and implies the Christian doctrine which it antagonizes." See *The Gospel According to the Jews, Called Toldoth Jesu* (London: R. Carlile, 1823) for the account.

11. See M. James Sawyer, *Charles Augustus Briggs and Tensions in Late Nineteenth Century American Theology* (Lewiston, NY: Mellen University Press, 1994), 102–8, for an extended discussion of Briggs's defense of the Virgin Birth.

12. Ibid., 106.

13. Machen, *Virgin Birth of Christ*, 342.

14. Raymond E. Brown, *The Virginal Conception and Bodily Resurrection of Jesus* (New York: Paulist, 1973), 62.

15. Ibid., 65.

CHAPTER 18: OSIRIS, FRANKENSTEIN, AND JESUS CHRIST

1. Edwin M. Yamauchi, "Easter: Myth, Hallucination, or History?" *Christianity Today* 18.12 (March 15, 1974): 4. This very helpful and widely circulated article originally appeared in *Christianity Today* (March 15, 1974): 4–7, and (March 29, 1974): 12–16. It is at leaderu .com/everystudent/easter/articles/yama.

2. Ronald H. Nash, *The Gospel and the Greeks,* 2d ed. (Phillipsburg, NJ: Presbyterian and Reformed, 2003), 126.

3. Gary Habermas and Michael R. Licona, *The Case for the Resurrection of Jesus* (Grand Rapids: Kregel, 2004), 91.

4. Henri Frankfort, *Ancient Egyptian Religion* (Mineola, NY: Dover, 1948), 28.

5. Plutarch *Moralia*, trans. Frank Cole Babbitt, Loeb Classical Library (Cambridge, MA: Harvard University Press, 1936), 5:32. Available at penelope.uchicago.edu/Thayer/E/Roman/Texts/Plutarch/Moralia/ Isis_and_Osiris*/A (accessed August 2005).

6. Ibid., 5.11.

7. Bruce M. Metzger, *Historical and Literary Studies: Pagan, Jewish, and Christian,* New Testament Tools and Studies 8 (Grand Rapids: Eerdmans, 1968), 20.

8. Yamauchi, "Easter: Myth, Hallucination, or History?" 5.

9. Except, of course, for one crucial difference: Frankenstein was assembled from human body parts, while Osiris was strictly a god. The ancient world knew nothing of the final resurrection of a *man* apart from the resurrection of Jesus.

10. See Nash, *Gospel and the Greeks*, 128–29.

11. J. Gresham Machen, *The Origin of Paul's Religion* (reprint, Grand Rapids: Eerdmans, 1976), 228.

12. Evgueni A. Tortchinov, "Cybele, Attis, and the Mysteries of the 'Suffering Gods': A Transpersonalistic Interpretation," at etor.h1.ru/tor-paper (accessed August 2005).

13. Nash, *Gospel and the Greeks*, 130–31.

14. Yamauchi, "Easter: Myth, Hallucination, or History?" part 1, p. 5. See P. Lambrechts, "Les Fetes 'phrygiennes' de Cybele et d' Attis," *Bulletin de l'Institut Historique Belge de Rome* 27.1 (1952): 141–70.

15. Edwin M. Yamauchi, "Easter: Myth, Hallucination, or History?" 5. See also Edwin Yamauchi, "Tammuz and the Bible," *Journal of Biblical Literature* 84 (1965): 283–90.

16. About twenty miles north of Beirut.

17. Yamauchi, "Easter: Myth, Hallucination, or History?" 5.

18. Robin Lane Fox, *Pagans and Christians* (New York: Knopf, 1987), 265.

19. Nash, *Gospel and the Greeks*, 160–61.

20. N. T. Wright, *The Resurrection of the Son of God* (Minneapolis: Fortress, 2003), 81.

21. Ibid., 80–81.

22. Nash, *Gospel and the Greeks*, 160.

23. Ibid., 160–61.

24. Ibid., 161.

25. Ibid.

26. Ibid. Cf. also Metzger, *Historical and Literary Studies*, 18: "In all of the Mysteries which tell of a dying deity, the god dies by compulsion and not by choice, sometimes in bitterness and despair, never in self-giving love. But according to the New Testament, God's purpose of redeeming-love was the free divine motive for the death of Jesus, who accepted with equal freedom that motive as his own."

27. Nash, *Gospel and the Greeks,* 161.

28. Walter Künneth, *The Theology of the Resurrection* (London: SCM, 1965), 58.

CONCLUSION: THE REAL JESUS

1. C. S. Lewis, *The Chronicles of Narnia,* vol. 1, *The Lion, the Witch and the Wardrobe* (New York: Collier, 1970), 75–76.

2. For those interested in finding out more about Jesus Christ, we recommend the Web site www.bible.org. For starters, go to the section called "Finding God." As well, a new translation of the Bible, the NET Bible, is available for free download at this Web site.

FURTHER READING

We recommend starting with resources marked by an asterisk (*).

PART 1: I BELIEVE IN YESTERDAY

Barnett, Paul. *The Birth of Christianity: The First Twenty Years.* Grand Rapids: Eerdmans, 2005.

*———. *Is the New Testament Reliable?* 2d ed. Downers Grove, IL: InterVarsity Press, 2004.

———. *Jesus and the Logic of History.* New Studies in Biblical Theology. Edited by D. A. Carson. Grand Rapids: Eerdmans; Cambridge, England: Apollos, 1997.

Blomberg, Craig. *The Historical Reliability of the Gospels.* Downers Grove, IL: InterVarsity Press, 1987.

*———. *Making Sense of the New Testament: Three Crucial Questions.* Grand Rapids: Baker, 2004.

*Bock, Darrell L. *Can I Trust the Bible? Defending the Bible's Reliability.* Norcross, GA: Ravi Zacharias International Ministries, 2001.

———. "The Words of Jesus in the Gospels: Live, Jive, or Memorex?" In *Jesus Under Fire: Modern Scholarship Reinvents the Historical Jesus.* Edited by Michael J. Wilkins and J. P. Moreland, 73–99. Grand Rapids: Zondervan, 1995.

*Bruce, F. F. *The New Testament Documents: Are They Reliable?* 6th ed. Grand Rapids: Eerdmans; Downers Grove, IL: InterVarsity Press, 1981.

Dunn, James D. G. *A New Perspective on Jesus: What the Quest for the Historical Jesus Missed.* Grand Rapids: Baker, 2005.

Stein, Robert H. *Studying the Synoptic Gospels: Origin and Interpretation.* Grand Rapids: Baker, 2001.

PART 2: POLITICALLY CORRUPT? THE TAINTING OF ANCIENT NEW TESTAMENT TEXTS

Bruce, F. F. *The Books and the Parchments.* 5th ed. London: Marshall Pickering, 1991.

Fee, G. D. "The Textual Criticism of the New Testament." In *The Expositor's Bible Commentary.* Edited by F. E. Gabelein. 1:419–33. Grand Rapids: Zondervan, 1979.

Metzger, Bruce M., and Bart D. Ehrman. *The Text of the New Testament: Its Transmission, Corruption, and Restoration.* 4th ed. New York and Oxford: Oxford University Press, 2005.

*Patzia, Arthur G. *The Making of the New Testament: Origin, Collection, Text, and Canon.* Downers Grove, IL: InterVarsity Press, 1995.

*Wegner, Paul D. *The Journey from Texts to Translations: The Origin and Development of the Bible.* Grand Rapids: Baker, 1999.

PART 3: DID THE EARLY CHURCH MUZZLE THE CANON?

*Bock, Darrell L. *The Missing Gospels: Unearthing the Truth About Alternative Christianities.* Nashville: Nelson, 2006.

Bruce, F. F. *The Canon of Scripture.* Downers Grove, IL: InterVarsity Press, 1988.

*———. *The New Testament Documents: Are They Reliable?* 6th ed. Grand Rapids: Eerdmans; Downers Grove, IL: InterVarsity Press, 1981.

Carson, D. A., and Douglas J. Moo. *An Introduction to the New Testament.* 2d ed. Grand Rapids: Zondervan, 2005.

*Green, Michael. *The Books the Church Suppressed: Fiction and Truth in* The Da Vinci Code. Oxford: Monarch; Grand Rapids: Kregel, 2006.

Metzger, Bruce M. *The Canon of the New Testament: Its Origin, Development, and Significance.* Oxford: Clarendon, 1987.

*Patzia, Arthur G. *The Making of the New Testament: Origin, Collection, Text, and Canon.* Downers Grove, IL: InterVarsity Press, 1995.

*Wegner, Paul D. *The Journey from Texts to Translations: The Origin and Development of the Bible.* Grand Rapids: Baker, 1999.

Part 4: The Divinity of Jesus: Early Tradition or Late Superstition?

*Allison, C. FitzSimons. *The Cruelty of Heresy: An Affirmation of Christian Orthodoxy.* Harrisburg, PA: Morehouse, 1994.

Bauckham, Richard. *God Crucified: Monotheism and Christology in the New Testament.* Grand Rapids: Eerdmans, 1998.

*Bowman, Robert M., Jr., and J. Ed Komoszewski. *Putting Jesus in His Place: The Case for the Deity of Christ.* Grand Rapids: Kregel, 2007.

Brown, Harold O. J. *Heresies: The Image of Christ in the Mirror of Heresy and Orthodoxy from the Apostles to the Present.* Garden City, NY: Doubleday, 1984.

*Habermas, Gary R. *The Historical Jesus: Ancient Evidence for the Life of Christ.* Joplin, MO: College, 1996.

*Harris, Murray J. *Three Crucial Questions About Jesus.* Grand Rapids: Baker, 1994.

Hurtado, Larry W. *At the Origins of Christian Worship: The Context and Character of Earliest Christian Devotion.* Carlisle, PA: Paternoster, 1999. Reprint ed., Grand Rapids: Eerdmans, 2000.

———. *How on Earth Did Jesus Become a God? Historical Questions About Earliest Devotion to Jesus.* Grand Rapids: Eerdmans, 2005.

Kelly, J. N. D. *Early Christian Doctrines.* Rev. ed. New York: Harper and Brothers, 1978.

Van Voorst, Robert E. *Jesus Outside the New Testament: An Introduction to the Ancient Evidence.* Grand Rapids: Eerdmans, 2000.

PART 5: STEALING THUNDER: DID CHRISTIANITY RIP OFF
MYTHICAL GODS?

Fox, Robin Lane. *Pagans and Christians.* New York: Knopf, 1987.
*Habermas, Gary R., and Michael R. Licona. *The Case for the Resurrection of
Jesus.* Grand Rapids: Kregel, 2004.
Machen, J. Gresham. *The Virgin Birth of Christ.* New York: Harper; London:
Marshall, Morgan and Scott, 1930.
*Nash, Ronald H. *The Gospel and the Greeks.* 2d ed. Phillipsburg, NJ: Presby-
terian and Reformed, 2003.
Wright, N. T. *The Resurrection of the Son of God.* Minneapolis: Fortress,
2003.
Yamauchi, Edwin M. *Persia and the Bible.* Grand Rapids: Baker, 1990.

SCRIPTURE INDEX

SUBJECT INDEX

preference of the harder reading,
90–92, 283n. 6; preference of
the shorter reading, 92–93;
transcriptional probability,
93–94
Textus Receptus (TR), 112–13
Theodore of Mopsuestia, 131
Theodoret, 131
Theology of the Resurrection, The
(Künneth), 228–29
Theonas of Marmarica, 213
Thomas, 18, 191
Thucydides, 276n. 8; *History of the
Peloponnesian War*, 267n. 6
Toland, John, 300n. 26
Tolkien, J. R. R.: *The Lord of the
Rings*, 91–92
Tortchinov, Evgueni, 253
Trullan Synod (691–92), 296n. 7

Valentinus, 296n. 14
Van Voorst, Robert E.: *Jesus
Outside the New Testament*,
313n. 3
Vetus Latina Institute, 281n. 14
Virgin Birth, 239–40, 246–47, 260,
324n. 8; biblical accounts of,
243–46; virgin birth of pagan
gods, 240–243, 246, 260
Virgin Birth of Christ, The
(Machen), 240, 246

Wagner, Günter, 223
Wettstein, Johann, 287–88n. 12,
289–90n. 23
"Words of Jesus in the Gospels,
The" (Bock), 36
Wright, N. T., 256–57, 266–67n. 3

Yamauchi, Edwin, 250, 252, 254
YHWH, 245, 251

Zechariah, book of, 98–99
Zindler, Frank, 75, 113–14, 283–
85n. 1

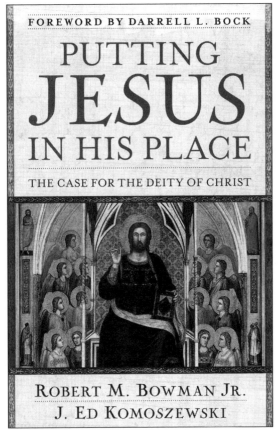

FOREWORD BY DARRELL L. BOCK

PUTTING JESUS IN HIS PLACE

THE CASE FOR THE DEITY OF CHRIST

ROBERT M. BOWMAN JR.
J. ED KOMOSZEWSKI

392 pages • paperback • ISBN 978-0-8254-2983-5 • Available September 2007

The central theological distinctive of Christianity—that Jesus is God incarnate—is frequently and openly called into question today. It's natural that those who reject the Bible also reject its exalted view of Christ. But surprisingly, many who embrace the authority of Scripture are quick to argue that Jesus' deity is found nowhere in its pages.

Putting Jesus in His Place demonstrates that the New Testament—from beginning to end—clearly reveals Jesus' divine identity. What's more, it shows that belief in Jesus as God was the conviction of his original Jewish followers, rooted in Old Testament theology and in what Jesus himself said and did.

In a manner that is both academically sound and spiritually engaging, the authors make a case for the deity of Christ that is easy to follow and hard to forget.